H. ALLEN SMITH

Life in a Putty Knife Factory

DOUBLEDAY, DORAN & CO., INC.

Garden City, New York 1944

Partial Dedication
Ten per cent of this book is dedicated to
Harold Matson

OWING to a favor I once did a cow, the Borden Company usually sends me a Christmas present consisting of cheese. One such gift came to me packed in an imitation-leather box about the size of second base. It was a perfect box to keep on the table next to my desk. That's where I put it, and then I spent several weeks trying to figure out what I would use it for.

Along about that time I finished writing a conglomerate mess of letterpress called *Low Man on a Totem Pole*. I sent the manuscript off to the publisher and went about my ordinary pursuits and frivolities.

Almost at once I began thinking of things that should have been included in that book—things that fitted perfectly here or there but which I had forgotten. As these things came up, I made notes about them and tossed them into The Cheese Box. Sometimes I'd sit down at the typewriter and peel off a dozen or so pages of stuff that should have been put into *Low Man on a Totem Pole*.

This sort of thing went on for a long time. Then one day last summer I found myself with nothing to do. The Dodgers had been rained out that afternoon and I had nothing to read except about fifteen hundred books. So I picked up The Cheese Box. By this time it had been stuffed so full of odds and ends that the lid wouldn't close. I sat down and began rummaging through its contents.

This book came largely out of The Cheese Box.

It is not, therefore, precisely a sequel to *Low Man on a Totem Pole*. It is more of a companion piece. If you could take the chapters of *Low Man on a Totem Pole* and the chapters of this book and riffle them together in the manner of an adroit card-shuffler, you'd come close to fitting them together properly.

I'm confessing, in other words, that this book is technically imperfect and, in fact, a botch. It lacks continuity. A chapter here and a chapter there . . . that's the way it was put together out of The Cheese Box.

If you are not a literary critic, you probably don't know that lack of continuity is a serious defect in a book. There are several recognized methods of correcting this defect—technical or mechanical devices which writers use to make their chapters flow together. I'm not going to bother about any of these corrective methods. I've been punching a typewriter for twenty years, but as of 1943 I take no particular pride in being a writer. The competition is getting to be too harrowing. The industry is being taken over by strip-tease gals who flap it three times at the customers and then dash for their dressing rooms to finish Chapter Eight. I have a navel, but there's no rhinestone in it.

Most of the lilting prose in this book has never appeared in print before. There are some fragments, however, which were written originally for newspapers or magazines—chiefly for the column I produced at the United Features Syndicate. These episodes and anecdotes appear here in a fancier and, I hope, a livelier form.

About the grammar in this book. It is, without question, atrocious. Grammar is a thing I never learned and, like most other human beings, I have nothing but contempt for anything I don't know. I play the typewriter strictly by ear and when the tune sounds all right to me I'm satisfied with it.

A couple of years ago I wrote a short article about New York City and it appeared in a national magazine. It happens that a young man of my acquaintance, attending school in the South, was assigned to write a composition on New York City. He took my essay from the magazine, copied it down word for word, and handed it in. His instructor graded it "50" with the further notation: "Too many common errors." That's how I am with syntax.

This project, then, dates back to a favor I did a cow —a cow named Bodicia Design Coupon.* Be kind to animals.

H. Allen Smith

*See *Low Man on a Totem Pole.*

Contents

Life in the United States of America should never be dull, and yet I have the sensation sometimes that I am living in a vast industrial establishment, devoted to the manufacture of putty knives. ESSAYS by Elmer Roessner

ONE EVENING during the summer of 1940—a period that now seems as remote as the Pleistocene Age—I came upon a filler item in a newspaper saying that the twenty-six letters of the alphabet may be transposed 620,448,401,733,-239,439,369,000 times. At the moment the thing struck me as a dreary piece of information—almost as dull as a conversation between two pipe smokers engaged in comparing tobacco blends. For some reason, however, it stayed in my mind, and I went back to it. Being wholly inept at ciphering, I didn't even consider proving or disproving the thing with a pencil. I did it with a typewriter. I transposed the twenty-six letters of the alphabet until I had some three hundred pages, and these pages became a book and the book became a best seller, continuing as such for more than a year.

The circumstance of becoming the author of a best seller brought a series of perplexities into my life. Some of these were pleasant and some were mildly frightening.

Among other things I appeared on half-a-dozen radio programs conducted by women during the morning hours, and each of these ladies started off with the same question: "How does it feel to be the author of a best seller?"

I can't reasonably complain about their lack of originality, because at least once I used the question myself. I used it on the late Thorne Smith, who was a great man though not very tall. Thorne's books had just started selling well when I went to interview him. He was living in a dingy basement apartment in Greenwich Village and the first thing I asked him was: "How does it feel to be the author of a best seller?"

"Well," he said, "it's a great thing. You see that shelf of books over there?"

He indicated a row of faded and ragged volumes.

"It used to be," he said, "that I could grab up all those books and carry them around the corner to a little bookstore, and the man who runs the store would give me enough money to buy a bottle of gin. Then when I got a job or sold a piece of writing, I'd go around and reclaim the books."

He turned and looked again at the books, and there was a sly grin on his face when he concluded:

"Now—now that I'm a best seller, I can go around to the bookstore and the man will give me enough money for a bottle of gin *and I don't have to take the books with me!*"

In the days of my floundering youth I once wrote a newspaper squib about the distribution of free carnival tickets in the town of Jeffersonville, Indiana. A lady proofreader came to me and pointed out, in my copy, this sentence: "These tickets may be had for the askance." The lady proofreader said she believed I had misused the word "askance" but I assured her it was correct and it got into the paper that way. The publisher of the Jeffersonville paper, Claude G. Brodhecker, bawled her out for letting the word get by, and she in turn gave me a blistering. I remember her closing words distinctly. "You," she said, "are the bummest writer I know of." Soon after that I resolved that someday I would write a whole book—a book that would make me mighty near as famous as Harold Bell Wright.

I didn't know, of course, how the writing of a successful book can complicate and gum up a person's life. I didn't dream that someday I would become An Influence. Yet that's what happened. The high quality of my writing has created a new pattern of life . . . for a dog.

In the earlier book I made mention of my dentist and his dog. The dentist, Dr. Bernard Adorjan, is deaf and his dog, Sookie, serves as his office assistant. When I ring the office doorbell Sookie opens the door and leads me into the waiting room, pointing with her nose at the chair I am to occupy. Then she waddles into the inner office and fetches the doctor. Once I am in the dentist's chair, Sookie climbs into my lap and observes all the blasting and riveting operations. Whenever Dr. Adorjan uses the spray to shoot that sweet stuff into my mouth, Sookie sticks out her tongue and gets a shot of it herself. When the dentist has finished with a towel he drops it on the floor, whereupon Sookie hops down, carries it across the room and deposits it in a hamper. The little dog does everything but run the drill and answer the telephone in that office.

That's approximately what I wrote in the other book. Soon after publication of the volume Dr. Adorjan was taking Sookie for a walk when a cop grabbed him and gave him a summons because his dog was not on a leash. In court Dr. Adorjan handed the magistrate a copy of my book opened at the page where Sookie's talents were described. The magistrate looked around to make sure the reporters were present, then quickly dismissed the case, and the story of how a book saved Sookie appeared in all the New York papers. Her picture also was printed and in the picture she was wearing sun glasses.

That episode wrought a great change in Sookie's character. She soon became the most-talked-about dog in Jackson Heights—a community on Long Island that appears to harbor more dogs than humans. Dr. Adorjan says that Sookie spent hours looking at her scrapbook, staring at the lovely photographs. Fame went to her head and she became temperamental. Nowadays she will not budge outside the house until Dr. Adorjan has hooked her sun glasses over her ears. She has excited so much comment that strangers with no cavities sometimes call at the doctor's office just to see her, and the doctor has had to teach her several new routines in order that she will not disappoint her admirers. The climax of her new repertoire is a salute. She'll be sitting on her haunches when the doctor sings out: "To hell with Hitler!" Whereupon Sookie's right forepaw comes up in a Nazi salute and she bares her fangs in a most horrifying way.

All of these antics are directly traceable to my literary gifts. I have influenced my life and times. No question about it.

I intend to deal with other weird consequences of authorhood in a later chapter. Right now I'd like to make note of the fact that as soon as I became a best seller I received a pleasurable amount of publicity in the press and on the radio. Almost at once I became an automatic s. o. b. to large portions of the population of Broadway and Hollywood. Some people who had been my friends even started calling me a revolving s. o. b. A revolving s. o. b., according to the late Iron Pants Johnson, is a man who's an s. o. b. any way you look at him. The movies didn't buy my book, nor did the Book-of-the-Month Club take it on, so as far as I know my friends have not yet started whispering it around that I am a swish.

This acquisition of an evil character brought me no great concern. The one thing that made me mad was the assault upon my genealogical background. It was a limited assault, to be sure, but it was brought to my attention, and an even dozen stirrup pumps couldn't have extinguished my burn. Certain people were flaring their nostrils at me because they considered me to be a nobody from nowhere. They were saying: "Who is this upstart? What right has he to be going around shooting off his typewriter? What about his family? What about his ancestry?"

My God! Ain't they never heard tell of the Smiths?

It is plainly up to me now to establish myself on solid ground. I've done considerable in the way of genealogical research and I intend, right now, to lay the evidence before the world—calmly, dispassionately, and with scientific detachment.

I can't start off with a long string of begats because I don't have the material at hand and have been unable to get it. Nonetheless, I can say without fear of contradiction that the Smiths have been as handy at the begat business as any other genealogical line in history. Maybe even handier.

My research has been rendered difficult by the fact that the Smiths have always been too busy (probably with begats) to mess around with family trees. When people ask after my ancestry, I simply tell them that I'm descended from an ape —a response that usually satisfies them.

Don't think a Smith never takes pride in his family. We have our little twinges of elation when we think of Kate's success, how Al got rich, Bessie's way with a blues song, Preserved's fame as a professor, how the angel Moroni appeared to Joe, Sophia's getting a college named after her, and how Ida runs the W. C. T. U. We have things to be proud about. I remember the day my old friend Sutherland Denlinger came back to New York from Washington, where he had gone to do a newspaper article on the Federal Bureau of Investigation. He told me:

"J. Edgar Hoover took me through the works. They have a tremendous file on criminals and shady characters. I thought you'd be delighted to know that seventeen big cabinets, each containing nine drawers, are devoted to the Smiths."

We hold the lead in so many things.

The greatest of all Smiths, to my way of thinking, was Sydney. Hesketh Pearson wrote a biography of Sydney under the title, *The Smith of Smiths*. I have read it, and I have also read an ancient volume called *Wit and Wisdom of the Rev. Sydney Smith Being Selections from His Writings and Passages of His Letters and Table-Talk with a Biographical Memoir and Notes*. It is by Evert A. Duyckinck. I mean the book is by Evert A. Duyckinck. It doesn't say who wrote the title but obviously Evert couldn't have written the book *and* the title.

This Sydney Smith was a caution. He's the fellow who first figured out about square pegs in round holes and vice versa—an experiment in which most of the world's Smiths indulge to this day. Sydney is also quite famous as the man who thought up the joke that first made Fred Allen famous —"It's so hot tonight I'd like to take off my skin and sit around in my bones."

Once this same Sydney Smith was asked to describe his family's coat of arms. He replied: "The Smiths never had any arms, and have invariably sealed their letters with their thumbs." He was just saying that to make a joke, as I'll presently prove.

Sydney had full realization, as early as the beginning of the nineteenth century, of the difficulties confronting a Smith afflicted with a common Christian or given name. When his daughter was born he named her Saba, after a king mentioned in the 72nd Psalm. Anyone with the surname of Smith, said Sydney, ought to have an uncommon Christian name by way of compensation. By this same logic, I have long defied my enemies and detractors and called myself H. Allen Smith.

I began parting my name on the side at an early age when I first started getting by-lines on newspapers. Ever since, I have been accused by many drunks and a few moderate drinkers of being affected and vain—a charge which I deny by citing that I neither say eyether or nyether. It was almost essential that I decorate up my Smith name with something fancy at the head end. I can agree that when a man named Archibald F. Throcklepidgeon begins calling himself A. Fieldstone Throcklepidgeon, he might be motivated by affectation and vanity; but when a Smith decorates himself up front he has reason and justice on his side. If he goes around calling himself Joe Smith or Jim Smith or Harry Smith he's likely to run into embarrassments. As it is, half the time when I'm introduced to someone merely as "Mr. Smith" the party of the second part always says, "What's your *real* name?" A Smith without a feather in his nomenclatural cap generally has one hell of a time getting a check cashed, and the way those hotel clerks look at you when you register as man and wife!

I know more Allen Smiths than I know dirty jokes. A fellow working on a newspaper in Passaic, New Jersey, once almost got his head knocked off by a lot of naked people on my account. It happened that I had visited a nudist camp back in the hills and that I had written an article about all the peculiar activities to be observed at the establishment. My story gave the nudists fits, and they descended upon the first Allen Smith they could find—the Allen Smith in Passaic. He convinced them that he was not the villain and escaped the humiliation of being assaulted by a band of nuts.

Then, too, I remember that during the Hauptmann trial in Flemington I was always bumping into the state trooper who was assigned as guard to the kidnaper of the Lindbergh baby. His name was Allen Smith. There's an Allen Smith living within ten blocks of my house—a major or captain or something—and occasionally I get phone calls from people asking me if I'm the same Allen Smith who used to be with the Knickerbocker Grays.

It must be apparent already that there's an argument on the side of a Smith who wants to call himself P. Judderwort Smith. Yet fancying up a name doesn't always work. Back in 1929 I was writing features for the United Press in New York. Out in Akron, Ohio, the members of the Liars Club read some of my pieces and swiftly elected me an honorary president of their group. They sent along the notification addressed simply to "H. Allen Smith, New York City."

Well, I was sitting there in the *World* building one afternoon when a young man walked in and, by chance, approached me.

"I'm looking for H. Allen Smith," he said.

"You're looking," I replied in that gay manner of mine, "at him."

He stuck out his hand.

"Glad to meet you," he said. "I'm H. Allen Smith."

I drew back a little, fearing that I was in the presence of a person whose atoms were poorly adjusted. When he reached for his pocket I had a feeling that he was going to pull a derringer on me, but he only handed me a card, which proved that he *was* H. Allen Smith and, as I remember, connected in some way with the B. & O. After that he explained that the letter from the Akron Liars had been delivered to him.

Having another H. Allen Smith loose in the same town was disconcerting, so some years later, when the opportunity arose, I became H. Allen W. Smith. This was during a visit at the home of my sister Lou, in Washington, D.C. My father and mother were visitors there at the same time and on an October evening we were sitting around telling lies about the old days when my sister said:

"Did you know Pop has been holding out on us for years?"

"In what way?" I asked.

"He's got another name," she said. "I just found out about it. He's got a third name—Wolfgang. Henry Arthur Wolfgang Smith."

Pop said it was true. He said that for several generations it had been the custom in his father's family to give one of the boys an extra name, over and above the customary two, and that the extra name was always Wolfgang.

"Well," I said, "that's a fine thing! Why didn't you give it to me?"

"Reckon we fergot about it," said Pop.

Then and there I decided I wanted that extra name. I told Pop that the matter should be rectified—that under the law he could still make me a Wolfgang. So on the following morning I took both my parents down the street to a notary public and swore out an affidavit. It certifies that my name is Harry Allen Wolfgang Smith. I have it buried away somewhere and find myself getting nervous about it now and then, visualizing the arrival of the G-men, a general ransacking of the house, discovery of the fatal paper, and then—handcuffs and leg irons and eventually a cold gray dawn against the wall. Wolfgang! A German agent! Convicted by his own sworn statement!

Don't get the idea that back yonder a little ways, when I talked of Sydney Smith, I was trying to make an Englishman out of myself. I'm no more a descendant of Sydney than you are. If my probings into the Smith genealogy had established me as an Englishman, I should have bowed before the verdict and taken it like a man. But they didn't.

For a long time I had been reading those ads in the magazines—"Is Your Name Here?"—followed by a list of surnames a mile long. At last I sent in my two dollars. I figured I'd throw those people into discord. I figured that if I asked them to give me a history of the Smiths, the Media Research Bureau of Washington, D.C., would come down with the triple fantods. They didn't blink an eye. They accepted my two dollars and came back at me with a fat envelope which contained a black-jacketed *Genealogical and Historical Sketch*. This sketch contained sixteen pages and there wasn't a word in it about me. There was quite a lot of information about other Smiths, but nothing about me or any of my kinfolks. There was mention of Captain John Smith, but I already knew about him. One paragraph in the sketch struck my fancy. It reads:

Recurrent traits of the family in America include, in certain branches at least, imagination, love of liberty, and a humanitarian interest in their fellow men, and in other lines shrewdness, quick wit, practical business ability, and capacity for leadership. Members of the family have displayed outstanding ability as statesmen, writers, and scientists.

According to that, we have everything, but I place little trust in it. I could have got that for less than two dollars. A penny, dropped into the slot of a weighing machine on a subway platform, would fetch a better report in better language.

While I was studying this document from Media, word came to me from McLeansboro, Illinois, making a semi-German out of me. My cousin Veronica, at my request, forwarded the information that my grandpa, Caleb Smith, was born in Baden on Armistice Day, 1846. His folks were Swiss and were named Schmitt. These Schmitts came from Basle, Switzerland, and the back of my hand to 'em! Why did they have to cross the border to Baden and make a Hun out of me? I wish an Alp had fallen on them before the moving van got to their hut.

Getting back to Caleb. His folks brought him across in 1856 and they went to Moweaqua, Illinois. Caleb became a cigar maker but later on acquired a brickyard in McLeansboro. I remember him. He was a short, pudgy man with a white goatee.

Theodore Dreiser thinks he has a sharp memory. He wrote a book of 589 pages about his infancy and adolescence. Among other things he remembers how he crawled across the floor to his mother and found that her shoes had holes in them, whereupon a great sorrow came upon him. I, too, have a good memory. I can remember going to Caleb Smith's brickyard. I remember precisely what it looked like. Just a lot of bricks.

Going back to the Media sketch, I now found that Sydney Smith was wrong. We have a coat of arms. The most ancient coat of arms for the Schmitts of Germany and Switzerland consists of the following:

Arms—*De gueules à un Pegase d'argent.*

Crest—*Un vol, d'argent et de gueules.*

I know nothing of the French language, so the thing has me stopped. I think I recognize, in that top part where it says *Pegase,* that the reference is to a horse. I'm a little afraid to investigate further—*d'argent* might turn out to be a three-letter word meaning beast of burden.

You can readily see how genealogical research might become fun. Here, in no time at all, I've got myself as far back as Switzerland and I've got a coat of arms with, I suspect, a horse's behind on it. But the quest doesn't end with *Pegase d'argent.* One more step needs to be reported.

In the midst of all my delvings I happened to encounter a female relative. She is a woman who can talk. She can talk and read a book and listen to the radio and knit a sweater all at the same time. All I had to do was close the windows, batten down all loose objects, and say:

"What do you know about the history of our family?"

I had trouble lighting a cigarette after that. Had to cup the match in my hands and bend away from the gale. I tried to make notes and now, a year later, I have them before me. It's the family history all right, and to make my report complete I must include it here. In the interest of accuracy, I'm setting it down just as my kinswoman poured it at me and as I scribbled it in my notebook. Here, then, is The Family History:

There was Caleb that was your grandfather you remember him used to have that brickyard in McLeansboro well he came, let me see now, he came from Baden and then he had some brothers, I think it was two, Dicker and Valentine, but first Caleb, somehow they got to Decatur and that's where he met your grandmother Maria Fitzpatrick, you remember all those Fitzpatricks in Decatur, lived on Eldorado Street I believe, you used to go over there when you were a youngun and mash down their bushes and tromp their vegetable gardens and one day, I remember, that was maybe in . . . All those Fitzpatricks were Irish, come from Kentucky, but I think Maria's mother, that is, I mean, that would be your great-grandmother, wouldn't it, I think she was English, at least I've always *heard* she was, though I myself never heard of any Irish people bragging about having any English people in the family, but as I remember it, and I'm more Irish than anything else, at least that's what I've been told, so they always seemed to say that Maria's mother—that would be a Mrs. Fitzpatrick—she would be an Englishwoman, at least they always said it, but anyway Caleb your grandfather married her and after that I think Dicker and Valentine . . . Valentine got his name from old Caleb's father, he was the one brought them over from Germany, and Dicker, that's a funny name, I've always thought it was a funny name, but Dicker wasn't his real name but Henry, and I suppose they called him Dicker because he liked to dicker except that as I remember him all he liked to do was sit in the front yard and spit, but you should be real interested in Dicker because his real name was Henry and that's what your own father was baptized, Henry Arthur, I don't know where the Arthur came from but the Henry was from Dicker, except that they never did call him Henry but Harry, I mean your father, he was Harry all his life so when it came to naming you they didn't name you Henry but Harry, but anyway it all goes back to Dicker and that's the way you happen to have the name Harry.

Now, as I said, Dicker and Valentine came to McLeansboro and started the brickyard and there were a couple of other brothers that were farmers around Springer, Illinoise, and they came down to Haw Creek Bottoms, but that has nothing to do with it, because Caleb is the important one, and he was back in Decatur, I think, making cigars, and finally he came down to McLeansboro and bought the brickyard from Dicker and Valentine. Dicker! I can't get over that name, Dicker!

There were four children, I mean Caleb and Maria, you always called him Grandpa but your grandmother you called Ma, they had four children, three beside Harry, and they were Vieve, she's a widow, and Roy, you remember your uncle Roy, been in the insurance and real-estate business in Decatur since who tied the pup, and Nellie, you remember Aunt Nellie, she was the wife of Doc Hassett, and Doc Hassett's the one brought you into the world, if I remember right, your own uncle, and they had four children of their own, or maybe five. But that's the Smith side.

Your mother's people date back to the Moores of South Carolina and your great-grandmother was a Hull, daughter of a Henry Hull, up around Carlisle, Illinoise, near East Saint Louis and she married Joseph Allen, he came from Memphis, and she brought him a lot of money, he was a real-estate speculator, and that's how they happened to be in McLeansboro, he had a grocery store and a drug store and he practically owned the whole county and gave the land for the public school, your own flesh and blood, you might say. They had four children and one of them was your mother's father. C. J. as he was always called, that's your grandfather, he was mechanically inclined and finally he had a sawmill up around Aiken, Illinoise, and that's where he met Almeda Lane, that's your grandmother, she was an orphan girl and the old lady postmistress at Aiken adopted her and that's where C. J. met her when he had his sawmill up there, he married her when she was fourteen years old, oh, I forgot to mention, the old lady postmistress was named Grandma Tyrrell and that's how your aunt Tyrrell got her first name, Tyrrell Allen, she was the youngest of the kids and your mother was the oldest and you can believe it or not, as Ripley says, but your grandmother was only fifteen years old when your mother was born, and then there was Willie and Sam and then Tyrrell. That was all in McLeansboro and C. J. had a machine shop there and after that a flour mill, it was quite a town in those days, McLeansboro, with stock shows in tents and there was the Grand Opera House, it was a town of retired farmers with two flour mills and a barrel-stave factory, and that's where you were born.

That's the way it appears in my notes, and a most adequate summary of family history it seems to be, though confusing in spots, even to me. On the surface it doesn't reflect much in the way of antiquity, though I'd like you to note the presence of Fitzpatricks in my line. There's a paragraph by Horace Walpole in a book of quotations which says: "The Fitzpatricks are so ancient that the best Irish antiquaries affirm that they reckoned many generations before the first man was created."

One other point can be clarified. The "Willie" mentioned down toward the end of the disquisition is Willie Allen, my mother's brother, the only member of the family on either side who ever distinguished himself in any way. He was, for a number of years, the leading steeplechase jockey in the country and lived at Laurel, Maryland. He made big money at his business and was always sending packages of things back to my mother in Illinois—chiefly his castoff clothes. Naturally he was a little man and I spent a large part of my boyhood in his clothes. Apparently he never wore a pair of jockey's boots more than half-a-dozen races, then he'd send them back to Illinois, and I'd wear them, though my mother would never let me wear them to school no matter how much I begged. Willie Allen committed suicide back about 1918 and not long ago I met an ex-jockey who used to ride with him.

This fellow, Jimmy Collins, said he was Willie's best friend and roommate for a number of years.

"So you're Butch Allen's nephew!" said Jimmy Collins. "Well, I'll be god damned. You don't look anything like him. Killed himself, Butch did. Some say he killed himself over a horse, and I believe it. He always rode a horse named

River Shannon, a great horse, greatest jumper in the country. Well, sir, River Shannon died, and right after that Butch
Allen took a gun and shot himself. Killed himself over a
horse."

That's my family history—the whole of it, so far as I'm
able to deliver it. I trust that in the future those people who
have seen fit to question my ancestry will examine these
pages before they speak. Let them note every line of it. Let
them note in particular how I got my name, indirectly, from
Dicker. Insofar as that coat of arms is concerned, they can
forget that.

CHAPTER II   *A Salute to Pop*

IN RECENT YEARS my father has been living at a
camp on the banks of the Potomac about twenty miles above
Washington. Until he grew weary of it, he was employed at
the camp as a sort of custodian, renting canoes and fishing
tackle to the customers, keeping the cabins repaired, and
looking after the establishment's little truck garden.

I visited Pop at the camp in the summer of 1941. It was
a pleasant setup, far from any main highway, and possessed
only a few drawbacks. The people occupying the dozen or
so cabins from early spring to late fall had to get along
without conveniences. The camp has no running water except that which flows past it. In order to take a bath it is
necessary to jump into the Potomac. Whenever a hard rain
comes, however, the river muddies up and nobody with any
sense would get into it. After such a rain, it takes at least a
week for the river to clear again.

The evening I arrived at the camp brought such a hard
rain; consequently, there was no bathing during my visit, and
before I left I had given the place a new name: Camp Armpit. Deprived of their bathing, the residents of the camp
turned into a colony of armpit sniffers.

I found Pop among his cronies. One of these is a gentleman employed as an assistant plumber in an insane asylum.
Another is a stiff-backed old man, around seventy, wearing

a drooping mustache and inhabiting a cabin back in the woods some distance from the camp. This old guy's name is Mose. He is the final remnant of an old Virginia family.

Mose often walks eight miles to a crossroads store to get some beer and many times Pop has made the sixteen-mile hike with him. Mose buys a case of beer when he has the money. Then he starts off for home with the cargo in his arms. He'll walk maybe two miles and then he'll remark to himself that his burden is getting intolerably heavy and maybe he ought to drink a bottle or two to lighten the load. He'll stop and knock off two bottles, walk another half mile, sit down under a tree, drink three more, walk another half mile, and so on—reaching his cabin at last with an empty case.

One day Mose drank a dozen bottles of beer at the store before taking up his full case and starting the long journey home. When he got into the woods he soon grew thirsty. He drank half-a-dozen more beers, moved on, and then tried to drink some more, but he couldn't get the caps off the bottles. He had no opener, and his condition was such that he was unable to devise another method of uncapping the bottles. He couldn't even bite them off. He had to weave all the way home before he could get another drink and, once in his cabin, he resolved that this dilemma should never be put upon him again.

Having nothing else to do, Mose got busy acquiring bottle openers, and when he had about fifty of them he went into the woods with a hammer and a pocketful of nails. He hung beer bottle openers on trees all along the eight-mile trail to the store and nowadays he never gets home with anything but an empty case.

Living in the neighborhood is a lady who writes novels, and she has long taken an interest in Mose and Pop. One day she came down to the camp to see Pop.

"Mose has lice on him," she told Pop. "I found it out today. Now, Mr. Smith, I want you to get him down here and give him a good scrubbing and get some food into him."

Pop went up and got Mose, who was full of beer, and led him down to the camp. He got some water and heated it and put it in a galvanized washtub. Mose sat and mumbled. He was ashamed of himself, but he swore that the man didn't live who could give him a bath. Pop gentled him and told him that if he submitted and behaved himself, they would have a nice mess of black-eyed peas after the bath. Mose is crazy for black-eyed peas.

Mose began to chant:

"Drunk and lousy and black-eyed peas! Drunk and lousy and black-eyed peas!"

He kept it up all during the bathing operation and finally, cleansed and depopulated and fed, went back up the hill to his cabin. The next day he came into the camp again. He had been to the store. He was chanting:

"Drunk and lousy and black-eyed peas! Drunk and lousy and black-eyed peas!"

"Mose," said Pop, "you're drunk all right, but I guarantee you, you ain't lousy."

Mose laid a forefinger against his nose and studied this intelligence for a while. Then he began a new chant:

"Drunk and *crazy* and black-eyed peas! Drunk and *crazy* and black-eyed peas!"

Pop is in his early sixties. He has always been a remote sort of person to me, because I left home when I was fifteen. When I decided to go to Virginia and visit him I approached the thing a little sadly. I figured I would find an old man, spiritless and debilitated. When I first came upon him he was wearing an undershirt. He looks a good deal like Harry Carey of the movies, though younger if anything. His arms and shoulders and chest were the equipment of an athlete. His biceps were as hard as mahogany. There was little gray in his black hair and he had his own teeth. He looked as though he could lick any man his size. He could take a rifle and, without glasses, outshoot anyone in the neighborhood. And though work is the thing he hates most in life, he has a reputation for being the handiest man in forty square miles.

He was born and raised in southern Illinois and speaks a sort of Ozarkian language. He is immensely profane but seldom obscene. He can tarnish the welkin with beautiful cussing and when I complimented him on his talents in this direction he said he learned it at a tender age, hanging around a poolroom in McLeansboro.

He is one of the most impatient men alive. The editors of *Time* magazine might be interested to know that Pop talks back to their publication. He subscribes to *Time* and each week reads it from cover to cover, talking and cussing a blue streak—not really at *Time*, but at the human beings whose antics are reported in its pages.

During my visit he was telling me about his impatience with his fellow creatures. He said he had always been that way and told me a story in illustration.

"You was the first boy," he said, "and I suppose I felt a little like other fellas about it at first. Maybe you don't remember this, but when you was about four er five years old I made you a kite. Be god damn if I didn't work half a day on it. Made the best damn kite I ever saw in my life. Then I took you over to a field alongside the brickyard and give you the string, and stretched 'er out, and I held the kite. Then I hollered at you to run. Well, you run a little ways and the kite started goin' up and got up about fifty foot and, 'y God, you stopped and turned around to look at it. It started comin' down, and I hollered at you to run, and you run a little piece and then you turned around and looked at it again. I was cussin' you and tellin' you to keep runnin', but you'd only run a little ways and then you'd stop and turn around to look. Fin'ly the kite come down and I was so god-damn mad I walked up to it and stomped it to pieces and went on home and cussed every step of the way."

He worked hard during the years his nine kids were growing up. He worked in his father's brickyard, then as a cigar maker, and later in various poultry houses. He'd work all day and then come home and work. He built better furniture than you could buy at a store. He had a cobbling outfit and always half-soled all the family shoes. And he was the family barber.

Up until I was about ten years old Pop always cut my hair. It was a harrowing operation—perhaps the most horrible memory I have of my childhood.

I would be jammed into the baby's high chair. A sheet would be tied around my neck so tightly that it is a wonder to me I didn't die of strangulation. Then Pop, who enjoyed the business no more than I, would begin.

It always took him an unconscionable time, or so it seemed to me, and he kept up a running commentary throughout the operation—a flow of bitter, acid language that kept my scalp free of parasites. He made disparaging remarks about my hair. He objected to its texture. His speech, as I said, has an Ozarkian flavor. The syllable "ire" becomes "arr" in his tongue. Thus he speaks of a thing being "hard as arrn," and of "buildin' a farr," and so on. During those horrendous haircuts he'd keep growling:

"Hair jist like warr!"

The actual cutting of the hair was akin to being broken on the rack, yet it was as child's play compared to the torture that came with the conclusion of the transaction. Throughout the snipping (he never managed to acquire clippers) I must admit that I had a certain amount of compensating enjoyment from my father's unorthodox use of the nine parts of speech. But the climax of a haircut at home was unleavened horror.

Having finished the actual scissorwork, Pop would stand off and sight at me with one eye and then the other, cursing a bad job badly done. Then he'd unfasten the sheet, and I'd bend my head for the furious assault. This was the job of removing particles of hair from my neck and its environs. He would clap his large left hand down over my skull, lean forward, and start blowing and puffing. As he blew he would flail my neck with the flat of his right hand—full, vigorous blows they were too—huffing and cuffing for what seemed like an hour. When at last it was over, I would get out of the chair, stagger into the back yard, collapse on the grass beneath the cherry tree, and just lie there. If a wasp stung me I wouldn't even notice it.

I wish my memory of other things was as sharp as the memory of those haircuts. I do know that in those days Pop became a sort of unassociated socialist. He never belonged to any political organization, but, being a have-not, and being a man who did more reading than most of his neighbors, the time came when he got to thinking about the theories of socialism. It has often been remarked in the family that his socialism dated from the day he saw a photograph of the late John D. Rockefeller on a golf course. That was back in an era when the common man snorted at golf and wrist watches and mixed drinks. Pop saw this golfing picture of Rockefeller in a newspaper. He sat and stared at it for a long time, mumbling cusswords. From then on we'd hear him, now and then, in a new theme song that always went:

"God damn Rockafella!"

He clipped the picture from the paper and, making some paste out of flour and water, fastened it alongside the mirror where he shaved. It somehow represented his discovery of a new social philosophy and he wanted to have it someplace where he could look at it every day. And whenever he was looking at it, whenever he was shaving, we could hear him muttering: "God damn Rockafella!"

Gradually he expanded his philosophy. "Rockafella" remained a symbol of a world that was all wrong. I think that, within himself, Pop had decided, even back in those days, that Fate had given him a backhand blow. Here he was—a man with no talent for ruling a family, no talent and no inclination for the job—trapped! He always enjoyed drinking, but he couldn't drink and hold onto his various jobs. So he plugged along, nursing his bitterness, losing his temper sometimes, until his children were beginning to grow up and go to work. Then he quietly quit. Just said the hell with it, and walked away from it all.

Not long ago, during a Christmas shopping season, I remembered something out of my childhood, something involving Pop's inventiveness. I was in the most famous toy store in America and I was marveling at the ingenuity of the men who fashion our modern playthings. They had dolls that would do everything human except live together as man and wife. There were mechanical contrivances much more intricate than the inside of a cow. Watching these things whirr and whizz and click and clack, I got to thinking about a straight pin. I agreed that the toymakers were clever, but never so clever as Pop.

At Christmas time, when I was a kid, we always managed to get a few toys, some purchased out of Pop's pay envelope and some contributed by relatives. These toys were never, however, of an enduring quality and by mid-January we had broken them beyond hope, or traded them off, or thrown them at a cat. The rest of the year we had to depend on our own ingenuity for playthings.

Pop, as I have suggested, was a man who enjoyed reading his newspaper in peace each evening—those evenings when he didn't have shoes to repair or furniture to fix. Peace and quiet, in a house containing eight or nine children and a dog, is well-nigh unthinkable. He tried yelling at us, but you can't quiet that many younguns by yelling. Maybe for a few minutes, but then the leapfrog and the pillow fights and the quarreling start all over again.

One evening six or seven of us were creating the usual bedlam and Pop was trying to read his newspaper. At last he had an idea. He took a penny out of his pocket, got down on the floor, and began to rub the coin vigorously back and forth on the rug. All of us gathered about him, wondering if he had suddenly been stricken daft. He rubbed the penny for several minutes, then held it up for us to see. One side of it glistened as it hadn't glistened since it left the mint.

Pop then handed each of us a penny and set us to work. We rubbed those pennies until they shone like bright gold, and we were quiet about it too. When we had given a glitter to both sides of our coins we took them proudly to Pop. He received each one, examined it on either side, and in each case grinned and said:

"Hm-m-m-m. Bee-yootiful!"

Then he put the shiny pennies back in his pocket.

For a time after that, whenever the tumult grew great in the house, Pop would summon us to his chair, give us each a penny, and say:

"Go shine."

This assured him at least a half-hour of quiet. He always took the pennies back, but one day he made the mistake of letting us keep them. From then on he realized that it would break our hearts if he took them back. He had to invent a new game.

Again he got down on the floor, this time with a magazine cover and a straight pin. On the magazine cover was an illustration of a girl's head and Pop placed it flat on the rug, face up. Then, with the pin, he began sticking holes around the outline of the head. He made the pinholes as close together as possible and covered almost every line of the illustration—eyes, nose, mouth, chin, hairline. It took him a long while, and when he had finished he got up, went to the lamp, and held the sheet up to the light. To us it was pure beauty—a girl's head lined in sparkling pin points of light.

Thereafter Pop's evenings were quiet. When the hubbub started, he'd call us around, hand us each a pin, and say:

"Go stick."

We'd lie on the floor and stick by the hour. We got magazine covers from the neighbors and Pop brought home all he could find. We'd spend a whole evening sticking a single cover, and when we were finished we'd take the result to Pop. He'd put down his paper, take the magazine cover, hold it up to the light, and say:

"Hm-m-m-m. Bee-yootiful!"

During my recent visit with him I recalled this "Gostick" business and asked Pop if he had actually invented the game.

"Don't remember," he said. "Don't think I ever invented nothin' in my life."

It had been my hope that, by spending several days with him, I'd be able to mine some stories out of him. I told my brother Sam in advance of my intentions, but suggested that he keep quiet about it. I figured that if Pop knew I was planning on writing about him, he'd be inclined toward reticence. My brother did tell him—told him about a month before my arrival at the camp that I was coming down and that I might want to write some stories about his early life. Sam told me later that Pop made the eight-mile hike that day but not for beer. He came back from the store with a handful of writing tablets. He shut himself up in his cabin and wrote for a week and a half, neglecting his work around the camp and telling no one what he was doing. Sam knew he was writing, but never said a word to him about it. Then one day Pop returned to his customary labors. A week passed, and Sam finally asked him about it.

"Did you get finished writing your life story, Pop?"

"Who told you I was writin' enything?" Pop demanded.

"Ah, I knew it," said Sam. "Where is it?"

"I threw the god-damn thing in the stove and burnt it up," said Pop.

"What did you do that for?"

"I couldn't git no good endin' for it."

When I got to the camp, Pop never mentioned the manuscript he had destroyed, nor did I say anything about it. Once while we were sitting on the front porch of the cabin, looking out over the Potomac, Pop said:

"Heard you wrote a book."

I confessed the rumor to be true.

"Does a fella make any jack outa writin' a book?"

I said that some fellas do and some fellas don't, but that I had made a little jack out of the book I wrote.

"Well," he said, "in that case, I'll leave you buy me a beer."

It being midsummer, the eight-mile trip to the crossroads store was not necessary, since bottled beer was sold at the next camp, less than a mile down the river. To reach this place it was necessary to enter the woods by way of a crude road filled with deep mudholes. We made that trip half-a-dozen times, twice in the dead of night, and Pop did some talking along the way.

He knew that trail through the woods like a storybook Indian and in the dark avoided every mudhole while I, trailing along behind him, managed to cover myself to my knees with mire. Thus there wasn't much chance for conversation during the night expeditions, but when we went beer-hunting by day Pop talked of many things. He told stories about his cronies, Mose and the assistant plumber in the insane asylum. And he talked about how he almost got rich.

When his father died the will gave Pop two acres of land on the edge of McLeansboro. It appears now that, in the last few years, oil has been discovered in the neighborhood of the old homestead.

"Fer all I know," said Pop, "there may be oil wells right this minute on my property. I been afraid to ask. I'm damn near certain about it, though, it's not my property any more. I didn't keep it six months. I guess I wasn't made to own property. I kept worryin' about it and worryin' about it and finally I jist got on a train and went to McLeansboro and sold the two acres to my sister. I took the money and bought me an old Ford and went drivin' off. I'm jist like anybody else when they git money. I decided I wanted to travel, so off I went in this old Ford. Did I ever tell you about that trip? Had the god-damnedest time I ever had in my life. Never fergit it as long as I live. I remember I was drivin' down in Tennessee, right in the mountains where they have all these here hillbillies. I was drivin' along this mountain road one day, takin' it slow and enjoyin' the scenery, when a kid come runnin' past the car, goin' faster than I was. He was about eleven or twelve years old and had on some old overhalls and was barefooted and he was bawlin'. I sped up a little and caught up with him and yelled at him and he stopped. I got out and ast him what he was cryin' about. He says, 'Hit's my maw!' and kept on blubberin' away. 'What's your maw done?' I ast him. He looks at me a minute and bust out cryin' again and says, 'Hit's my maw! God damn her, she's a-tryin' tuh wean me!'"

Pop looked at me and grinned, and his manner seemed to indicate that he didn't think I believed him. I believed him. I told him about Leon Kay's little adventure in Louisiana. Leon Kay is an old friend of mine and in recent years has been making a big name for himself as a war correspondent. He is unique among war correspondents because he has not written a book and consistently refuses to even consider writing a book. Late in 1941 he was on a sort of furlough in New York and the United Press decided to send him into Louisiana to see United States troops in training.

One day Leon was driving along a quiet back road in the bayou country when he came upon a shack that might have been lifted off the stage of *Tobacco Road*. The house had a porch and on the porch sat a man and woman and six or seven children. Leon stopped because he needed water for his radiator. As he approached the porch, he noticed that all the people were barefooted except the old man. The old man's feet were wrapped in dirty bandages.

Leon asked for water, and one of the kids led him to a well at the rear of the house. Before leaving, Leon stopped again by the porch, to utter his thanks. Just to be sociable, he glanced at the old man's bandaged feet and said:

"Hurt your feet?"

"Shoe poisonin'," said the old man.

The old woman, who had been silent up to this point, now spoke:

"We all warned him. Tole him he'd git it effen he tried to git fancy and put on them shoes."

The old man grinned. "Yep," he said, "I shore got it. And listen." He bent forward and spoke confidingly, proudly. "Maybe you didn't know it," he said, "but shoe poisonin' is worsen blood poisonin', and that's a fack."

This anecdote set Pop to talking more about his travels, and then he got off on the subject of women. He's a misogynist. From all I've ever seen and heard and from all I can find out, he has always been a highly moral man in matters of sex. His magnificent cussing is blasphemous in character, never lewd. He simply dislikes women and refuses to pay them the compliment of talking about their questionable charms.

He got started on the subject by condemning the widespread use of the expression, "Like Mother used to make." He himself is an expert cook and he won't concede that women are talented in the same direction.

"You hear people talk," he said, "about how good their mothers could cook, but it ain't true. Kids will eat anything and think it tastes good. Almost all kids are that way. A growin' kid will eat the bark off a tree and think it's good. So when kids grow up and start losin' their appetites, they remember back when they used to eat their mothers' cookin' and how good it used to taste, and they think from that their mothers was marvelous cooks. Prob'ly nine tenths of them couldn't cook as good as old Mose can."

From that point he went to a discussion of feminine beauty.

"It's all the way you look at them," he said. "If you give some thought to it, you won't decide women are so beautiful. Men are always talkin' about how beautiful a woman's breasts is. Go look at one. Suppose women were built different than they are today. Suppose all the women in the world had only one breast apiece and it was right in the middle and had tits on it like a cow. What would the men say? Beautiful! They'd go around grabbin' at that unsightly thing and talkin' about how lovely and round it was, and how pink, and so on. All right. Suppose that's the way it was, and along come a woman with two breasts like they got now. Good God! That woman would be a circus freak and men wouldn't be able to look at her without getting sick at the stummick. So I got it figured out that a woman's breasts are unbeautiful, not to mention downright ugly."

I never, myself, thought of it in quite that way. Too late to start now.

Pop kept on talking about women and, I think, let go with his fundamental grudge against the sex.

"When I was a young fella," he said, "I got to thinkin' one day about the setup between women and men. There wasn't no justice in it. A man has almost always got to chase the woman. Maybe in some cases the woman is actually chasin' the man, but she don't let on that she is and pretends like she is hard to git. I got to thinkin' that the whole arrangement was wrong and oughta be changed. It oughta be switched around so the women would always be chasin' the men and tryin' to rape them. It oughta be that a man couldn't go out at night alone without women tryin' to pick them up, and he'd always be fightin' for *his* virtue. When I got to thinkin' about that, a long time ago, I got so all-farred god-damn mad at women that I never got over it. I wouldn't chase a woman if somebody offered me a whole case of beer to do it."

With this I agree. I don't suppose Pop's Utopia will ever come to pass, but it is pleasant to think about.

CHAPTER III *Wild Liars I Have Known*

OF ALL the talented liars the world has seen, I believe I have known a few of the most dazzling. Moreover, in the event a Liars' Rodeo were summoned in Madison Square Garden, I believe I could organize a team from the ranks of newspapermen and that team would meet and beat all comers, including talent agents, movie starlets, used-car salesmen and columnists.

The one salient characteristic of a newspaperman's lying is theft of material. He doesn't invent his lies—he steals them. Let me illustrate.

Eight or ten years ago the Chinese actress Anna May Wong arrived in New York from Europe and, as was the custom in those olden times, she was greeted at Quarantine by a group of reporters. They asked her all manner of questions about conditions on the Continent, and she gave them a few gay anecdotes. The interview was concluded and the gentlemen of the press departed in quest of other celebrities on the boat. One fellow, however, hung behind. When he and Miss Wong were alone, he said:

"Uh, Miss Wong, uh, well, you see, there was—— I mean, uh, well, Miss Wong, to be frank about it, there was one other thing I wanted to ask you, and——"

Miss Wong smiled and didn't give him a chance to finish.

"It's not true," she said.

I have heard no less than six different newspapermen tell that story and every one of them told it as having happened to himself. I'm pretty sure that the adventure actually belongs to John McClain, yet he is not one of the six I've heard claiming it.

The public, or part of the public at least, has long had the notion that newspapermen are romantic adventurers, and newspapermen seem to suffer the delusion worse than anyone else. Since the time of Richard Harding Davis there has been a tendency to associate newspapermen with the adjective "picaresque." The association is not too far-fetched. The dictionary defines picaresque as: of, pertaining to, or characteristic of, rogues or rascals.

When newspapermen get into the society of other people, at parties or other social functions, they sometimes get the itch to glamorize themselves. They seem to feel that it's expected of them, so they start telling lies. They appropriate stories belonging to other newspapermen, casting themselves as protagonist in each of the stolen dramas. I've stolen stories belonging to other reporters and I've had stories stolen from me. I'll never forget the time I had a dream stolen from me.

A dozen years ago that ex-harum-scarum redhead, Henry

McLemore, was one of my close friends. Henry was, and is, among the most eloquent of all God's creatures that possess mouths. He and I contributed in many ways to the public misconception of newspapermen. We worked together at the United Press, with offices in the *Daily News* building in New York. The *News* building has a circular lobby, featuring a huge terrestrial globe. This lobby is usually crowded with tourists, and Henry and I sometimes gave them a little show. We were young and gay then.

We'd come up Forty-second Street and enter the lobby through the main entrance. I'd come through the revolving door first, spinning the thing like a top. I'd have the brim of my hat turned up in front, a wad of paper in my left hand, a pencil in my right. As I charged into the lobby, I'd cry out:

"Gangway! Scoop! Scoop! Scoop!"

Then I'd rush through the bug-eyed tourists, toward the elevators, and into the lobby would come Henry, equipped the same as I had been and screaming:

"Stop the press! Stop the press! Stop the press!"

Henry and I were friends for a long time, but we drifted apart, and sometimes I think it was all because of my error in telling him about a dream I'd had.

It was a dream concerning two newspapermen named Ferguson and Morris. In the dream Ferguson and Morris quit the newspaper business and opened a pet shop. I went into the shop to offer them my best wishes for success and they immediately began showing off their specialty—the Bouncing Interchangeable Pussy Pups. Ferguson reached into a cage and pulled out a kitten. Remember, now, I'm still dreaming.

"Suppose," he said, "you want a kitten. All right. You got a kitten—a nice, fluffy, grade-A kitten such as this kitten I hold in my hand. But suppose you want a dog for a change. Now, watch it closely."

He threw the kitten to the floor, just as if it were a tennis ball. It bounced like a tennis ball, too, but when it came back to his hand it was no longer a kitten—it was a tiny pup. Another bounce, as he quickly demonstrated, changed the pup back into a kitten.

In the dream I told Ferguson and Morris that they had a

mighty neat article there, a nice piece of merchandise, and I even bought one—on time.

That was the extent of the dream. As I said, I told it to Henry McLemore the next day and he said it was as pretty a dream as he'd heard tell about in years. He began telling me about how he dreamed in serials—continued stories which picked up each night where they had left off the night before. I never suspected the larceny that lay in his black heart.

One day, perhaps a week after that, I was sitting in a tavern with a radio producer. We were waiting for Henry McLemore.

"Did Henry tell you about his dream?" the radioman asked.

Little suspecting what was to follow, I said he had not.

"Darnedest dream I ever heard of," he went on. And he proceeded to tell *my* dream of the Bouncing Interchangeable Pussy Pups. It was exactly as I had dreamed it, save that Henry had improved the utility of the Pussy Pups. The kitten turned into a pup on the first bounce, all right. But after that, the way Henry McLemore was spreading the dream around, the pup could be hurled to the floor and would bounce back as a ripe cantaloupe.

I listened to this tale of bald-faced thievery and said nothing whatever until Henry himself joined us. Then I flung it in his face.

"Henry," I said, "you stole my dream."

"What dream?" he demanded.

"My dream," I said. "My dream about the Bouncing Interchangeable Pussy Pups. You stole it, you dirty rat!"

I was astounded at his reaction. Right in front of that radio producer he had the effrontery to turn the accusation back against me.

"*Your* dream!" he cried. "What do you mean, *your* dream? That's *my* dream. I dreamed it. I never heard tell of such a thing. Trying to steal my dream from me. You know damn well I dreamed that dream and told you about it. I'll certainly never tell you another one of my dreams!"

I was so mad that I got up and walked out of the place. I stewed for a week. How was I going to get back proprietary right to that dream? How was I going to establish, before the world, beyond all doubt, that the Bouncing Interchangeable Pussy Pup dream was mine and mine alone?

Then the grim and bitter truth came in upon me. I would never be able to prove anything. The law of our land does not provide a shred of protection against the evil depredations of a dream thief. No jury on earth would ever be able to say, conclusively, whether Henry McLemore dreamed that dream, or whether I dreamed it. I had no witnesses.

I was exposed to lying journalists at an early age. One of my most vivid memories is concerned with Harold J. Trisker, who came on the scene during the days when I was employed on my first newspaper job back in Indiana. Harold J. Trisker arrived in Huntington one summer day and applied for a job as reporter on the *Press,* where I worked. He was a small man with something of the look and manner of Stanley Walker. I think he was more than a little mad. He had darting black eyes that never seemed to rest, and he was a pathological liar. I doubt if he ever had worked on a newspaper before, because he was the most incompetent hired hand ever taken on at the *Press.* Yet, to hear him tell it, he was the hottest reporter in the North Temperate Zone.

The moment Trisker had been placed on the pay roll he sat down and started lying. He began telling stories about newspapers on which he had worked. We were all greatly impressed for an hour or so, and then he gave himself away.

"You fellas ever heard of Pennsylvania?" he asked.

"Sure."

"Ever hear of Pittsburgh, Pennsylvania?"

Certainly we had.

"Well," he said, leaning forward and letting his eyes dart around, "my father owns the biggest newspaper in Pittsburgh, Pennsylvania, and that makes it the biggest newspaper in the world."

We weren't exactly cosmopolites, but we looked at one another and then let him continue.

"It's the most wonderful newspaper in the world," he

went on, "and I was the editor of it for a long time. It is the only newspaper in the world that *everything about it is marble*. The building is marble, the floors is marble, the wastebaskets is marble, the telephones is marble, and—*even the typewriters is marble!*"

From then on Harold J. Trisker was ours. We gave him his head, never smiled in the face of his fantastic stories, and awaited an opportunity. He couldn't write a simple birth announcement, and he couldn't approach the job of writing a simple birth announcement without saying:

"Y'know, fellas, this here reminds me of the time I was the star reporter on the New York *Times* and . . ."

It went on for a couple of weeks, and the more the Trisker lied, the more he was encouraged by our seeming gullibility. Then we framed him.

It was an elaborate plot, requiring the services of the advertising manager, the two circulation men, and three of us in the newsroom.

It began at ten o'clock one evening. I was, according to plan, away from the office and I telephoned Don Sullivan, the managing editor. He was alone in the newsroom with Trisker. It was a phony call, and Sullivan's conversation went like this:

"Oh, my God! In the Italian section? But I can't! I haven't anybody to send! How many dead? Oh, my God!"

Harold J. Trisker's eyes were darting like mad. A big story was breaking—he could tell that much. Sullivan hung up the receiver, grabbed his head in his hands, and began to groan. Then he got up and started pacing the floor.

"Biggest yarn in years," he said, "and here we're caught with no way of handling it!"

"Wh-wh-wh-what is it?" from Harold J. Trisker.

"Big shooting out in the Italian section, east of town. Some guy ran amuck, killed four people already. Oh, my God!"

"Let me go!" demanded Trisker. "Let me cover it. Please! Please let me go, Mr. Sullivan!"

Sullivan stopped and looked him up and down.

"Think you could handle it?" he asked dubiously.

"Just you give me the chance!" said Trisker.

"Well," said Sullivan, "there's no other way out. Go

ahead. Take a taxi at the corner and tell the driver to rush you to the Italian section. And above all, *be careful*. That's one of the most dangerous sections in the state of Indiana."

Harold J. Trisker went out the door like a cat escaping from a tennis-racquet factory. He fell halfway down the stairs and at the bottom slammed into Joe Gallagher, one of the circulation men, who was waiting for him. Gallagher wanted to know where Trisker was going in such a mighty rush, and Trisker, already winded, gasped out:

"Big shooting! Italian section! Gotta get a taxi!"

"Wait a minute," said Gallagher. "I got my car right here at the door. Come on, I'll take you."

They got into Gallagher's Model-T and drove eastward, out the Roanoke road. They were a mile or two beyond the city limits when Joe stopped the car. It was a black night.

"This is it," whispered Joe. "Off to the right of the highway there. We'll leave the car here and walk down that side road. The Italian section's just over the hill."

They got out of the car and started down the side road. Trisker was scared, but he was trying to act nonchalant. They were plodding along through the dusk and Trisker was saying:

"This makes me think of the time I was murder reporter on the Chicago *Tribune* and they sent me out to——"

Just then a loud voice, coming from a field off to the left, interrupted Trisker's reminiscences.

"THERE'S THE SON OF A BITCH! GIT 'IM!"

Two fiery flashes pierced the night as the shotgun roared. Joe Gallagher gasped, groaned, and dropped to the roadway.

"They got me!" he mumbled. "Run for your life."

His final phrase was wasted. Harold J. Trisker was already running for his life. He didn't turn and run back down the dirt road toward the car. He took a straight line toward town. A fence knocked him down, but he got up and rammed through it, and crossed a pasture with the speed of an antelope. Somehow he got back on the main highway and in another fifteen or twenty minutes dragged himself into the *Press* newsroom.

"Poor Joe!" he was wailing. "They got him! Poor Joe! Murdered him in cold blood!"

Don Sullivan forced him to get control of himself and write the story of the gory adventure. Trisker was clumsy enough at the typewriter under normal circumstances and now he was trembling like an old-time bride; yet he managed to turn out a magnificent piece of prose, full of the hysteria that was in his own soul. Naturally, it never got into the paper. There was another fake phone call. The police wanted the entire affair hushed up for the time being, pending capture of the mass murderer.

The deception was carried on for two days after that. Joe Gallagher had to stay away from the office. Trisker was told that Joe lay at the point of death in Huntington Hospital. There were frequent phone calls to and from the hospital. Zip Mason, the circulation manager (who had handled the shotgun), would walk solemnly into the newsroom and ask for the latest word.

"He's sinking," Don Sullivan would say.

Then Zip would start weeping. He was a good actor, and the tears would stream down his face past his mouthful of gold teeth.

"Dearest friend I ever had," he'd blubber. "And think of his poor wife and those eleven kiddies. No insurance. No food in the house. Bastard at the grocery store won't give them any more credit. No coal in the cellar. Oh, if it could only of been me instead of Joe!"

And then Trisker's eyes would fill up and he'd begin swallowing hard and turn his face to the wall, so we couldn't see his great grief.

On the third day Trisker was sent to the county jail on a routine assignment, to get the story of a man who had been arrested for beating his wife half to death with a cornet. At the jail he happened to run into the sheriff and began talking to him about the big shooting out in the Italian section. The sheriff quickly concluded he had a maniac on his hands. He spoke soothingly to Trisker.

"Yes," he'd say, "and so after that this Joe Gallagher did what?"

Trisker went over the entire story and then the sheriff lost his patience.

"Listen, you feeble-minded bonehead," he said. "There

ain't no Italian section and there ain't been no shootin'. Now, git outa here before I jerk a knot in yer tail!"

Trisker stared at him for a long time, then turned around and walked out. Nobody saw him after that—nobody, I mean, at the Huntington *Press*. He went to his room, and spent a couple of hours writing. Then he packed and left town, and Huntington has never seen or heard of him since. In his own way, however, he got his revenge.

The morning after he disappeared the Fort Wayne paper, which had an extensive circulation in Huntington, carried a front-page story. Harold J. Trisker's by-line was on it. The date line was Huntington. It started off something like this:

> *Joseph Gallagher, assistant circulation manager of the Huntington* Press, *lies at the point of death in Huntington Hospital, his body riddled by shotgun slugs, fired by an insane Italian, who ran amuck last Tuesday night and killed four persons. The mad killer is still at large.*

The thing went on from there, through all the gruesome details. Harold J. Trisker had written his big story and telegraphed it to Fort Wayne before taking his departure from Huntington. It reached the Fort Wayne paper just before dead line, and they put it on page one without ever questioning its authenticity. This proved quite embarrassing to the conspirators, especially after a Fort Wayne staff man arrived in town for a follow-up on the frightful Italian Section Massacre.

We were a daffy bunch around the old Huntington *Press*. I was the baby of the family, while at the other end of the age scale the patriarch of the tribe was John Darl. John was a linotype operator with a wolf complex. A wolf complex, back in those days, was not the same as a wolf complex today. John Darl saw wolves where other men could see nothing. And he saw wolves *before* he went on drinking sprees. He would come into the office, look significantly at everyone in the newsroom, and then say:

"Saw a wolf today."

There was nothing sinister or dramatic in his manner as he said it. He simply announced that he had seen a wolf, just as other people might mention the weather, a crick in the back, or the price of side meat.

Having said it, John Darl would pass on into the composing room and we, in the newsroom, would look at one another and grin. John Darl was ready for another brannigan. He would be orry-eyed before nightfall.

John had another peculiarity beyond his ability to see wolves. He was one of the few men I've ever known who actually enjoyed the ministrations of a barber. He was the world's champion barberee. The day seldom passed that he did not make at least one trip to the barber. For all I know he never ate, and his salary seemed to be equally allocated between barbers and bootleggers. You can imagine how he smelled.

Though John had his little eccentricities, he was a wise man. He denounced the cruel thing that we had done to Harold J. Trisker. He was a handy man with an epithet and he blistered us with hot language when we turned our attention to a young man named Ben Chiffriller.

Ben Chiffriller came from God knows where and got a job as night dishwasher at Tommy Ellis' restaurant on Jefferson Street, just around the corner from the *Press*. Ours was a morning newspaper and most of us worked until one or two o'clock in the morning. After that we'd adjourn to the Ellis establishment for food. John Moynihan, then a reporter on the *Press*, discovered Ben Chiffriller.

Ben was in his early twenties. He was a long, lanky fellow, built about like Jimmie Stewart, and it would have been necessary for him to think twice to qualify as a half-wit. He had long, greasy black hair that was forever falling over his face, which was just as well, because he had the face of a pure goon.

He hid his beautiful personality in the Ellis kitchen for a while and then one night, when John Moynihan was seated at the counter, Ben Chiffriller emerged from his steamy lair. He walked up to Moynihan, crooked his arm, and said:

"Feel that there muscle." Then he laughed like Mortimer Snerd.

Moynihan felt the muscle and passed a polite, complimentary remark about it, whereupon Ben Chiffriller laughed again like Mortimer Snerd and said:

"Watchy this here."

He threw his arms around Moynihan's middle and lifted him off the stool, amidst great gruntings.

"I'm strong as a horse," said Ben, punctuating the remark with another laugh and then fading back into the kitchen.

Moynihan told the story at the office and the rest of us became curious. We wanted to see Ben Chiffriller in action. He had become bold now and it was a regular thing for him to emerge and demonstrate his strength. There would be five or six of us lined up on the counter stools, and Ben would go from one to the other.

"Watchy this here," he'd say, and then he'd wrap his arms around us and lift us off the stools. It was amusing for a while, but after a few weeks his antics began to get on our nerves. Zip Mason had the idea. . . .

One night after he had submitted to being lifted a couple of times, John Moynihan remarked to Ben that he ought to take up prize fighting. He said that Ben had the perfect physique for the fight game and ought to be able to make a lot of money at it. Ben got all excited. He wanted to know how he might go about it.

"Why," said John, "didn't you ever hear of Zip Mason's reputation? Zip is an old prize-fight manager. Used to manage Jack Dempsey and put Dempsey where he is today. Maybe I could get Zip interested in you."

Zip did get interested in him. There was a conference the next night in the kitchen of the restaurant. Ben Chiffriller took off all his clothes and Zip walked around him, eying him critically, pinching him here and there, thumping him.

"Well," said Zip at last, "I believe it could be done. I think I could make a champion out of you. It'll take a lot of training, but I believe I could get you a match with Elmer Dempsey."

"Elmer Dempsey?" Ben repeated.

"Elmer Dempsey," said Zip, "is Jack Dempsey's brother, and Elmer happens to hold the wagonweight championship of the world. Have you got guts, Ben?"

"Uh-huh," said Ben, "and stren'th."

Thus began the training period. These incidents took place in the dead of winter. The first thing that Zip Mason had Ben do was get that mop of hair removed—shaved off. Meanwhile we enlisted the services of a linotype operator (not, to be sure, John Darl) and I began writing flowery articles about the new fighter, Battling Ben Chiffriller. The linotype man would put these articles in type, then we'd pull proofs, back the proofs up so they'd look like real newspaper clippings, and take them around to Ben.

Day by day there were new developments. All the stories I wrote were dated out of "Christmas, Indiana," which we described to Ben as the prize-fighting capital of the Middle West, and the home of Elmer Dempsey. Gradually the fake newspaper stories built up Battling Ben as contender for the wagonweight title. And Zip Mason went ahead with his training routine.

The thing eventually got out of hand. Almost everybody in town knew about it. Zip told Ben that his shoulder development was inadequate, and said that the time-tested way of strengthening shoulder muscles was to wash windows. That poor misbegotten moron would wash dishes all night, dreaming of the day when he'd be champion, and then when morning came he'd go up and down the block volunteering to wash the windows of the stores for nothing.

One night Zip showed up at the restaurant with a log chain. He told Ben that he'd have to start skipping the log chain around the block twice each night—with his shirt off. And Ben would do it. He'd take that chain out on the sidewalk with snow a foot deep and, stripped to the waist, skip it around the block. One night he came around the corner by the Huntington Hotel, skipping his chain like mad, and ran straight into the arms of old John Johnson, the cop. John Johnson was as big as a brewery horse and a man of tremendous sarcasms. When he got himself untangled from the log chain he stood off and looked at Ben and said:

"What in the name of holy Christ do you think you're doin'?"

"I'm in trainin'," said Ben.

"In trainin' for what?" demanded John Johnson.

"I'm in trainin' to win the prize-fightin' champeenship of the world," said Ben. Then he laughed like Mortimer Snerd. John Johnson glared at him a half minute, then said:

"I seen some squirrels in my life, but you got 'em all beat. Now, listen to me. You get the hell offa the street, and if I ever catch you out like this again I'll take that chain and ram it down your fool throat."

Ben came chain-skipping back to the restaurant and told of his encounter with the cop. Zip Mason decided to eliminate chain-skipping from the training schedule.

Came the great night when Elmer Dempsey arrived at the restaurant for the ceremony of signing the articles. Elmer Dempsey was impersonated by the linotype operator who had been setting up all the fake stories. This printer, whose name I've forgotten, was a heavy, muscular man with a face that could pass for a pugilist's.

Before the arrival of Elmer Dempsey, Zip told Ben not to take any guff off the champion. It was two o'clock in the morning when the linotype operator, engulfed in a heavy overcoat and his face half hidden by mufflers, strode into the Ellis Café.

The contract was a fearsome document which I had written and "Elmer Dempsey" had set in type. It was filled with clauses protecting Elmer Dempsey in case he killed or crippled Ben. It was a long and wordy instrument and after Elmer Dempsey had growled and shaken hands with Ben (almost ripping the boy's arm off) Zip Mason cleared his throat and read it all the way through, pausing now and then to remark to Ben out of the side of his mouth:

"Don't let this big bum scare you."

Ben stood up well under the ceremony and even tried to bluster a bit. At one point he crept up behind Elmer Dempsey, flung his arms around him, and lifted him off the floor. Then he laughed that laugh.

Back on his feet, Elmer Dempsey whirled on Ben, throwing his arms into fighting position, and I thought Ben was going to faint dead away. After Elmer had gone Zip Mason complimented Ben on his behavior.

"But," said Zip, "you look a little nervous to me. There's only one way to cure the nervousness of a killer like you. That's an asafetida rubdown."

The next day they gave Ben an asafetida rubdown.

Then, as might have been expected, Zip carried the thing too far. The day for the big fight at Christmas, Indiana, was fast approaching. One night Zip had Ben strip in the kitchen of the restaurant, looked him over, sadly shook his head, and said:

"I guess we'll have to cancel. You're twenty pounds overweight."

Battling Ben was overwhelmed with grief. He'd do anything, absolutely anything, to get that championship and all the money that came with it.

"Well," said Zip, "I hate to ask you to do it, but there's only one way in the world you can lose twenty pounds quick. I hate to ask you do it . . ."

"I'll do it," said Ben. "I'll do whatever you say. I'm gonna git in that ring and I'm gonna bust that ole Elmer Dempsey right in two. Tell me what I gotta do."

"You know where the livery stable is?"

"Sure," said Ben.

"Well," Zip told him, "there's only one way you can shed that twenty pounds. You go over to the livery stable and bury yourself in horse manure up to your neck. Tell the guy over there you want a big pile of it, and it's got to be warm horse manure. Bury yourself in it up to your neck and sit there for two hours. You'll lose the twenty pounds."

That killed it. Battling Ben finished work and went to the rooming house where he lived. Apparently a small doubt had crept into his mind, because he sat down and told his landlady all about it, and what he was supposed to do at the livery stable. The landlady was smart and saw at once what was going on. She tried to break it to him gently. And he— Battling Ben Chiffriller—packed his clothes as Harold J. Trisker had packed his clothes and departed, leaving no forwarding address.

CHAPTER IV   *Flight from the City Room*

TWENTY YEARS is not such a long time to a carp, because a carp lives to be one hundred fifty and doesn't worry much, being just as dumb at the age of one hundred forty-nine as he was at the age of two. Twenty years is, however, a long time in my estimation, for it represents the period I spent as a newspaperman.

During the first ten years I suffered from the common delusion that it was romantic and full of high adventure. Today I regard it as about as exciting as the melancholy stuff that comes out of an oboe. I have many friends who remain in the newspaper business and who believe that it is noble and heroic and honest. The thing baffles me just as much as it baffles me to see people standing in line waiting to have some feeble-headed ex-waitress foretell their future by the manner in which tea leaves settle into a cup. And I grow wary of those guys who used to be newspapermen themselves and who slobber into their beer about the good old days.

Generally speaking, a man who is adroit at posterior osculation is in a stronger position on a newspaper staff than the man who has competence but no taste for human ham. I've never had any talent for politics, and a newspaper city room is today a sort of political chamber of horrors. This is due, in large measure, to the arrival of the Newspaper Guild.

Up until I left my last newspaper job I was a member of the Guild and always voted on the "communist" side. By this I mean that I always supported the Newspaper Guild against its nasty enemies, and sometimes I think I did it simply because of the assortment of dyspeptic old ladies who made up the opposition. It always seemed that the nice guys were the strong Guildsmen, i.e., communists, whereas the "Rightists"—actually those who busied themselves trying to sabotage the Guild—were people who wouldn't say spit if they had a mouthful.

Personally, I've never admired communists because they operate on the theory that human beings are nice people. And I dislike reactionaries because they wear garters and go to the bathroom to pick their teeth.

Wrong Westbrook Pegler, the human saddle sore, is a prominent example of the type of mind that fought the Newspaper Guild with all the viciousness at his command. I've always considered Pegler to be one of the great writers of our day, but he has a foggy noodle. His handling of the language is a beautiful thing to behold, yet his thinking apparatus is warped; nine tenths of the inhabitants of Matteawan are his intellectual betters. Maybe he's sincere. Maybe he just doesn't know any better. I wouldn't know.

Please pardon me for writing about things that some people might consider to be serious, but I do want to recall one more thing. I remember back when the newspaper *PM* was being organized. A guy came to me one day and gave me a long talk. He said that my name had come up in a conference of *PM* editorial people—that they were talking about offering me a job. But, said my friend, they had strong misgivings about me. I wanted to know about those doubts, because I'm a good speller, write pretty fast, and try not to get cockeyed more than once a month.

"They don't think you're socially conscious," he told me.

I grinned and then asked him what I should do to rectify this failing of mine. He gave me the old song-and-dance, and when he was finished, I said:

"Listen. I don't like to see people shoved around either, but the crusader instinct is not in me. If they're gonna be shoved around, that's too bad. I've been shoved around a lot myself. So what? I'm not socially conscious by nature and I don't intend to take a course in it. I dislike capitalists and bosses just as much as you dislike them, but I also dislike the masses. The hell with them too."

The trouble with this world is . . . Also the hell with that.

There's a point about newspaper work that I've never seen discussed in print before—the weight of all the prejudices that go into the making of a newspaper story. Let us suppose that I have settled myself at my typewriter in the city room, prepared to compose an account of an interview. Do I think of the ultimate consumer? Do I think of the man or woman for whom this whole enterprise, in theory, is designed? Do I think of the guy who's going to lay down his three pennies for a copy of the paper? Faugh! If there is such a word.

I think first of the newspaper's general policies and then I think of the advertising department. After that I contemplate the personalities of the seven or eight men who might possibly handle my copy once it is finished. There are four assistant city editors. My story will pass through the hands of two and maybe three of them. I can't tell which of the four will get his hands on my masterpiece, so I must consider all of them. One is an ex-sailor, and if I can manage to work in some mention of a ship or the sea, he'll get out of his chair and whop me on the back and tell me it was a grand piece. Woe betide me, however, if I misuse a nautical term.

Move on to the next fellow. He's a veteran of the First World War. Get something of a military nature into the story and he'll smile and say it's fine, just fine. If at all possible, drop a little compliment for the gallant men of the American Legion, and he'll go to bat and demand a banner head for the piece. And the next guy. A complete nut about flowers and gardening. Get some flowers into the copy somehow, if only in a couple of similes, but get 'em right. Don't use such obvious things as roses or violets. Go look up a couple of good ones, and he'll beam all over the place and maybe, two or three days later, let you off work an hour early.

Now we come to the fourth man. He married a registered nurse and he fancies himself an authority on medical matters. He is a font of misinformation on the ills of the human body and I have seen him, in ten minutes' time, come close to killing men suffering from a common cold or a beer hangover. So, for this one, work in a medical term or two and he's in the bag.

The copy goes now to the news editor. He is an authority on the Far East and on aviation. Get one or the other or both into the story, somehow, even if you have to drag them in clumsily. Put the word "Orient" or "Oriental" somewhere in a paragraph and the moment he sees it, he'll mark the piece down for a good position in the paper and send it along to the copy-desk slot man—meaning the man at the head of the copy desk. Here's a tough one. This guy's hobby is collecting and reading the works of George Jean Nathan. If you can mention George Jean Nathan in your story—a difficult thing to puzzle out sometimes—he'll write "Don't trim" at the top of your essay, toss it to a copy-reader, then come straight to you and regale you with quotations from the works of Nathan.

As for the copyreaders—well, any one of perhaps a dozen might get your story. It's useless to carry the precautionary campaign beyond the George Jean Nathan man. Needless to say, all the copyreaders hate and despise George Jean Nathan and would throttle him on sight, simply because they have to sit there all day and listen to their immediate superior babble about George Jean Nathan. If you manage to get George Jean Nathan into your copy, the slot man will issue orders that the story is not to be cut, but those copyreaders will figure out some way of messing it up without appearing to butcher it. And they are, almost all of them, men with bitterness in their hearts and prejudices pouring out of their ears. They sometimes develop colossal hatred for a single word or phrase. I once knew a copyreader who suffered from a peculiar phobia. He could not bear the sight of the word "ergo." Whenever "ergo" popped up in a piece of copy in his hands, he would scream like a water buffalo brought to childbed, rip the paper to shreds, hurl his scissors and paste pot to the floor, knock over his chair, and start kicking the metal cabinet containing the atlases. I used to put "ergo" into stories now and then just for the pleasure of watching him run amuck.

So, what do we have here? If the story I write is handled tactfully, if it is written in such a manner that it will pass unscathed straight through to the copyreader, it will be a composition containing mention of the might of the merchant marine, the glory of the American Legion, the beauty of rare blossoms, the magnificence of the modern tonsillectomy, the mystery of the Orient, the horsepower of our fighting planes, and the wisdom of George Jean Nathan. To achieve this result is quite difficult when writing, say, an interview with Lana Turner.

I neglected to mention that as the author of the article in question I might conceivably have a few million prejudices myself and that I would be inclined to pile as many of them as possible into my copy. Newspapermen *do* have prejudices.

One of the best-known feature writers in New York has, in his desk, a little memorandum book which he calls his private son-of-a-bitch list. Let's call him Morton. His book is filled with names of people and institutions, and he is forever adding to the list. Maybe he will be walking up Broadway and he passes an author or an actor he may have met casually, two years earlier, at a party attended by two thousand other people. The author or actor doesn't speak to our friend, Morton. A note is made of this seeming snub, and the man's name goes into the son-of-a-bitch book. If ever the opportunity arises for Morton to take a crack at that guy, he takes it.

This Morton is a cantankerous fellow at times and holds cosmic grudges. Five years ago he had a date to meet a chorus girl in Times Square, and impure notions were in his mind as he started for the rendezvous. Just above Fourteenth Street his subway train stopped, due to some mechanical difficulty. Morton was ten minutes late reaching his destination and the chorus girl was gone. He was so furious that he went back down into the subway station, confronted the poor innocent attendant in the change booth, and shrieked imprecations at him. And to this day Morton hates the entire subway system, giving it top position on his son-of-a-bitch list. He enjoys nothing more than the minor assignment of writing a story about a suicide in the subway. He is a clever writer and he'll spend forty-five minutes deftly twisting the phraseology to suggest that the subway people are scoundrels, werewolves, and Peeping Toms.

A big insurance company is on Morton's list, for a purely personal reason, and so is the telephone company; he once had a fiery argument with an operator who wouldn't return his nickel.

He is a marvelous specimen of the human race and there's something tragic about him. He never goes through a single day without some kind of temperamental outburst. He lives forever in the belief that he is being put upon. Waitresses tell me that he is the most difficult customer they ever served, for he has never been known to eat a meal without complaining about it. He consistently accuses bartenders of watering his whisky and, when they deny it, he assaults them with language that scorches the varnish on the bar and explodes the brandy bottles.

I remember one evening when Morton walked into Dominic Settiducatti's tavern, ordered a martini, and settled down at one of the tables for a few games of knock rummy. It is Morton's custom to continue drinking until he is finished for the evening, at which time he pays the tab. Always, however, he howls against the reckoning, charging that he is being swindled and threatening to notify the State Liquor Board. Mr. Settiducatti knows Morton and his habits only too well. It is Mr. Settiducatti's unvarying custom to keep a careful, accurate account of the number of drinks served to Morton.

On this particular evening the card game continued for hours, and Morton ordered martini after martini. Back of the bar, Mr. Settiducatti kept a count through a series of white chalk marks on a baseball bat—an instrument he keeps handy for packing ice in the beer cooler and for quieting unruly rewrite men.

At last Morton finished his session at knock rummy. He got up from the table, walked to the bar, pulled out his wallet, and asked for the reckoning. Mr. Settiducatti counted the marks on the baseball bat and announced that Morton had consumed seventeen martinis.

The guy nearly exploded. He achieved new heights of acrimony. He grew hysterical as he denounced Mr. Settiducatti for a highwayman and a heel. Then he seemed to get control of himself. He stood there at the bar, glaring his hatred at Mr. Settiducatti, and when he spoke again it was in icy accents.

"You'll never get it from me. As long as I live, I'll never pay you. I'm walking out of this filthy joint and, so help me, I hope I drop dead if anybody ever catches me in it again. You are a cheap, petty thief, and you've robbed me for the last time. Trying to charge me with seventeen martinis! The proof is right there. No man living could drink seventeen martinis and stay on his feet. Good-by, you guinea gangster!"

He turned, walked halfway to the door, and fell on his face.

Most of Morton's troubles are purely imaginary, yet he remains one of those ill-starred fellows who seem always to be blundering into difficulties.

One day a man prominent in the theatrical world got in touch with Morton about a job. The theatrical man was going to give him a marvelous job, paying twice the salary he was getting on the newspaper. They arranged to meet in a booth at a quiet restaurant just off Times Square.

This was Morton's great opportunity—the thing he had dreamed about. Here it was, coming true. He sat in the booth, opposite the theatrical man. They had a couple of drinks and then they ordered dinner. Morton got a plate of clam spaghetti. They talked on as they ate and things were going swimmingly. Then something happened. Morton had his mouth full of clam spaghetti. Before he could catch himself, before he could even turn his head, a tremendous paroxysm seized him, his mouth flew open, and he sneezed a mighty sneeze, splattering that theatrical man from chest to scalp with clam spaghetti. The Savior himself wouldn't have hired Morton after that.

☆   ☆   ☆

While I always stood on the side of the Newspaper Guild, there is one crime for which it is responsible. Before the coming of the Guild there was usually a certain fraternal spirit among the members of a newspaper's staff. They had their individual quarrels and sometimes they were long and interesting feuds, but, for the most part, they all worked together and played together.

Nowadays newspaper shops are split into two warring groups—the Leftists versus the Rightists. The bitterness of this political vendetta is a wonderful thing to behold. The quarreling and fighting go on interminably and people work in the same room with one another for eight hours a day without speaking. The enmities that arise are not transient in character, but endure.

Let's examine the case involving Herb and Vince, two rewrite men on a New York paper. They occupied adjoining desks, and after edition dead lines were accustomed to sit and gab about the world, mankind, women, the Dodgers, Saroyan, and even the Guild. Herb was a Leftist and Vince was a Rightist, but they got along all right, arguing the question without venom, playing saloon together after work, respecting each other's talents, and keeping their hands off each other's wives.

One morning Vince arrived at his desk with a grim look on his face. After a while Herb said something to him. Vince didn't answer—didn't even look up.

"What's eatin' you?" asked Herb.

"Don't speak to me!" snapped Vince. "Keep away from me and don't speak to me!"

"Hey!" from the startled Herb. "What's come over you?"

"Listen," snarled Vince, "I know what you called me behind my back and I want no more to do with you and your kind. I'm getting my desk changed today."

"Hold it!" said Herb. "Whadda ya mean I called you something behind your back? I don't get it."

"You called me a Fascist bastard and you know it."

"You're a liar!"

"Ned Purdee told me all about it—you called me a Fascist bastard in Nick's last night."

"Ned Purdee's a god-damn liar!"

"And you're a stinking communist pimp!"

"Okay. Okay," from Herb. "If that's the way you feel about it, then you *are* a Fascist bastard."

"Take your glasses off, you dirty Red!"

They both wore glasses and they both whipped them off, and what followed was one of the most peculiar fistfights in history. Once they had removed their glasses, both boys were virtually stone blind. They began swinging wildly, but they could neither see each other nor anything else, and Herb slugged a big stone pillar three times before he realized it wasn't human. Not a blow was good in the wild minute of activity before the thing was broken up.

From that day forward Herb and Vince ceased to be friends, and around their office, among the other members of the staff, it became a joke to say, whenever an argument developed: "Put your glasses on and I'll beat your brains out!"

There were rousing fights in the pre-Guild days, but they were usually over women or the spelling of a word or other trivial matters, and quite often they were carried out on something of a heroic scale. Let's go back to the Denver *Post,* as of 1928, for another fight story—the epic of Bosquet versus Whipple's proxy.

Both Jean Bosquet and Sidney Whipple were reporters on the *Post* staff. Whipple is a little man and Bosquet is twice his size. As I remember it, Whipple was writing a story one day when Bosquet came along and picked up his first sheet of copy.

"Listen, Sid," he said, "why don't you put the lead on——"

"Put that down!" said Sid.

That was the beginning. They quit speaking, and pretty soon they were saying nasty things about each other, and it was inevitable that the thing should soon reach a grand climax of some sort. Provocation followed provocation, and at last Bosquet announced one night in the Denver Press Club that he was going to maim Whipple, who declared that if Bosquet ever laid a hand on him he, Whipple, would kick Bosquet in the crotch till he bled.

Bosquet sent a courier to Whipple, challenging him to a death grapple at the Press Club on the following evening. Whipple returned word that he'd be there at nine o'clock and that Bosquet should get right with God.

All these flamboyant negotiations were carried on with the aid of certain stimulants distilled from sugar beets, but when the next day dawned, both men knew that there had to be a fight that night.

Obviously Whipple was no match for Bosquet—it would be much the same as putting Roy Howard in a ring with Joe Louis. So Whipple took steps. He decided to hire a proxy. He approached Barney Cohen, a stalwart young man employed in the *Post's* reference department. Barney was as big as Jean Bosquet, if not bigger. Sid came to the point at once. He would be willing to engage Barney as a mercenary—pay him money to fight Bosquet. They haggled a bit, then settled on ten dollars cash plus whatever medical expenses might be incurred. The compact was made.

Came ten o'clock that night at the Press Club. Most of the *Post* staff had assembled in the club lounge. Bosquet was there, brooding over the wrongs he had suffered at the hands of Sid Whipple, speaking of his sorrow that he should have to do this thing to Whipple's family.

Then the front door opened. In came Barney Cohen and behind him, almost hidden from view, was Sid Whipple. They proceeded to the center of the room. The rest of us formed a big circle and inside the circle a fantastic conference took place. It was all done in dead pan. Sid announced that he had hired Barney Cohen to fight for him, adding that if Bosquet was any kind of a man he'd accept the situation. Bosquet was in a fury—so much of a fury, in fact, that he did accept it.

The entire company adjourned to the alley at the rear of the Press Club. Automobiles were brought up to furnish floodlights. Bosquet and Barney Cohen removed their shirts, squared off, and then ripped into each other. It was a beautiful fight. They slugged and grunted and bled and slugged and bled and cursed, and all that time little Sid Whipple was scampering around at the very border of the battle, crying:

"Hit 'im, Barney! Kill the son of a bitch!"

They fought for a good twenty minutes and neither man gave ground. By that time, however, they were both exhausted. Suddenly they stopped slugging and fell into each other's arms, sobbing. We led the gladiators back into the club and there were drinks all around, and then more drinks all around, and more after that, and pretty soon Bosquet and Whipple were hanging on each other and vowing eternal friendship.

"Jean, old pal," Sid Whipple was saying, "if you'll only do one thing for me. Sing 'The Rosary.' You sing it lovelier than anybody on earth."

So with Whipple at the piano, Bosquet sang "The Ro-

sary." It was—particularly after all that juice of the sugar
beet—one of the most touching scenes I have ever witnessed. Yet if one had been a "Fascist" and the other a
"Red" they'd be fighting to this day.

CHAPTER V   *Chiefly About Hugh Troy*

PRACTICAL JOKERS are as common as bum spellers
around a newspaper shop. Hoaxing, in fact, seems almost a
part of the business. I have worked on more than a dozen
newspapers and each of them had at least one practical
joker on the premises.

My initiation into Journalism was by way of a fairly common joke. It came on the second day of my employment at
the Huntington Press. I remember that it was a steaming
afternoon and I was applying myself to the hen scratches
used in proofreading when Mr. George Wood, foreman of
the composing room, stepped into the editorial department
and engaged the managing editor in conversation.

"I've got to have that nonpareil spaceband," said Mr.
Wood, "and I've got to have it right away. You'll have to
find somebody to send."

The two of them looked at me, and I was all eagerness
to serve. At last they decided I was trustworthy and the
managing editor told me to trot down to Rox Cartwright's
print shop and get a nonpareil spaceband for Mr. Wood.

Rox Cartwright's print shop was a good half mile away
but I got there in handy time. Mr. Cartwright was a tall,
solemn man, and when I told him I had come to get a nonpareil spaceband for Mr. Wood, he looked me up and down
and said:

"Where's your truck at?"

I assured him I had no truck, whereupon he sighed heavily and led me around to the rear of his shop. There he dug
an old wheelbarrow from a pile of junk and pointed out a
huge piece of machinery as being the nonpareil spaceband.
I helped him load it on the wheelbarrow, thanked him, and
started off with it.

The nonpareil spaceband proved a greater burden than I had ever been called upon to handle before, but I tugged and shoved and sweated until, at last, I arrived in the alley alongside the newspaper office.

Mr. Wood came into the alley, took one look at my unwieldy cargo, and began to purple the neighborhood with strong language.

"Take it back!" he cried. "Take it out of my sight! Take it back to Rox Cartwright and tell him for me that he's gettin' old. I said nonpareil spaceband, and what does he send me! A pneumatic slug line! Heavenly God!"

The trip back with that pneumatic slug line was much worse than the original journey. I could only make it a few feet at a time, and nothing but a single hope bore me up. I figured that the genuine nonpareil spaceband would not likely be as heavy as the pneumatic slug line Rox Cartwright had given me by mistake.

Finally I reached the print shop, gasping for breath, barely able to tell the proprietor what Mr. Wood had said.

Rox Cartwright shoved the wheelbarrow to the rear of the shop and dumped the huge hunk of iron—actually part of an old flat-bed press—onto the ground. He was looking over an even bigger chunk of machinery when human compassion caused him to turn and examine me.

It must have been fairly obvious that I would never be able to stand up under another trip with a nonpareil spaceband. Rox Cartwright stood and studied the thing over in his mind a bit, then he spoke:

"You better go on back to the shop. This is a little joke they played on you. You go on back and tell George Wood that enough is enough, and also tell him for me that he's an old goat. There is no such thing as a nonpareil spaceband, and if there was a nonpareil spaceband, it wouldn't be no bigger than the blade of a pocketknife. Now, go on back."

Since that day I have witnessed the perpetration of innumerable practical jokes. I could write a book about practical jokes and I'd do it except that I am a physical coward and have no appetite for being hanged. There is an immense popular prejudice against practical jokes. Kindly people look upon playful hoaxing as criminal and classify the practical joke with the pun. I'm not altogether in agreement with them. I won't undertake to defend the practical joke, but I will speak for the pun. Its enemies usually employ the old aphorism: a pun is the lowest form of wit. Yet the pun has had some distinguished champions. Charles Lamb, for example, wrote:

"A pun is a noble thing *per se*. It fills the mind; it is as perfect as a sonnet; better. I never knew an enemy to puns who was not an ill-natured man."

A practical joke can be wantonly cruel—as in the case of Battling Ben Chiffriller—and again it can be an innocuous work of genius. Years after the affair of the nonpareil spaceband it was my privilege to make the acquaintance of the most accomplished practical joker of the contemporary scene. He is a thirty-five-year-old artist named Hugh Troy. At the present writing he is in the Army. I began hearing vague stories about him almost from the moment of my arrival in New York, but I didn't meet him until ten years had passed.

Hugh Troy stands five inches above six feet, which may account for his becoming one of New York's leading muralists. The day I first met him I lunched with him beneath one of his murals in the café lounge of the Savoy-Plaza and I noticed that the headwaiter scrutinized him carefully as we entered the room, as though he expected Hugh to break forth a bundle of Roman candles or turn loose a chipmunk.

At first Hugh tried to argue me out of a project I had in mind—writing an article about his career as a practical joker. He was well aware of the stigma that seems to attach itself to the business.

"My reputation as a practical joker," he said, "is affecting my reputation as an artist. I get a commission from some big company to do a mural, and then the president of the company finds out about me. They have me under suspicion from that moment on. When I get through with a job they come around in committees and go over my paintings with magnifying glasses, looking for gags. I've always tried to soft-pedal my extracurricular activities."

Later he changed his mind and we adjourned to a less

fashionable gin mill where he spent the afternoon remembering his exploits.

Hugh Troy's father was a professor at Cornell and Hugh's penchant for pranks dates back to his boyhood in Ithaca.

"When I was a kid," he said, "the people next door closed their house and went off to Europe for six months. They had a big cherry tree in their back yard. We heard they were coming back two weeks before their arrival in Ithaca. My brother and I spent those two weeks hard at work. We filled that cherry tree full of apples, fastening them onto the limbs with bits of wire. We used two barrels of apples, and when the people came home and saw their cherry tree bearing apples, they called in half the town to look at the miracle before they found out it was a hoax."

Hugh's parents usually spent a couple of months away from Ithaca each year, leaving the two boys home with Grandma and a maid. Grandma Troy, whose great age kept her indoors, was pure Irish and believed implicitly in the little people. She became the victim of a game which Hugh invented, called Getting Grandma Behind.

"As soon as my father and mother left," Hugh explained, "I would begin on Grandma. Chiefly by manipulating the newspapers, I would mix up her calendar, first getting her a day behind so that she believed Friday was really Thursday and finally getting her to the point where Sunday, at our house, was actually Wednesday.

"On Wednesday morning my brother and I would bring out the Sunday papers, which we had kept hidden for four days. The maid would cook up a chicken dinner and Grandma would lead us in prayer. It was even more difficult to bring Grandma back up to date when the time approached for the return of my mother and father. But we always managed to do it, and Grandma never found out."

Hugh attended Cornell, and his years at the university were made up of a succession of gags. The skipper of a dinky trolley car came to resent Hugh's presence in town. Whenever the car approached, Hugh would step forward and signal it to stop. Then, with easy nonchalance, he would place one foot on the car step, tie his shoelace, utter his thanks to the motorman, and wave the trolley on its way.

A certain professor of architecture at Cornell—prototype of the absent-minded pundit—habitually wore rubber overshoes to class if the weather report even hinted at rain. One very wet day Hugh purloined the rubbers for a few hours and painted them to resemble human feet. He then covered them with lampblack and put them back in the locker room. That afternoon the unsuspecting professor started home in the rain. He had walked no more than a block before the lampblack was washed away and such citizens as happened to be abroad were startled to see him sloshing along, so it appeared, in his bare feet.

When he had finished college Hugh Troy came to New York to make a name for himself as an artist. Usually he shared living quarters with other college men and usually they were up to no good.

Early one morning Troy led four companions down Fifty-fourth Street to Fifth Avenue. They wore overalls, carried picks and shovels, and had provided themselves with red lanterns and "Men Working" signs.

Opposite the old Rockefeller town house they set to work ripping up the pavement. They labored through the morning and by noon had dug quite a hole in the street. Hugh posted flags and signs and they knocked off for lunch. He led his fellow laborers into the dining room of a fashionable hotel near by. The headwaiter was horrified as the grimy workmen tramped into his sedate precincts. Hugh quickly identified himself and whispered:

"It's all right. It's a little joke the manager wants us to put over."

After a hearty meal, during which many of the other guests sniffed in the general direction of the chandeliers and then stamped out of the place, Hugh led his boys back to the diggings. They worked through the afternoon until they had a hole big enough to drop a Buick into, then they put up their lanterns and signs and quit. Their gaping excavation was not officially discovered to be a fake until nightfall of the following day, and a couple of years went by before the identity of the gang foreman became known, by which time anger had abated and there was no prosecution.

Another time Hugh and one of his friends were sitting on a bench in Central Park. They sat quietly until they saw a policeman approaching. Then they got up, picked up the bench, and started walking away with it. The cop, to be sure, came charging down on them, demanding to know what in the name of heaven they thought they were doing with that bench.

"Oh," said Hugh Troy airily, "we're just taking it home."

"Takin' it home, are ya!" roared the cop. "Well, I'm takin' ya to the station house."

At the Arsenal Precinct in the Park the lieutenant changed color when Hugh placidly produced a bill of sale showing that the bench actually belonged to him, that it had been built to order for him and he had paid for it.

The lieutenant was in a fury but could do nothing beyond sending Hugh and his friend away with their bench. They hurried at once to the north end of the Park. This time they hid in the shrubbery with their bench until they saw a cop ambling in their direction. They came out of the bushes carrying the bench, but this time they were running, looking furtively in all directions except that where the startled cop was standing. He caught them.

Back in the station house they again faced the livid lieutenant. He blasted them with profanity and assigned an officer to escort them out of the Park and to their home.

"I don't know what the law says about it," the lieutenant declared, "but I know that if you come back in this Park with that bench, I'll make a personal issue out of it, and I'll tear that bench up and beat your brains out with the planks."

In those days Troy lived in Greenwich Village and often patronized Loew's Sheridan Theatre, where he preferred to sit in the rear of the balcony. He is so extraordinarily tall that one day his head got in the way of the beam from the projection room, messing up the picture on the screen. The audience hooted and stamped and the manager came on the run. He gave Hugh an expert tongue-lashing, which was an error.

A week or so later the film in which Garbo first talked opened at the Sheridan. Hugh took a seat off to one side of the balcony. He waited until the picture was well started, then he quietly opened a small can he had been carrying in his pocket. Out flew a dozen moths, and they made directly for the beam of light and stayed there. Garbo not only talked—she blemished.

Hugh has baffled and confused many citizens who have had the misfortune to call a telephone number and get his phone by mistake. If they were calling the druggist, he'd be the druggist. Or the butcher, or the boy friend, or the Committee for the Protection of the Holders of Bonds Sold through G. L. Miller & Co., Inc. (Rector 2-3289). Hugh always played all the parts ad lib.

During one period he was continually getting calls intended for a bookmaker. Hugh accepted bets and quoted odds and had a magnificent time inventing horse names.

"Who win the fifth at Belmont?" a caller would ask.

"Belt Buckle," Hugh would say.

"Who?"

"Belt Buckle win it."

"I don't get it. Sounds like you said Belt Buckle."

"I did say Belt Buckle. Belt Buckle win the fifth at Belmont. Crotch Cricket run second."

Then Hugh would hang up—leaving the horse player bewildered and convinced that, at last, he had begun to hear strange noises.

There was a woman in Queens who repeatedly got Troy on the phone when she was seeking some other number. For a while he tried arguing with her, but she was stubborn, insisting that she had the right number. Hugh tried all sorts of things, but the nuisance would not abate. At last he resolved on vengeance. He considered the thing for a long time before he acted.

"I'll drive her crazy," he said. "I'll drive her crazy on one single subject."

He chose turkeys as the subject and he set out deliberately to make the woman turkey-conscious. He knew her identity and her address. He bought a huge carton of Thanksgiving Day greeting cards all bearing turkey illustrations. He began mailing these so she would receive one in every mail delivery. He showered her with reams of literature concerning poultry shows, with entry blanks for prize turkeys. He sent her, now and then, a cheap roasting pan with instructions on how to cook a turkey. And about once a week he'd dispatch a telegram to her, saying:

GOBBLE GOBBLE GOBBLE

"I kept it up for six months," he said, "and then I began to get sick of turkeys myself. I don't know what effect it ever had on her."

On election night in 1932 Hugh was walking through Times Square when his eyes fell on a stack of tabloid extras carrying big black headlines:

ROOSEVELT

ELECTED

He could think of nothing to do with the papers at the moment, but the notion struck him that someday they might be useful. He bought a dozen copies, took them home, and stowed them away in a closet.

Three years later he invited a few friends to his apartment for a New Year's Eve party. After a few cocktails the crowd decided to range around town in quest of adventure. There were no definite plans and at the last minute Hugh remembered his election extras. He got them out, gave a copy to each of his guests, and they hurried to the nearest subway station.

For three hours they rode the subways, always standing in the aisles, each with a copy of the old newspaper. Passengers in the seats would look up and see a man reading a newspaper which proclaimed, ROOSEVELT ELECTED. Farther down the car would be another man reading the same paper. It was confusing no end.

Being one of the tallest men in New York City, Hugh Troy has a little trick that often startles his companions. All over town he has twenty-five-cent pieces hidden on ledges. He'll be walking in Times Square with some acquaintance. Suddenly he'll say:

"Excuse me just a moment."

Then he'll step over to the wall of a theater or a hotel,

reach up to a ledge, and pluck a quarter from it. I suppose he collected his hidden wealth before he went off to war.

"If I ever get rich," he told me that afternoon of the long talk, "I'm going to buy a yacht and call it the *Great White Also*. When I was in elementary school, back in Ithaca, I came upon a line in my geography which said:

"The Arctic is inhabited by the brown bear, the black bear, and the great white also.

"It worried me. At home I asked about the Great White Also. The family let me go on believing that a Great White Also was some horrible, child-eating beast, and whenever I misbehaved they used to tell me that the Great White Also would get me. I think it would be a wonderful name for a boat."

He confessed to one great frustration and one great ambition.

He was walking on Fifth Avenue one day when the window display in a fashionable beauty salon caught his eye. It was a representation of a "Temple de Beauté." In the foreground was a single flickering flame—the flame of eternal beauty or some such thing. For a long time Hugh schemed and plotted ways of getting into the salon window unobserved, but he never made it. He wanted to hang a frankfurter over the eternal flame.

It's unlikely that he'll ever achieve his remaining ambition. He wants to buy out the entire orchestra of the Metropolitan Opera House on opening night and issue the invitations for all the seats in that section.

Every person in these seats, by prearrangement, would have thick black hair save only a certain number of bald men, who would be placed in such a manner that, viewed from the boxes and the balconies, their bald heads would spell out a four-letter word.

The dot over the *i* would be provided by no less a person than Dr. Nicholas Murray Butler.

CHAPTER VI   *Dissertation on Strong Drink*

SEVERAL YEARS AGO a St. Louis scientist who is personally allergic to liquor conducted an extensive survey among drinkers and non-drinkers. He wanted to find out the essential differences between a guzzler and a teetotaler, and he reported his conclusions to the American Psychological Association.

He found that drinkers like:

1. Attending murder trials.
2. Poker.
3. Boxing matches.
4. Quail shooting.
5. Women.

And his report showed that teetotalers like:

1. Attending graduation exercises.
2. Using a typewriter.
3. Swinging in a swing.
4. Looking through telescopes.
5. Hunting wild flowers.

At the time this report was published I was already a drinker of long standing. If I hadn't been, I'd have switched over at once. I'm not much of a hand at quail shooting, but the rest of the qualifications fit.

There is only one rule governing my own drinking. I never sing while engaged in tilting the flowing bowl. This self-imposed restriction is a precaution against sudden death—not necessarily because I'm a lousy singer. There was a time when three highballs would invariably set me to wailing about "My Melancholy Baby," but no more. I have a small phobia about singing during drinking hours. It dates from the time I was reading a book on Greek history and came to the story of Terpander.

This Terpander was a Greek poet and musician and, according to tradition, invented the *scolion,* or drinking song. Having invented it, he had to show that he was proud of his invention. He had to go around singing drinking songs and to do that he had to get drunk. Consequently, Terpander was generally plastered and singing *scolia*. One day in Sparta he crawled out of bed, took a couple of bromos, and staggered around to another drinking party. (Greek civilization was glorious.) As soon as Terpander got a few under his tunic he began singing *scolia* as usual. The book doesn't tell us the name of the song he was singing but we do know that somebody at the party didn't like it. Terpander was warbling away when this unknown critic picked up a fig and threw it at him. Just at that moment Terpander was reaching for a high note. His mouth was wide open and into it flew the fig, whereupon Terpander choked to death, everybody applauded, and all hands had another snort.

Let that be a lesson to you, as it has been to me. Don't ever sing while you're drinking.

In my casual explorations around New York City I've seen the inside of many saloons and I'm thoroughly in favor of them. When I say saloon I mean saloon—not night club. A night club is no fitten place to go for serious drinking. I was a working newspaperman in New York for twelve full years before I ever stepped inside the most celebrated of all New York clubs—the Stork. Perry Charles, the movie magnate who cuts his own hair, took me to the place one afternoon to meet an actress. It was altogether too elegant and refined for my tastes. The Stork is definitely not an establishment in which a man might fall down without attracting attention. Customers in the Stork say "Hodja do?" and the males sometimes kiss the hands of the females right in front of everybody. It is not at all like Harry's Palace Bar & Grill.

I had long been interested in the personality of the Stork's proprietor, Sherman Billingsley, but I had never met him. Mr. Charles produced Mr. Billingsley and Mr. Billingsley sat down at our table. I had anticipated a suave, superior sort of guy, but he wasn't that way at all. He is an easy-mannered fellow with a Middle Western drawl and a frank manner of talk.

Mr. Billingsley is and has been for some years a virtual social dictator in New York City. Lots of society people consider being barred from the Stork Club as the greatest disgrace that can come upon them. Playboys have been cut off without a cent simply because Mr. Billingsley put the rope up against them, and debutantes who incurred his disfavor have been shipped off to convents by their humiliated parents. So, sitting in the presence of such a powerful force, I wanted to know one thing.

"Do you come from society people?" I asked Mr. Billingsley.

"Lord, no!" he said. "I'm a hillbilly. I grew up in Oklahoma—a town named Enid. My mother and father came out of the mountains of Tennessee and they never had anything. My father was an odd-jobs man when he could find any odd jobs. There were nine kids, and I was the youngest, and I had a tough time of it. If I wanted a dime, I had to go out and scratch for it. I worked at all kinds of jobs. I can even remember how I used to collect old bottles and sell them to a junk dealer to get a few pennies. If you call that society, then I'm society."

While Mr. Billingsley was engagingly amiable, I still didn't care much for his joint. The people who go regularly to the Stork have a good time, no doubt, but it's altogether synthetic. Their talk is affected and their moments are filled with pretense and posturings. Most of them are nothing more than oil slicks on the sea of life. In the Stork Club I heard a girl greet a guy with: "Dahhhhhhh-ling! How clevah of you to guess I was here!" At Harry's Palace Bar & Grill a girl's greeting to a guy is more likely to be: "Gitcher gahddam hands offa me, yuh filthy heel!"

Well, some people like one thing and some people like another.

The Stork would never have fitted the drinking personality of a man like Joe Carroll. Joe was a newspaperman who weighed over three hundred pounds. When he fell off a bar stool he shook the entire neighborhood and it required the labor of four strong men to pry him loose from the floor. He always drank double scotches and at times would offer an explanation for that habit. He said he had once been compelled to submit himself to a psychiatrist, and the psychiatrist had decided, after diagnosing his noggin, that he was a schizophrenic.

"I am a split personality from wayback," Joe would say. "I got a split personality and I always order double scotches—one for each of my personalities."

He was cured of drinking by a miracle. One summer afternoon he was throwing his tremendous weight around in a water-front saloon. He lurched over to the pinball machine, managed to fumble a nickel into it, and started a game. His body-english must have been at fault, for he lost his balance and fell on top of the machine. One elbow crashed through the glass cover and struck one of the bumpers. This created some sort of a short circuit in the house and set off a loud burglar alarm bell on the front of the building. In Joe's fuzzy mind, he had hit the greatest jackpot of all time. Beyond that he couldn't reason. It was a pure miracle. He staggered out of the place and went home, and from that day to this has not touched liquor. He won't even talk about the stuff.

A few blocks from Mr. Billingsley's place is a restaurant and bar where I sometimes go for a slice of life. It has a deceptive appearance. There's a small bar at the front but the rest of the place has a tea room atmosphere. On entering this establishment the first impulse is to turn around and go out. Then you notice the bartender. The bartender is a gray-haired old gal wearing a beret. She gabbles incessantly in the harsh voice usually found in veteran actresses. Her talk seldom makes any sense yet it's almost as exhilarating as her booze. She seems to suffer the delusion that all her male customers are aviators.

"Well," she'll say, "where the hell you been flying lately?"

The boys who stop regularly at her place usually have fictitious stories all ready for her—wild tales of heroic flights. She listens to these fantasies with no suggestion of either enthusiasm or doubt, and when they are finished, she generally leans across the bar and says:

"You ought to have your head examined."

Her customers delight in ordering cocktails from her. She is capable of mixing a few of the more common monstrosities, but when someone asks for a dubonnet or an orange blossom or a pink lady, she throws up her hands, and, after calling the customer a few salty names, tells him if he wants a drink like that he can get behind the bar and mix it himself.

The lady bartender is not the sole attraction of this establishment. There is Hilda. Hilda is the restaurant's fortune-teller. She makes the least noise of anyone in the place, sitting quietly at a small table and advising customers about their future.

She is a nurse at one of New York's leading hospitals during the daytime and spends her evenings at the restaurant. She tells fortunes for the sport of it and for desserts. Customers usually offer her a cash gratuity but she pushes it away and says:

"I don't want your money, but I'll let you buy me some dessert."

Then she picks out a dessert from the menu and orders it. Hilda is dessert-daffy. She has been known to eat fourteen desserts, ranging from butterscotch pie to banana splits, in a single evening; yet she still weighs less than one hundred and twenty pounds.

I first heard about Hilda from one of the lady bartender's "aviators." But I didn't believe she was a nurse because nurses don't generally go in for the occult. One evening I gave her a play. As soon as I sat down opposite her she began her goofy chatter, turning over cards and telling me about trips and investments and deaths in the family. I paid little attention to this stuff but just sat back and waited until she had finished with my destiny. Then I offered her a dollar. She pushed it back at me.

"I'll let you buy me some dessert," she said.

After she got busy with a hunk of chocolate ice cream, I asked her casually if it were true that she works days as a nurse.

"Sure," she said. "That's why I'm all out of sorts tonight. Had another falling-out-of-bed epidemic at the hospital today. That's a thing medical science has never figured out. Nobody understands it. I think it proves something, but I don't know what it is."

She seemed willing to let the matter rest there, being out of sorts, but I urged her on and she continued:

"In the first place, when a patient falls out of bed in a hospital, it's like an international crisis. Everybody connected with it has to make out a long report. Under some circumstances you are not permitted to put the patient back into bed until you've gone through a lot of red tape. House doctors, the patient's own doctor, and head nurses have to be called. It's something like a murder case.

"Well, the strange thing is this: hospitals have epidemics of this falling out of bed. We'll go along for maybe a month or two without a single case and then—thump, thump, thump, thump all over the place. You'll get four or five in a single day, and three or four the next day. It's beyond me what causes it.

"We had two women and a man fall out of bed today. It put everybody on edge. Looks like the beginning of an epidemic, and those things drive the whole hospital nuts. Ask any nurse or any doctor. They'll tell you. I hate to think of tomorrow. Probably get half a dozen more."

By this time she had finished her ice cream and I figured I was cutting in on her time—preventing her from earning more dessert—so I got up and left. The lady bartender yelled at me before I got to the door.

"Hey!" she sang out. "Did Hilda treat you okay?"

"Sure," I said. "Fine."

"Where you flying to now?" she asked.

"Burbank," I said.

"Well, happy landings, you jerk!" she shouted, adding a few more names as I went through the door.

A lovely place. I know of only one other bartender in New York who can be more entertaining. His name is Hector, and for years he worked in a downtown saloon frequented by newspapermen. He is a small man with dark hair and sharp black eyes. He has a fierce, impassioned manner of telling a lie about himself.

One night in 1936 Hector left the saloon at his customary hour of departure and nobody in the neighborhood saw him or heard anything of him for four years. Then on a summer day in 1940 he walked into the place, nodded casually, took off his coat, tied on an apron, and stepped behind the bar.

"Was home with my sick whale, name Bill," he said to

his old boss, and his old boss shook his head in perplexity and let it go at that.

Hector's monologues are never boring even to a bore, and the most famous of them concerns his head. Whenever he makes an error in drinks or in giving change, or drops a glass, he smacks his forehead with the palm of his hand and cries out against Fate.

"This head!" he exclaims. "You see the mistake I make dumb? It is not me. It is this son-of-a-gun head. It is not my head. Long time ago I am in the war fighting. I am on Italian side. Was twelve o'clock. Was guns go bang all around. Bang! Is shot off my head. I look around to find him, but I cannot see nothing because I forget my eyes is gone too.

"Then I hear the captain he yell to charge. I do not like to disappoint. I feel on the ground and find this head and put him on. It is all right head for fight but when I look in glass, it is not my head. It is Austrian's head with big mustache. Look, I show you."

He lifts his chin and points to his throat. There is a thin scar on his neck.

"I do a good job putting him on, no? But he is a bad son-of-a-gun head. He is head for a young man, not me. He is always talk crazy. What can I do about? How can I tell Austrian head to stop talk too much? Maybe would not be so bad but for one thing. Head always is looking at ladies. Make me go crazy. Is bad."

Among many stories told about the late Ring Lardner is one in which he was approached by a newspaper friend who said:

"Hey, Ring. Let's get drunk tonight."

"What day is it?" Lardner asked.

"Wednesday."

"Can't. Got an appointment next Tuesday."

Mr. Lardner was thinking of that delicious affliction—the hangover. Westbrook Pegler has written extensively about hangovers and to my mind he is competent as an authority on them. Miss Elsa Maxwell once remarked that she doesn't drink alcoholic beverages, explaining that she doesn't have to drink because she was born intoxicated. Mr. Pegler was born with a hangover. In his several disquisitions on the jeebies, or feebles, he has nonetheless missed an important point. A hangover is the worst infirmity known to man because it excites no feeling of sympathy. Let a man show up for work with the sniffles or a sprained ankle or half his ear bitten off and his bosses and associates are full of solicitude for his well-being. But let him come in with the inside sweats and the feeling that a moose is having a baby in his head and he becomes an object of scorn. The boss punishes him with extra work and his associates creep up behind him and yell "Boo!" and otherwise torment him. It is no wonder that, when the sun gets over the yardarm, he heads for the hair of the dog. There is simply no such thing as commiseration for a man with the black-butterfly ague.

I remember the case of a young man known around Broadway as a playboy. One night he got vigorously lit and in the early hours reeled to his room in a midtown hotel. His friends knew that when he awoke he would be feeling far from chipper. It happened that the circus was in town and the young man's "friends" went to work. Early in the morning they arrived at his room and with them came a troupe of midgets. The little people were given their instructions and left there.

It was almost noon when the young man awoke with the complicated trembles. He groaned and grunted a bit, felt around in the air for enemies, rolled over in bed, and opened his eyes. He saw a dozen tiny men and women scattered over the room, calmly going about the business of getting dressed, reading the morning papers, sipping from tiny coffee cups, mending socks, and paying no heed whatever to him. The young man gave himself a few extra shudders and shut out the view by closing his eyes. Soon he went back to sleep, and when he awoke again, everything in the room was as it should be. When he finally was able to drag himself out of bed he swore off drinking forever and a day. Before long, however, his pals revealed the joke to him and that made everything all right. He canceled his pledge.

It may be pure legend, but I've often heard the story of the rich man who has a "hangover room" in his mansion. In one version the mansion is located outside Lima, Peru. In another it is on Long Island.

The "hangover room" is constructed with every detail upside down. The floor is the ceiling with an elaborate chandelier thrust upward from the center. The rugs and furniture are fastened to the ceiling, upside down of course. Pictures are upside down. The fireplace is upside down. The windows with their shades and drapes are upside down.

The proprietor of this remarkable room often entertains at parties where the wine flows freely. As might be expected, his guests sometimes pass out. What happens then shouldn't happen to a dog. The insensible guest is carried into the trick room and placed on the floor (ceiling) midway between the chandelier and the wall. Put yourself in his place and imagine his sensations when he regains consciousness.

He finds himself lying on the ceiling, looking down at the floor. He sees ash stands with cigarette butts resting in their bowls. Flowers are in the vases, magazines are scattered on a table, a desk top is littered with assorted inkstands, books, papers, pencils.

I have no idea what the victim's thoughts might be. He probably figures at first that the law of gravity has been repealed overnight. Then he must recognize that such reasoning is illogical, since nothing else in the room has risen to the ceiling. He moves his body cautiously and finds that he is neither nailed nor glued to the ceiling. What to do? Should he begin crawling across the ceiling to the chandelier and achieve an anchorage there until help comes? Or should he creep toward the wall and try to crawl down it to the floor?

Personally, I'd rather have the midgets.

Of all the hangover stories I've ever heard I believe Lejaren Hiller's is the most novel. Mr. Hiller is one of New York's leading commercial photographers. About twelve years ago he went to the home of a prominent man, Mr. L., in Greenwich Village. Mr. Hiller wanted to take a photograph of Mr. L. and use it in a testimonial advertisement.

Mr. L. told him he never went in for that sort of thing—that the proposal was out of the question.

"But," he said, "let's not have any hard feelings about it. Sit down for a while and we'll have a drink."

They had a drink and then another, and pretty soon they finished the better part of a bottle and they were feeling quite good about everything. Mr. L. was rich as well as prominent and had a closet full of liquor. He suggested that maybe they ought to invite some more people in. He then called up a couple of his friends and invited them over, and Mr. Hiller phoned two or three of his own pals, and they came, and before long the joint was jumpin'.

Some time during these proceedings Mr. Hiller passed out cold. When he opened his eyes it was morning and he was lying on a divan in Mr. L.'s living room. He felt terrible. He prowled around a bit on the ground floor but found no sign of human life so, dazed and bewildered, he got out of the house, into a taxi, and went home. In his own apartment he collapsed on the bed without even bothering to take off his clothes.

Later in the day the telephone awakened Mr. Hiller. It was one of his friends who had been at last night's party. The friend was excited.

"Didn't you hear?" he yelled over the phone. "Mr. L. committed suicide this morning!"

Mr. Hiller threw some cold water on his face and straightened his necktie and hurried over to Mr. L.'s house. Sure enough, Mr. L. had done away with himself and the house was swarming with cops. Mr. Hiller sat down and told them his story. The cops said there was no doubt that it was a suicide and told Mr. Hiller he could go home.

Arriving back at his own apartment, Mr. Hiller decided it was about time he took a shower. He was removing his shirt when he saw something that shocked him to attention. There was writing of some kind all over his bare chest. Looking down at it, he couldn't quite puzzle it out, being still slightly fuddled. He got a couple of mirrors and fixed them so he could read it.

Someone had used India ink and a brush to write on Mr. Hiller. He almost fainted when he read it. It was Mr. L.'s last will and testament. And it was signed by two of the guests who had attended last night's party.

Mr. Hiller gathered up his galloping thoughts and wisely called a friend who was a lawyer. The lawyer listened to his story and then said: "Good God! Never heard of such a thing! Stay right there and I'll be over."

The lawyer came over and examined the chest writing. Mr. Hiller wanted to wash it off and forget about it forevermore.

"You can't do that," said the lawyer. He pointed out that witnesses had signed the epidermal testament.

They got in touch with a surrogate and went to his chambers where Mr. Hiller peeled off his shirt and showed him the chest testament. The surrogate was duly impressed and after studying the thing awhile said to Mr. Hiller:

"Were you a witness to this will?"

"No, your honor," said Mr. Hiller in all truth.

The situation was without precedent, but the surrogate handled it nicely. He had a photographer called in, Mr. Hiller bared his chest, and the last will and testament of Mr. L. was photographed. After that Mr. Hiller rendered an affidavit, telling his story, and the surrogate said he could go home and wash off the will.

When Mr. Hiller told me the story of his hangover, he said he was certain that the decoration of his chest started out as a joke after he had passed out. From his friends he learned that Mr. L. himself wrote the will and appeared to be having a lot of fun while doing it. Had he already decided to kill himself? Or, having written the testament on Mr. Hiller's chest, did the idea of suicide occur to him later? Mr. Hiller doesn't know the answer. Nobody does.

I don't vouch for the authenticity of the story, but Mr. Hiller swears it is true. I had one semi-scientific question to ask after he had finished his narrative. Did he, after that weird adventure, go on the wagon?

"Not for a minute," said Mr. Hiller.

Before I have done with the subject of bibbing I want to set down a confession. It is a confession made and rendered in the interests of historical accuracy. It is undertaken with a humility that amounts almost to shame, for it involves the admission that I once double-crossed a good friend.

Some months ago that amiable codger Benjamin DeCasseres chose to recall in his newspaper column certain events that took place on the twelfth floor of the Waldorf-Astoria on the afternoon of December 5, 1933.

Mr. DeCasseres wrote with unconcealed personal pride and with a total disregard for true facts. There are two reasons why truth was abused in his essay. In the first place, he does not know and could not possibly remember, with any degree of clarity, precisely what happened that afternoon of December 5, 1933. And in the second place, it would be well-nigh impossible for him to know the truth. For ten long years Benjamin DeCasseres has been living a lie.

A week prior to that December day in 1933 it came to my attention that Prohibition was approaching its end in the United States. I was then employed as a feature writer in the New York offices of the United Press. I knew that I would be called upon to write some sort of fancy report on the death of Prohibition, so I cooked up a stunt.

With the facilities of the United Press at my command, I decided to make it possible for a single individual, selected in advance, to take the first legal drink swallowed in the United States of America in thirteen years. I wanted to get H. L. Mencken for the enterprise but Mr. Mencken, who leans to beer, was in Baltimore. Then I thought of Ben DeCasseres, whose home I frequently visited and who was always fond of discussing his alcoholic capacity.

Mr. DeCasseres fairly leaped at the chance to make history, get a free drink, and get his name in the newspapers. I arranged for him to meet me at the Waldorf-Astoria immediately after lunch on December 5.

Before going to the hotel myself I had to check all the arrangements. The end of Prohibition was to be accomplished in Salt Lake City where the Utah Constitutional Convention was voting that day to ratify the Twenty-first Amendment, which repealed the Eighteenth Amendment. Ratification by three fourths of the states was necessary, and Utah was the thirty-sixth state to vote.

The United Press had, of course, a direct wire from the Salt Lake City convention hall into its offices in New York. I arranged to have another wire set up between the office on Forty-second Street and a room in the Waldorf-Astoria. The flash would come from Salt Lake City to New York and then would be swiftly relayed to us in the hotel suite and Mr. DeCasseres would hurl the first legal drink down his hatch. A telegraph operator was installed in the hotel suite and at the other end of the wire, in the United Press office, sat Alfred D. Greene, night wire chief of the United Press. Mr. Greene was to relay the flash to the hotel the instant it bounced off the wire from Utah.

I had a brief whispered conversation with Al Greene before I left the office for the hotel.

Arriving at the Waldorf suite, I found Mr. DeCasseres with an illegal highball in his hand and an expression of beatific abandon on his face. The hotel management had agreed to furnish a bottle of liquor for the stunt, but a marvelous mistake had been made somewhere along the line and an entire case of scotch stood on the floor beside a divan.

Mr. DeCasseres and I, with two hours to go before the flash from Utah was due, began making inroads on that scotch. After a while Mr. C. V. R. Thompson, New York correspondent for the London *Daily Express,* telephoned and asked if he might chisel in on the stunt. He wanted to have Mr. DeCasseres interviewed, over the transatlantic telephone, by one of the editors of his paper in London. I agreed to this, being already in an expansive frame of mind, and before long Mr. Thompson joined us and was assigned to a bottle of scotch, at which he began taking heroic belts.

The telegraph operator was making a show of testing the hookup with Al Greene, but I could see him casting envious glances at us, so he was invited into the party. Mr. DeCasseres, who once described himself as an intellectual faun, was in good form, as he usually is, and was making an effort to remember how many times he had been hurled bodily out of Jack's restaurant in the old days.

Around four-thirty the brass sounder began chattering and Al Greene informed us that the Utah delegates had assembled and that the flash would be upon us within the next ten minutes. Having given us this warning Mr. Greene telegraphed an off-the-record query:

"Have them bums started drinking yet? Wish I was there."

The telegraph operator was in his place at the table and Mr. Thompson began putting his call through to London. Mr. De-

Casseres sat across the room in an overstuffed chair and said:

"Whose house are we in? The bounty of the Lord! Columbia, the gem of the ocean! God giveth and God taketh away! Vengeance is mine, sayeth the Lord! Hard work never hurt anybody!"

I directed Mr. DeCasseres to the chair he was to occupy during the historic ceremony. He was across the table from the telegraph operator. The London connection had been completed and a telephone was placed in Mr. DeCasseres' left hand. He began talking to the British editor as though the transatlantic telephone were a fake and a fraud, as though he were actually shouting across the bosom of the sea. I fixed him a fresh highball and another for myself.

We settled into our assigned places. Off to one side stood Ted Saucier, of the Waldorf staff, wondering if he hadn't made a horrible mistake by permitting such goings on in these austere precincts. I stood directly behind Mr. DeCasseres. Mr. Thompson was at his side and had taken the telephone away from him.

"In a few moments," Mr. Thompson was saying into the instrument, "we shall have the flawsh from Utah. Then Mr. DeCasseres shall take the first drink, and then I shall put Mr. DeCasseres on the wire for the interview."

It was 4:39 P.M. We were all tensely quiet, though weaving a little. Then the telegraph instrument sounded.

Click pause. Click pause. Click.

Unobtrusively I raised my glass to my lips and took a long swig. At once the instrument broke into a chatter.

"Flash!" yelled the operator. "Prohibition repealed!"

Mr. DeCasseres drank—drank fiercely, pouring part of the highball over his chin. He put down his glass and Mr. Thompson handed him the telephone.

"Hurrah for Tom Paine!" cried Mr. DeCasseres across the ocean. "This is the second Declaration of Independence! Bang the fieldpiece, twang the lyre! Whoooooopeeee! Gimmy another drink, boys, I'm thirsty!"

The man in London tried to get in some questions but Mr. DeCasseres wouldn't stop. He was bursting with patriotic fervor and international brotherhood. He spoke feelingly of Thomas Jefferson, George Bernard Shaw, Wayne B.

Wheeler, and the Gaekwar of Baroda. He declared his personal love for all the peoples of the world and scotch whisky. He was still going when Mr. Thompson wrenched the telephone from him and rang off to save money.

After that I had to write a report of the affair for immediate use on the United Press wires. It was not the most intelligible piece ever written but it had words in it. When I had finished with it, we sat around and had some more scotch, and then I had to return to the United Press offices to write a story for the night wires.

I left Mr. DeCasseres trying to remember for Mr. Thompson and a couple of visitors—Lou Wedemar and Forrest Davis—the number of times he had been thrown out of Jack's in the old days.

So that is actually what happened on the afternoon of December 5, 1933, in the Waldorf-Astoria. Mr. DeCasseres never suspected that he had been double-crossed. He could not know that when the telegraph instrument clicked three times, those clicks were a signal to me. Al Greene was telling me that the flash had come in, that Utah had voted, that Prohibition was no more. Al Greene was giving me the better part of a second to quietly take the first legal drink. And I took it.

☆   ☆   ☆

If Al Greene's role in the foregoing episode seems secondary, that would be misleading. Mr. Greene seldom plays a secondary role in anything. He is one of the rare characters of this earth. I worked alongside him for five years and had dinner with him almost every night during that period. In all that time, however, I never had a single luncheon with him. Al Greene does not eat lunch, and for an interesting reason.

"When I was about twenty," he once explained to me, "I worked in the depot at Wichita, Kansas. I was the telegraph operator. Well, it was a pretty good job for a young fella so I got married. Beautiful girl. We took a little bungalow about a mile from the depot and I bought a bicycle.

"At noon each day I got forty-five minutes off for lunch. I'd rush out of the depot, jump on my bicycle, and pedal like mad for home, get there, jump off my bike, and run into the house. Then, with about five minutes to go, I'd come running out, get onto the bike, ride down to the depot, and go back to work. I didn't eat a bite of lunch for a whole year. Got out of the habit, I guess. From that day to this I've never been a lunch eater."

CHAPTER VII   *Sports Section*

BEING AT HEART a non-joiner, I have succeeded in attaining the age of thirty-five without accepting membership in more than three organizations. These are the American Newspaper Guild, the Lions Club, and the North American Committee for the Suppression of Classical Music.

The North American Committee for the Suppression of Classical Music was founded by a newspaperman, Bert Mac-Donald, who quickly appointed me first vice-president. We sought no further members but held a meeting at once and drew up our program. It follows:

1. Refuse to read when "Music to Read By" is being broadcast.

2. Snicker, on all occasions, at Met deficits.

3. Attend Carnegie Hall concerts and cough all through them.

4. Get Toscanini off the air.

5. Demand that the house buy every third drink.

This organization withered and, for all I know, may have died. As for the Lions Club, I became a member of this group when I was editor of the local newspaper in Sebring, Florida, back in 1926. The Lions met once a week for luncheon at the Hotel Nancessowee, and I lasted one meeting. I arrived five minutes late and found that the club inflicted a penalty for tardiness. I was compelled to mount a chair and sing a little song. The song went like this:

> *I'm a litt-tul prairie flower,*
> *Growing wilder every hour;*
> *Nobody cares to cultivate me.*
> *I'm as wild as wild can be.*

While singing this song I had to place my right hand above my head with the middle finger pointed downward, and then I had to revolve slowly on the chair until the song was finished. I did it.

This matter of the Lions Club is brought up because it marks the climax of my career as an athlete. Two days after that first meeting the Lions Club baseball team played the Sebring Volunteer Fire Department. A young man named Payne Sebring was supposed to pitch for the Lions, but when time came for the game to begin he could not be found. Somebody asked me if I knew how to pitch and I said certainly and took the mound.

So far as I know they are still playing the first inning and the firemen are still at bat. They hit every ball I threw at them. I'd try throwing them ten feet out in front of the batter, but those firemen would simply run out of the box and slap them. All this time one of the head Lions kept running up and down the side line. He was a man with a crippled back and he walked or ran in a bent-over posture. As he moved up and down the side line he kept crying out in an agonized voice:

"Pain! Pain! Pain!"

For a while, out there on the mound, I thought the poor fellow was suffering physical torment. Then it dawned on me that he was actually hollering:

"Payne! Payne! Payne!"

He was yelling for Payne Sebring, who still hadn't shown up.

Naturally, this continual crying for the Lions' regular pitcher didn't do my control any good. When the score reached nine to nothing with nobody out and the bases loaded, they yanked me. The shortstop took over the pitching job and the man with the bad back went in at short. I went home. I didn't attend the next Lions Club meeting, or any after that, and I'm sure nobody minded.

In a land where major emphasis is placed on sports, it seems I have always missed out completely or got going in the wrong direction. In the parochial schools I attended I can recall but four athletic pursuits: fist fighting, throwing rocks at telephone poles, running around the block, and burn-ball.

The game of burn-ball was a variation of baseball. It was played with a hollow rubber ball slightly smaller than a tennis ball. The pitcher delivered with an underhand swing and the batter used his fist, knuckles forward, for striking. It was permissible to pull the sleeve of the shirt or sweater down over the fist, or wrap a handkerchief around it, to take out the sting. After the batter hit the ball, he pursued the usual course toward first base, though it wasn't necessary for the fielders to throw to the first baseman. All they had to do was hit the runner with the ball. I hurt all over just thinking about it. Nobody ever *tossed* the ball at the runner. It was thrown always with full force, and the most capable fielders were those who could hit a runner in the face. Getting hit in the cheek, or even on the arm or leg, was as painful as an earache on an elephant. If you were ever stung on the cheek by a wasp, or hit in the leg by a shotgun blast, you have some idea of what it meant to be put out in burn-ball.

Once or twice a week Father John, our parish priest, was accustomed to play burn-ball with us. He was a man in his forties, a stern, frightening figure to most of us. Though we didn't know the word tyrant, we considered him to be one, and he knew that we did. I know now that he was a good man and a reasonable one. He proved it by forgetting old scores and coming out regularly to join in that brutal pastime of ours.

He made a little game out of getting into the game. He'd come out of his house and wander into the schoolyard, reading his office, pretending he wasn't aware of the burn-ball game. After a while he'd close his book and stand and watch us a bit. Then he'd ask if he could get in, and we would joyfully welcome him into the contest. He'd shuck himself down to his shirt, even removing his collar, and he'd play until he could no longer stand the punishment.

How we gave it to him! At all other times Father John was in the driver's seat, but in burn-ball we had him where we wanted him. Meaning no disrespect, I am impelled to say that Father John was sensitive where he sat. He was inclined toward pudginess in that direction and his black britches had no slack at the hips. It was a glorious experience to get a square shot at that bottom, and an ignominious thing to miss it. Father John rarely hit the ball out of the infield and the fielder who got it almost always ran forward so he could get a good bead on Father's sensitive spot. We rarely missed, and I can see him now, scampering toward first base and, on coming within a few feet of it, hunching his shoulders a little against the awful stab that he knew was coming. He was well aware of our sadistic intentions but he never complained, and I don't think he ever padded himself against those painful assaults. Nonetheless, he couldn't stand up under them for more than four or five direct hits, at which point he'd make his excuses, pick up his clothes, and head for the house, never giving us the satisfaction of rubbing the sore places while in our view. It was great sport to have him in the game for a while, but it was a relief when he departed because we could never take the name of the Lord while he was around. There was only one proper remark for a boy to make when, running the bases, he was stung with a full-bodied hit. That was: "Jee-zusss Kay—ryst!" Father John's presence placed us under severe restraints.

My athletic background was meager, then, when I left school and went to work on the Huntington *Press*. After a time they put me to work covering basketball games and, a little later, somebody on the paper got the notion of making a sports editor out of me. This project failed because of a sort of stubborn iconoclasm on my part. The fellow who had been serving as sports writer was going away somewhere and he was told to break me in for the job.

We had a semi-pro baseball team in Huntington and a nice enough ball park for a town of its size. I knew the fundamental rules of baseball but the job was to learn score-keeping. The retiring sports editor took me to the park one Sunday afternoon and set me to work scoring a regular game. It was simple enough until we came to the first strike-out. He told me to put down a *K*.

"Why?" I wanted to know. "Why a *K*?"

"Because," he said, "a *K* stands for a strike-out."

To this day I don't understand what caused me to rebel. I told him that *K* didn't stand for strike-out to me and didn't make sense to me. He argued that baseball scorers from the time of Abner Doubleday had been using a *K* as the strike-out symbol, and that I would have to use a *K* whether it appealed to me or not. I said the hell I would. I said I would use *SO* for Struck-Out, or *FA* for Fanned, or *WH* for Whiffed, but I was not going to fly in the face of all logic and use a *K* when the *K* didn't even suggest a strike-out. He explained to me that the scorebook beneath my hand was the team's official scorebook and for that, if for no other reason, I'd use *K* and like it. I lost my temper and he lost his and we ended up with his taking the scorebook away from me and finishing off the job without further conversation. Back at the office he went to the boss and told him that I'd never, never, so long as I lived, make a sports writer because I had no respect for tradition. So they hired another fellow as sports writer and left me to get in trouble in other directions.

As for football—I choose to ignore it as I have ignored it for twenty years. Again it is a case of stubbornness. How a man can go through life in America ignoring such a phenomenon as football is almost, of itself, a phenomenon. I am prepared to state my case.

There was a time when I was a football enthusiast and knew the shoe sizes of every member of the first four teams at Notre Dame. That, however, was a long time ago. I have been bitter about football for so long that there's only one way my mind can be changed. I intend to continue ignoring football until such time as the Buttolph System is put in general use. When that day comes, I'll be famous. Sports writers will interview me and people will point me out on the street and say, "See that old guy? First quarterback that ever played the Buttolph System. Don't look it, does he?"

The master mind of the Buttolph System was a short, pudgy bachelor around forty years of age, bearing the name of Bill Buttolph. He stood up poorly under the title of athletic director of the Y.M.C.A. in the town where I lived. Where he came from, how he happened to have the job, how he subsisted on the meager salary they must have given him, are mysteries I am unable to penetrate at this late date.

The Y.M.C.A. in our town occupied quarters above a

garage. There was a gymnasium large enough to swing a cat in—well, maybe a little larger—large enough to swing a puma in. And there was a room for sitting and reading wholesome magazines and the Scout manual.

I was not a member of this organization but as a neophyte reporter on a local paper I was given the privileges of the place and spent many hours among the dumbbells, preparing myself for the larger contacts of later life. We played compressed basketball during the winter and in the summer we went on occasional hikes and held picnics and little track meets. Bill Buttolph had charge of all activities involving exertion and it was a thankless job. I remember the track meets, devoted chiefly to foot races and broad jumping, events which demanded no equipment other than boys and flat ground. In the foot races Bill Buttolph always served as starter though he had neither gun nor whistle, and it was his custom, after we had crouched at the starting line, to send us away by slapping two shingles together.

One late summer day Bill (we always addressed him as Mister Buttolph but I'll call him Bill now) sat down beside me at the "Y" and asked me if I'd like to play football. He said he was going to get up a team among the "Y" boys and he wanted me because he knew I was a fast runner. I told him I certainly did want to be a football player. My participation in "Y" affairs was a sort of seeking for athletic activities which other boys of my age were getting in high school. I asked him could I be a halfback?

"I got you in mind for quarterback," said Bill, "because you're fast and brainy."

In those days I was fast and brainy.

We met the next afternoon at the "Y" and Bill Buttolph told us he had been unable to arrange for automobiles, so we'd have to walk. There were an even dozen boys, all about the same age, and Bill led us on a long hike to a horse pasture a couple of miles beyond the edge of town.

All during the hike Bill seemed preoccupied. He was not his usual self. Normally, he was full of pleasantries such as, "Hey, fellas, did you ever see a cigar box?" Or, "Did you ever see a brick walk?" Not this day. He made no effort to be jovial and he didn't respond to questions. Now and then as we trudged along the dusty road he would take a paper from his pocket, unfold it, glance at it, frown, then put it back again. The rest of us just walked. We were not Quiz Kids. If we saw a bird we made no attempt to identify it or recite its habits. We just threw a rock at it.

At last we reached the pasture, and Bill led us to a big tree on the edge of the field and had us sprawl out in the shade. Then he looked at the sky, and at the turf, and began pacing up and down before us, saying nothing, obviously lost in heavy thought. Finally he reached into his pocket and pulled out a cigar and lit it. We all stared at one another in astonishment, for Bill Buttolph had always preached the evil of tobacco. But we said nothing and watched him in silence as he paced a bit longer. At last he stopped walking, turned to us, cleared his throat, and spoke.

"Fellas," he said, "this is a great day in the history of sport. This is a famous day in the annuals of football. Your names will go ringing down the corridors of history just as sure as God made little green apples."

On my honor, that's what he said. He must have rehearsed it, "annuals" and all, for he didn't talk like that ordinarily. It was, to us, intensely dramatic. We sat there and stared at him with our adenoids exposed.

"One thing I got to ask you," he went on. "I want each and every one of you to trust me and keep the faith. What happens here today, what happens on this field today, must be a secret between us. Don't even tell your fathers and mothers. Just put your trust in Bill Buttolph, as I put my trust in you. Is it a bargain, fellas?"

We all nodded eagerly and there were murmurs of a cross-my-heart-and-hope-to-die nature. We were pleased with the prospect of having our names go ringing down the corridors of history.

He took the paper out of his pocket, unfolded it, and studied it a moment. Then he told us. He had worked out a sensational system of football offense. We were the chosen few who would be the first in all history to play it. He tried to explain it to us as we lay there on the grass, but his words were not adequate, and soon we were on our feet, working out the basic formation.

Attend closely, now, and I'll do my best to clarify it. The Buttolph Formation can best be described through a diagram Here it is:

```
         Q
  H            H              Opponents.
         F
E T G C G T E                 Line of scrimmage.
         C
         G  Q
         G
         T
         E                    Buttolph Formation.
         E
         H
         H
         F
```

The opponents, an old-fashioned football team, are lined up according to Hoyle, or Camp, or whoever. Not so the Buttolph Line. The center occupied his customary position over the ball. Directly behind him stood the right guard. Directly behind the right guard stood the left guard. Behind the left guard was the right tackle, and so on—straight back, Indian file, to the fullback. The only man missing from this line was the quarterback, or me.

The quarterback stood, as the diagram shows, to the right of the Buttolph Line, facing away from the line of scrimmage. He leaned forward in a crouch, his hands resting on his thighs. His signals were not delivered orally. He signaled with his hands, like a baseball catcher. Perhaps he would have two fingers of the right hand extended and three of the left. His teammates, standing in the Buttolph Formation, could easily see his hands. Suddenly the quarterback would wiggle his thumbs. That was the signal for swift and furious assault. The men of the Buttolph Line would go charging off in all directions.

"The idea," Bill Buttolph explained over and over again, "is that you come out of that line like Christmas presents falling off a Christmas tree."

Somehow, somewhere, in all this churning movement, one of the Buttolph men would get the ball and, still falling like a Christmas present, go zipping off through the opposing team whose members, to be sure, would at this point find themselves in a state of unutterable confusion. Such, at least, was the theory.

Bill Buttolph drilled us over and over, not alone on that first afternoon, but many afternoons thereafter, and each day he renewed his plea for absolute secrecy. He was afraid word would get out. He was certain that the Buttolph System would take the football world by storm, that Buttolph would become a name to rank even above the name of Rockne. Oh, he was sure of it! And so was I.

All this time we were practicing as a unit with no opposition. But finally, in late September, Bill figured he was ready. He made an arrangement with the football coach at the local high school to let us play a team of scrubs. The contest was scheduled for a Friday afternoon on the field where the high-school team usually played its home games.

There was, thank heaven, virtually no audience when we gathered at the field for the cataclysmic event. Bill Buttolph hadn't told anyone about his system and we, the members of his squad, had kept the faith. Nobody knew that a mighty event in football history was impending.

We wore nondescript uniforms, but so did the high-school scrubs. Bill asked, as a favor, that the game open with the scrubs kicking off to us. He wanted to start his great offensive on the first scrimmage.

They kicked and we returned the ball to midfield. The scrubs lined up laterally in the time-honored fashion, little suspecting what was to come. Then we went into the Buttolph Formation. Our line stood straight back from the center and I was in position, fixing my hands for the signal. Then I heard a mighty shout from the side lines and saw the high-school coach tearing onto the field, demanding to know what in the name of hell went on. Bill Buttolph joined him, argued with him, soothed him with talk, told him to keep his eyes open, and got him off the field. Then I went to work.

This time I gave the signal. I wiggled my thumbs. The

Christmas presents fell out of the Christmas tree. And high-school scrubs swarmed all over us.

The game lasted just long enough for us to try four plays. By this time the confusion was so great as to be sheer chaos. Then the high-school coach came onto the field again, swearing quite eloquently and declaring that he would have no further part in such god-damn foolishness. He called off his scrubs and told Bill Buttolph that he ought to be committed. He spoke of some fundamental football rule requiring a certain number of men to be at the line of scrimmage. We, the Buttolph players, just stood there. Bill didn't look at us for a while. When he did, it was just a shifty glance, a glance that reflected his inner hurt. Then he walked away without saying a word. His spirit was broken. Within a few weeks he left town and I have never heard a word of him since.

Thus the Buttolph System and its ignominious failure. Okay, it failed. It was laughed at. But don't tell *me* it didn't have merit. Down through the years I have cherished the notion that Bill Buttolph had something there. I've never abandoned the thought that someday the Harvards and the Yales, among others, will play football like Christmas presents falling out of Christmas trees. And year by year I renew my resolve. I'll have nothing whatever to do with football until the people who run the business get some sense in their heads and take up the Buttolph Offense.

Then and then only will I yell razz-muh-tazz.

Since the ancient incident of the scorebook and the *K* my interest in baseball has been casual, almost academic. Yet, during the last couple of years I managed to work myself into a mild lather over a baseball controversy, to wit: Is there such a thing as a curve ball?

As I recall it, the argument started with a piece in the *New Yorker* magazine. An old baseball scout let loose "the secret." He said that there was no such thing as a curve and that everybody in baseball knew it. He added that the secret had been guarded because the fans would lose interest if word got out that Cooper and Feller and Hubbell and Higbe were incapable of throwing anything but a straight ball.

Newspapers took up the argument and I remember hearing Waite Hoyt broadcast a vigorous denunciation of the no-curve theory. Hoyt is called "Hurt" in Brooklyn. Once when he was struck by a pitched ball, a fan cried, "Holy Jeez! Hurt's Hoyt!" Well, Hoyt was bitter about the curveball argument, but don't forget he was once a big-league pitcher, and a pitcher would be the last person on earth to admit a pitcher can't throw a curve.

Life magazine assigned a high-speed photographer to investigate the dispute. He came away with a series of pictures showing the flight of baseballs pitched by Carl Hubbell and Cy Blanton. All these photographs failed to show the existence of a curve.

It soon developed that the curve question was an old one and that various tests had been made in the past. Baseballs had been thrown through a series of hoops covered with thin paper, to show that they curved. Tall stakes had been driven along base lines and pitchers had thrown balls that curved out and in and in and out. Yet, to my knowledge, the argument was never clearly settled to the satisfaction of all concerned. Personally, being a skeptic, I'm on the no-curve side.

My specific interest in having a decision made is minor. In my files I have a notation concerning "the first deliberate curve ever pitched in baseball." This historic event occurred, according to the memorandum, back in 1866 and in Brooklyn. The pitcher was a gentleman named Arthur Cummings, who played with the Brooklyn Excelsiors.

Mr. Cummings' performance that day back in 1866 has interested me for a long time. It gives me something to speculate on when I have nothing else to occupy my mind. I've often tried to reconstruct the scene where Mr. Cummings pitched the first deliberate curve in all history.

How did he happen to make up his mind to do it?

Let's visualize Mr. Cummings out there on the mound. Let's assume the Excelsiors were trailing. Mr. Cummings, as the saying goes, was in the clutch. What did he do?

"Well," he may have said to himself, "I reckon I'll have

to try something new on these bums. Lemmy see, now. Mebby if I threw a ball down there and made it sorta curve on the way, then they couldn't hit it. Yep. That's what I'll do. Wonder how a feller oughta fix his fingers to make a ball curve. This way—this oughta do 'er. Okay. Here we go. Look out, you big bum, here comes the first deliberate curve ever pitched in history."

After that, what? Did the batter know it was a curve? Did the catcher know it was a curve? Did the spectators know it?

I think it's improbable that any of these people knew Arthur Cummings had deliberately thrown a curve. I believe he was the only person present who knew it. Having thrown the ball, I can picture him swaggering down to the plate, chuckling to himself as he approached the batter.

"Hey," I can hear him saying. "Hey, dopey. Know why you wasn't able to hit that last'n?"

"Sure," says the batter, "I got dust in my eyes and my hind foot slipped and your catcher jabbed me in the side with his glove and I got a bad head cold."

"Like hell," says Arthur Cummings. "You didn't hit it because it curved. I throwed a curve. Deliberate."

"No kid," says the batter.

"Swearta God I throwed a curve," says Arthur Cummings. "And listen. Soon as you're out, run up an' tell th' boys in th' press box about it, will ya? I don't wanna do it myself. Wouldn't look good."

Maybe that's the way it happened but, so far as I can learn, the actual details are lost in time. I do think, however, that it would be a lovely thing, after all these years, to learn that cocksure Arthur Cummings outsmarted himself—that his first deliberate curve in all history was as straight as a hoe handle.

CHAPTER VIII   *Adventures with the Angels*

IT IS IMPOSSIBLE for me to recall a single detail of the ceremony yet I am positive that when I was an infant I was baptized in the Roman Catholic Church. About ten years later I was dipped by the Dunkers. If I don't go straight to Heaven, something's wrong somewhere.

The Dunkers, more popularly called Dunkards, had a church in Decatur, Illinois, and Eddie Abbott, who was my closest friend, was a member of it. He was a normal boy in most respects. His father was a huge, frowning man who worked as some sort of telephone linesman and his mother, who always wore a black bonnet, had a butter route. By this I mean she had the agency for a certain brand of butter, which she delivered by means of a horse and wagon.

When I first found out about the facts of life, particularly as regards the origin of babies, I hurried to Eddie, to let him in on the discovery. An older boy had furnished me with the information and I had it correct as to fundamentals, though a bit confused as to details.

I told Eddie about it and he sat and looked at me a long time, and then he began to blubber. Suddenly he turned to me fiercely and cried:

"That's a lie!"

I didn't know what was going on in his head, but I defended myself, just as other scientists have defended themselves down through the ages.

"You mean," he demanded, "that my mother and father did that?"

"They sure did," I said.

Whereupon he beat hell out of me.

Our friendship was interrupted for several months, but after a while his anger cooled and we became pals again, though we never mentioned the hateful thing.

At this period I was around eleven years old and, with my brothers and sisters, attended Mass every Sunday at St. Patrick's. I have no idea how my friend Eddie ever converted me to the Dunkard church. It wasn't an all-out conversion. Most certainly it must have been an important event in my pre-adolescent life, though my memory of it is hazy. Perhaps I was in some sort of religious ecstasy and things appeared as in a dream. In any event, it was my custom for several weeks to attend early Mass on Sunday morning, then hurry over to the Dunkard church for services there.

Then came the Sunday when the Dunkards had a baptismal ceremony, and they got me. I was taken into a little room where I stripped. They gave me a white nightgown which I put on. Then they led me out, with half-a-dozen others, to the rostrum. At the rear of the platform were large sliding doors. These doors had been shoved back, revealing a small concrete pool full of water. Somebody took hold of me and lowered me into the pool. I can't recall whether the water was warm or cold. I suppose I was whooping and praising the Lord and otherwise carrying on. They gave me my triple dunking and I became a Protestant Catholic, practicing both religions simultaneously and to the best of my ability.

This confusing double allegiance went on for several weeks. I kept my Dunkard affiliation secret, inasmuch as I attended a parochial school. Then one day the mustard seed that serves me as a conscience began troubling me and I decided that I ought to make up my mind and abandon one or the other religion. I needed advice, and I searched around until I found the person I thought I could question safely.

This was Old Joe, sexton of the Catholic church I attended. Old Joe had one eye and a twitch surrounding the other. I came upon him one winter day sitting on the basement steps of the school, picking his teeth with his pocket-knife. I sat down beside him and chattered nonsense for a while. Then I got down to business.

"Joe," I said, "I was just wondering—could a fella belong to a Protestant church and the Catholic church at the same time?"

Old Joe turned and twitched his good eye at me. He twitched it a long time and scared me silly, for I had a feeling that he could read my thoughts. He didn't say a word to me, but finally got up and started away. After a few steps, he turned and beckoned for me to follow. I was trembling all over. To me he seemed to be acting in a most mysterious manner. Actually, he was simply slow-witted. I thought he had been able to read my thoughts—that he had divined my ecclesiastical duplicity—and that he was going to take me to Father Murphy. I pictured myself being excommunicated and hammered on the head.

The old man led me out of the school building and to the

rear of the big church where we entered a sort of subbasement—the furnace room. Using an iron hook, Old Joe opened one of the massive furnace doors. Then he seized me roughly by the arm and led me to a spot directly in front of the door.

"Look in yonder," said Old Joe.

I looked in yonder. It was an inferno—solid fire—and the heat came beating out at me in waves that had me gasping for breath.

"You see it?" said Old Joe. "Now, lemmy tell you sum-pem. That there is ice cold. That there is ice cold alongside the hell you would go to ef you was so much as to set foot in a Protisan church. That there is ice cold alongside the hell the Protisans go to. Don't never go in no Protisan church."

Old Joe's illustrated lecture did the trick. I had never fully appreciated the high warmth of hell before. I never went back to the Dunkards.

Spiritualism—the belief that a living human being can gabble back and forth with the dead—is one of the most delightful frauds mankind has put upon himself. I have a sincere envy for those people who honestly believe in spiritualism because they must surely have a lot of fun.

I'd like very much to be able to talk with Thorne Smith, if only to ask him if he's getting enough to drink. I'd give up radio if, at will, I could tune in Grandpa Smith, the last Czar of Russia (he'd have to talk English), Giacomo Casanova, Hitler's papa, Noah, Fatty Arbuckle, Lola Montez, and Adam.

If I could get in touch with these people and others I might mention, and if I could spend my evenings talking with them, I'd never have to worry about material for books. I could get a complete book that probably would retail at $3.50 or maybe even $5.00 in a limited signed edition out of Adam alone, if he'd talk. I mean if he *could* talk. Maybe that's why the spiritualists have never brought Adam through. He never stayed around long enough to learn the language, and I'm pretty certain he wouldn't know how to write on a slate. If I could acquire this spiritualistic ability, problems such as that involving Adam's means of communication would come up, but I'd handle them someway. I attended a séance once in which Otto H. Kahn came through and talked in Italian dialect. This was all the more remarkable because Otto H. Kahn, at that sitting, was still alive. So if he could emerge from the spirit planes and chat with me in Italian dialect, surely Adam, considering all the time he's been out there, should be able to talk something.

I attended my first séance soon after I arrived in New York, back in 1929. The medium was a Negro woman, and after she had brought back sundry kinsfolk for the customers, she came through with a horse. No question about it. A man in the audience spoke up and said that he'd like to communicate with a dear horse he once owned—a horse named Edna. Within thirty seconds there was a heavy clumping about the dark room and then the man who had asked for Edna let out a sharp cry. Edna had given him an affectionate kick on the shin.

For a couple of years after that I almost lived at séances, always attending them in the company of Joseph Dunninger. Dunninger is the man who offers a fortune in cash to any spiritualistic medium he cannot expose or debunk. Dunninger was for years one of the leading American magicians, and I always liked him because he never pulled a half dollar out of my nose. I have a nose that is large enough to hold perhaps $6.50 in half dollars and I have known other magicians who have embarrassed me in public by reaching up and pulling large objects out of it, including hard-boiled eggs. Dunninger never pesters his friends with such stuff.

One of the chief ghost-conjurers of that period in New York was a little Italian named Nino Pecararo. He's the one who brought back Otto H. Kahn in Italian dialect. All his spirits, in fact, spoke in dialect. Dunninger and I attended a number of Pecararo's spooky shows. The Italian boy enjoyed a large following because, some years earlier, he had helped convince Sir Arthur Conan Doyle that spiritualism is true.

We were in the elegant apartment of a spiritualistic architect one evening and Nino, concealed in his cabinet, was fetching back spirits as fast as he could talk. It was a lively show, and when it was over, I found myself standing against a wall between two middle-aged women Believers. One of these women turned to me and said:

"Wasn't it *simply* miraculous!"

"No," I said.

Both women came at me then, demanding to know what I meant.

"Well," I said, "I'd never be convinced unless I could be inside that cabinet with him during one of his séances."

It was a foolish thing to say. Before I knew what was going on, another séance had been scheduled for a week later and Nino had agreed that I could enter the cabinet with him. I tried to withdraw, but those women demanded that I go through with the bargain, since I was such a smart aleck, and Dunninger egged me on.

The special séance was held in the office of a Broadway lawyer and Nino was quietly sullen when he arrived that night. A goodly crowd was there, including a noted orchestra leader and a society woman with a high-pitched chest. Nino's wrists and ankles were bound and his body was placed in a sack of heavy black netting. Then he was tied securely to a straight-backed chair and placed in the cabinet. Next they tied me to a chair and settled me alongside Nino, perhaps two feet away from him. The lights were doused, the people in the audience formed themselves into a semicircle in front of the cabinet, and the séance began.

Nino and I sat in the darkest darkness I have ever known and faced a heavy black curtain which separated us from the audience. The people outside made not a sound, and Nino scarcely moved a muscle for thirty minutes. During those thirty minutes my small supply of courage began to ebb. I started thinking as follows:

"This bastard is crazy. He's crazy and he's mad as hell at me for presuming to get into this cabinet with him. He's even crazy enough to kill me. I know he's able to wiggle himself out of those ropes and out of that sack. He's so mad, so crazy, that he's going to get loose and pick up that chair and brain me with it."

My thoughts raced along like that and I started to sweat.

Still no sound from Nino—no audible indication that he was escaping his bonds. Then, without warning, he let go with one of the most piercing shrieks ever heard on earth. It was enough to frighten a fence post. Coming as it did after that long, awful, black silence, the shriek even scared the members of the audience out front. And me—I was too weak and limp to shudder. All the strength drained out of me and my body, at that moment, didn't possess enough energy to have put forth a pimple. I just sat there and waited for him to strike, figuring myself as a sure thing for the Great Beyond. He let half a minute go by after the shriek, then he spoke:

"That . . . was . . . Theodore . . . Roosevelt."

I didn't believe in spiritualism then, and I don't now, but if that was Theodore Roosevelt, a pox on him. What a thing to do!

For a while I debated the advisability of getting the hell out of that cabinet, but then I thought of the embarrassment of facing the people outside and resolved to stay a bit longer. What followed was another long period of silence. I could hear Nino squirming a bit now and then. This time he'd get me. This time it would be the chair on my head. Those were the longest minutes of my life—about forty of them—and at last it came again. Another shriek, worse than the first. I leaped a foot and a half off the floor, chair and all. Then came Nino's voice again:

"That . . . was . . . King of . . . Italia."

And that was enough for me. They hadn't tied me securely and I managed to get the ropes off. I didn't care any more about the shame of it. I simply got up and parted the curtains and got out of that damned place, away from Theodore Roosevelt and the King of Italia. The people outside understood and were silently sympathetic, and nobody chided me for leaving the cabinet. I simply took a place at the rear and stood there trying to think up a foolproof murder plan, a way of killing that devil Nino without getting caught.

The spirits that came after that were much less noisy and seemed, in fact, to have a certain jubilation in their voices. Nino began bringing back dead grandmothers and uncles and cousins and the like. My departure from the cabinet had turned him into a spiritualistic ball of fire. Then Ed Wolf, the radio producer, spoke up and asked if he might have Napoleon Bonaparte on the line. There was a groaning and grunting inside the cabinet and suddenly Nino came plunging through the curtains, carrying them with him. He was free of the chair but still in the net, and he began threshing about on the floor. He had kicked the legs off two chairs before someone got the lights switched on. Half-a-dozen men piled on top of the writhing medium and someone got a bucket of cold water and poured it on him. Then he quieted down and they cut the net and ropes off him. Soon he opened his eyes, looked all around, and muttered:

"Whatta happen?"

By good fortune I didn't have a club in my hand, or I'd have then and there put him into the deepest of all trances.

The spiritualists said that my adventure in the cabinet disproved nothing. They contended that Teddy Roosevelt and the King of Italy actually had come back. I was in no mood to argue with them. I went home.

Subsequently Nino Pecararo confessed himself a fraud. Dunninger got him to sign a confession in which he admitted that he was nothing more than an escape artist, able to extricate himself from bonds. The spiritualists answered this by saying that Dunninger had hypnotized Nino into making such a confession.

I wrote stories for the United Press about the various séances I attended and one day J. W. T. Mason came to me and began questioning me about spiritualism. Mr. Mason, who died two years ago, was a famous journalist, author, psychologist, philosopher, and an authority on Oriental culture. He was a handsome man with tremendous dignity, much given to deep thinking. He gave me one of his books, and I still have it though I've never been able to read it. A dozen times I've lowered my head and plowed into it, but it's too much for me. I don't even understand the long inscription he wrote in it for me.

Mr. Mason worked at a desk near my own and, as I say, he became curious about my adventures among the spiritualists. He wanted to know what I thought about the whole thing and I said I thought it was a lot of ordure. He said I should never take such an attitude. He told me how he had spent years studying various religions and he spoke of Keeping an Open Mind. I always liked him and respected him, but he could never put that frightful malady on me—the disease of the Open Mind. He asked me if I would someday take him to a séance. I said I would.

A week or so later Dunninger put on a séance of his own. His idea was to play medium himself for an evening and demonstrate that he, through sheer trickery, could achieve all the manifestations produced by spiritualists, and then some.

I went to Dunninger and told him about Mr. Mason and we cooked up a little plot. Dunninger asked me to dig up some obscure fact out of Mr. Mason's past history—some incident that would likely be forgotten now.

It was a tough job, but after considerable research I came upon an old biographical sketch of J. W. T. Mason which made mention of a youthful journalistic exploit. Mason, it seemed, had attracted international attention around the turn of the century by obtaining an interview with Leopold II of Belgium. The interview was a lengthy affair and dealt chiefly with Leopold's exploitation of the Congo Free State. This was the obscure fact I handed over to Dunninger.

The phony séance was held in a Manhattan office building, and by prearrangement I arrived with Mr. Mason just as the show was about to start. We sat down with the other invited guests and waited. Mr. Mason, you must understand, thought he was attending a real séance.

Dunninger put on a good performance, slopping ectoplasm all over the place, jingling bells, producing raps here and there, and babbling in half-a-dozen "spirit-control" voices. Mr. Mason just sat there in the darkness, eagerly taking it all in. The thing went along for about twenty minutes and then there was a long silence and, after that, a heavy, throaty voice came from the black curtains.

"Is Mason present?" it asked.

I could feel my companion tighten up at my side. For a moment he seemed unable to answer and then, in a strangely timid voice, he said:

"Which Mason?"

"Mason," said the hollow voice from the cabinet.

"J. W. T. Mason?" asked J. W. T. Mason.

"That is right," said the voice.

"Yes," he called out. "Yes. I'm—yes, this is J. W. T. Mason speaking."

He sounded as though he had a telephone receiver at his ear.

"Do you know me, Mason?" came the voice.

Mr. Mason hesitated a long while. He had spent many years among Englishmen and had acquired certain British mannerisms of speech which he employed particularly when under stress.

"No," he finally said. "No, I can't say I do, old man. Who are you?"

"I am an old friend of yours, Mason. An old, old friend. Think back. Think far back. You must remember me. You must remember Leopold."

By now Mr. Mason was sitting on the edge of his chair, leaning forward, taut as a banjo string.

"Haw!" he said.

The ghostly voice continued:

"Do you remember, Mason, the long talk we had? Do you remember?"

"Haw!" from Mr. Mason.

"Can you remember, Mason, what we talked about?"

"Haw!" A long pause. "Yes, Your Highness, I remember quite well. It was——" The voice from the cabinet interrupted him.

"Yes," it said, "it was about the Congo. It was a good long talk and I wish—I wish . . ." The voice began to grow faint and then, fading away, concluded: ". . . and I wish we could continue it."

"Haw!" said Mr. Mason. The voice had faded into what sounded like the indistinct mumblings of an old man, then there was quiet in the room, and the lights came on. I had to act quickly. Mr. Mason was sitting there on the edge of his chair, blinking, and appeared to be in some sort of a trance himself.

"Come on," I said, seizing him by the arm. "Let's get out of here."

We were in the corridor and headed for the street by the time Dunninger had emerged from the cabinet.

"Extraordinary!" Mr. Mason kept saying as we walked down the street. Then he'd crinkle up his brow and puff furiously at a cigarette and think. At the corner he mumbled a good night and got into a cab.

When I reached the office the following day I noted that he was not at his desk. I explored around and finally found him. He was standing at a window, staring out over Brooklyn, smoking, thinking. He stood there for half an hour, then he began to pace up and down the office. Several times he started toward me as though to ask me a question. Then he'd change his mind and resume his pacing, or go back to the window and stare out at eternity (which is over Brooklyn).

I let the thing go on for a couple of hours and then I decided I'd better tell him. He was worrying himself sick. Perhaps he was now faced with the prospect of revising his whole philosophy, calling in all his books and doing them over. He had to be told, so I told him.

He'd have been justified in picking up the nearest copy spike and letting me have it, but he didn't. He put on his spectacles, which he wore attached to a black ribbon, and stared at me for a long time, and then he grinned.

"I couldn't puzzle it out," he said. "The peculiar thing —the amazing thing—was that voice. It was exactly like Leopold's voice. Haw!"

The Mason adventure came in 1930, and while I attended a few séances after that I soon lost touch with spiritualistic matters. Then in 1941, when I was engaged on a brief career as a syndicated columnist, I wrote a piece kidding the ghost-grabbers. An avalanche of mail came down upon me. The letters arrived from spiritualists all over the United States and not a single one of them denounced me. A columnist who attacks dogs or chrysanthemums or stamp collectors or Abbott & Costello will get mail that is filled with bitter invective. Yet the spiritualists startled me by their serenity. Their letters could be divided into two groups—

those attempting to prove through personal experience that spiritualism is true, and those containing the following theme:

"You poor boy! You are simply deluded. God has not made the way clear to you. If you could only understand! If you could only see! And you will someday. You will see the light!"

In the former category was, for example, a letter from a lady in St. Louis. She wrote:

All my life I have been told what was coming to pass by falling into a trance and see it come. I saw the war start and saw the Japs take control of the world. Conan Doyal appeared to me while I was sitting in the Odean Theater. Once I was alone in bed in my apartment when I heard a slight movement in the next room and sat up in bed, and there in the next room was a big black man dressed in black from head to heels and was looking at me as though awaiting my orders. One look was enough for me, but I was not so frightened but what I remembered what to say to dismiss him, and I lost no time in saying: "Depart in the name of the Lord Jesus Christ and come no more." And he was gone. My life has been so full of these visions that I am used to them.

I'm glad I don't have them because I'd never get used to them. I don't want that black guy around my house, night or day, and I don't want Conan "Doyal" getting in the way when I'm looking at a movie, and, most important of all, I don't want to see any Japs taking control of the world.

As another consequence of that column I wrote about spiritualism, somebody in San Francisco sent me a subscription to a weekly newspaper called the New York *Spiritualist Leader*. It was a lively periodical and I enjoyed every issue I got.

The *Leader's* star reporter for a while was Elbert Hubbard (1856–1915). Mr. Hubbard in 1942 was writing a weekly piece from the spirit world, dictating it to one Irene Remillard, a medium. He said that he had organized a Universary Defense Program with himself as chairman of the board of directors. All the members of this board were "out there" with Mr. Hubbard and among them was William T. Stead, who went down on the *Titanic*.

Another contributor to the paper was Will Rogers (1879–1935). Will turned out his column through "automatic writing" translated by a lady in Charlotte, Michigan. He soon ousted Elbert Hubbard as star of the *Leader* staff and, just as it happens to earth newspapermen, Will's success went to his head. He started out writing a column of normal length, but before long his stuff was running into two full columns of type and then three. I remember that one of his pieces contained an apology for repeated delays in getting his copy to the editor. Will explained that he had been extremely busy lately. Said he'd been hanging around Washington, D.C., quite a bit. With Abraham Lincoln.

While I looked forward to reading the post-posthumous writings of Elbert Hubbard and Will Rogers each week, I also enjoyed the workings of a new institution, "The Spiritual Post Office for Earth." This department in the *Leader* was conducted by a medium named Alexander De-Chard. Mr. DeChard places an "untreated blank white card" between slates and waits five minutes for the letter to be written. People in the spirit world can write home regularly to their friends and relatives through this, shall we say, dead-letter office? If you want to get in touch with a spirit, you can write in and Mr. DeChard will send your letter along, somehow, and later you will get your answer, if they can locate the party.

Some of the sample letters from out yonder were printed in the *Leader*. One of them was to Wilbur from Lillian. She told all about how it felt when she woke up after dying. Said she smelled flowers. After that, she wrote, she saw Mr. Bruce (a spirit) and his eyes were still troubling him. Then she went to her own funeral, and liked it, though she admitted that she felt sad.

Another letter was from a Deacon Jones, addressed to some kinsfolk in Hartford, Connecticut. Deacon Jones wrote his spirit letter in Negro dialect. From it I quote:

It is necessary dat all ob de people should know de truf about coming back. I ask you, be you gwine to allow yourselves to be so extemporaneously bigoted in dis ere fashion? Am I here or is I not? Why so when you see de glorious cause of Nature when you can't see da beauties ob dis Spiritualism? Open the doors in your heart, Robert! Your brother is here, also Mama, Papa, Lillian, Celia, George West, and Rev. White. All send love.

Sure sounds convincing, doesn't it? Of course I didn't see the original as canceled by Postmaster DeChard. The original, according to de *Leader,* came on a decorative letterhead. At the top was "a psychic picture of the handsome colored deacon in gray and green." The gray was the deacon, no doubt, and the green was his dialect.

Several of my letters from spiritualists went into the matter of dreams, suggesting that if I examined my dreams closely I might find that they were really communications from the Beyond. This I did, but got nowhere. Then one day I saw a note in one of the papers saying that a lady named Marta had been elected Queen of the Somnologists. A somnologist, according to the item, is a dream reader, though the term did not show in any of my word books.

Marta was boss of a gypsy tearoom across from the New York Public Library. The tearoom itself was unprepossessing and Marta, who had to be hauled out of the kitchen on my arrival, proved to be an elderly, nervous lady with a suggestion of witchery about her. She had me sit down at a little red table and subjected me to long scrutiny. She suspected I was a cop.

While Marta scrutinized me I scrutinized the rest of the room. There were other little red tables around the walls and above each table was a card giving the name of the reader, such as "Jean" and "Lee." The tables were all occupied. Some of the readers were working with cards. Others were staring into cups and telling their customers stuff about tall dark men, short dark men, middle-sized dark men, and to be careful what you do next Thursday. This sort of commerce has always fascinated me because of the number of people, looked upon by the world as intelligent, who go for it. Personally, I'm a good customer of the fortunetellers simply out of curiosity, and among the honors that have come to me in this life was the distinction of being the first person on earth to have his fortune told in beer suds. I forget the name of the guy, but he turned up in Manhattan early in 1930, got some wax for the ends of his mustache, acquired a press agent, and went into business. The press agent phoned me and I hurried over to get my future mapped out and some free beer. The man with the mustache simply had me drink off a glass of beer, then he took the glass and examined the patterns formed by beer suds on its inner surface. He said it was much more reliable than tea leaves—that tea-leaf readers sometimes cheated by jiggling the cup, whereas all the jiggling in the world wouldn't displace the patterns made by the beer suds. He said I would live past seventy and that three is my lucky number.

Getting back to Marta's tearoom. When she decided I was not trying to trap her into a pinch, she said I could ask her anything, since I had identified myself as a reporter.

"But first," she said, "just to show you how I operate, what did you dream last night?"

"Well," I said, "I didn't exactly come here to get my dreams read. I didn't intend to do any free-loading on you, but it happens that I had a strange dream last night. I was sitting in the bathtub and a green goat suddenly came out of the drain and started talking in a foreign language."

Marta didn't bat an eye. "What language?" she asked. I said I didn't know.

"Hmmm-m-m-m," she said. She seemed to be thinking the thing over, and finally she leaned forward and in a voice that was almost a whisper said:

"Think hard, now. Was there any water in the tub at the time?"

"Yes," I said. "A little. Not enough to drown a goat."

"Think back," she went on. "Was it clean water or dirty water?"

"Clean water," I said.

"Ah! I knew it! Now, can you remember seeing any fruit, or any berries, in this dream?"

"No," I assured her. "No fruit, no berries."

"Well," she said, "a green goat is a new one on me, but the clean water is the significant thing here. Very, very significant. Let me see, now. No fruit. No berries. Tell me, did you see any butterflies?"

"No butterflies," I said.

"Thank goodness!" she cried. "I'm getting sick and tired

of butterfly dreams. A while back everybody was dreaming about butterflies. The draft caused it. A butterfly dream means a loved one has gone away. When the draft began and the boys started going away to camp, everybody started dreaming about butterflies. Now we don't get many butterflies. It's mostly all water now—clean water."

"What does that signify?" I asked her.

"Strength, money, and power," she said. "Only this week I myself dreamed of Niagara Falls. Clean water means an element of good. If you analyze the person who dreams of clean water, you'll find he's right on the edge of a big deal. Usually a big money deal. The faster the water is moving, the quicker it will come and the more bountiful it will be. Now, *your* clean water was in a tub, not moving. You see the difference between *your* clean water and *my* clean water? Yours was standing still in a tub. Mine was coming over Niagara Falls."

She straightened up and smiled triumphantly. Somehow I felt a little depressed. Here she already had a nice tearoom, with plenty of dreamers coming in, and now this Niagara Falls thing. Them that has, gits. I asked her if she did much in the way of dreaming.

"I'm a heavy dreamer," said Marta. "Dream all the time. But I never in all my life ever dreamed about a green goat. I think it indicates something very definite. I think it indicates you have a fine type mind. I really do."

CHAPTER IX　*Taking Pride in My Profession*

IN SOME RESPECTS an author is the lowest expression of human life. I make this statement with full realization that it will not set well in some quarters. I'd like to see a composite picture of all the authors in the world today, though I'd want to be in good physical condition when I looked at it. Such a picture would refute every claim that God created Man. And if a sound track were added to the portrait, ten days could not pass before a world dictator would arise and the publication of books would cease.

My friend Jack Woodford of Hollywood, himself an author, has made a lifetime hobby of authors. Mr. Woodford is the most successful of all writers on the subject of how to write. He collects authors, studies them, and writes about them. In addition to this depressing side line he has turned out fifty-odd novels and he has raised his daughter Louella to be an author, permitting her to write her first book at the age of thirteen. Mr. Woodford is himself a handsome guy and Louella, at twenty-four, is a beauty, and if you sat down and listened to them talk, you'd get the impression that they were bright and intelligent and civilized. Yet Mr. Woodford has certain peculiarities when it comes to theorizing about writing. For one thing, he has long contended that an author should practice absolute celibacy whenever engaged on a writing project. He can have that one. And for another thing, he claims that he writes with his subconscious. I read somewhere not long ago that Katharine Brush does this too. In his efforts to explain his technique, Mr. Woodford confuses me no end.

He sits down at a typewriter and starts writing—with his conscious mind operating. He goes along for a few pages and suddenly he slips into the subconscious, and then whammety-whammety-wham for hours at a stretch. I suppose, when he finally finishes for the day, he gathers up his copy, climbs into a chair, and says: "Now. Let's see what I wrote. Wonder what it's about. Sure hope it's fiction."

I'd like to try the Woodford system but I don't know how to go about it. For one thing, I've got to stay fairly conscious while I'm writing because I have to get up now and then to look at the dictionary or go to the bathroom. And I've never been able to interpret the psychological considerations that enter into my writing. I don't want to waste my time figuring out what's going on in my head that makes me write the way I'm writing because then I won't have time to write anything except what I have figured out is going on that makes me write down on paper *what I have figured out*. The hell with that.

Some months ago a young man came to my house and made my life full and complete. For a dozen years I had been going around New York interviewing people, poking my ungainly nose into their affairs, asking them impertinent questions. And then this young man came along and interviewed *me*. He was from a college paper and first off he gave me a little shock by demonstrating the vast strides that have been made in the technique of the interview. He came briskly into my house with a leather thing under his arm—a sort of cross between a brief case and a knapsack.

When he got settled on the couch he placed this contrivance on his lap and began unflapping it all around. Almost immediately he had a desk. It flapped out on all four sides, with the rear flap standing upright. There were little racks containing pen, pencil, eraser, ruler, a tube of ink, paper clips, a little calendar, Kleenex, a book of stamps, and the hanging flaps at the sides furnished pockets for the storage of other office equipment—possibly a telephone, the World Almanac, and a wastebasket.

The young man made his preparations in a businesslike manner, finally picked up a freshly sharpened pencil, poised it over his portable office, raised his eyes to mine, smiled like Don Ameche, and said:

"Now! I want you to tell me about your writing habits."

Well, I couldn't tell him much about my writing habits. I did ramble around a while on the general subject of writing habits. I told him about the time Percy Hammond, the dramatic critic, was asked what single thing he would like most to do in the world. He replied, "Not write." And I told him how so many writers groan and bellyache about the awful chore that writing can be.

I told him how I used to observe Westbrook Pegler at work in the ball parks—how Mr. Pegler sweats and whinnies and grinds his teeth in the throes of beautiful letters, taking hours to produce a single page of his deathless prose.

Then, for contrast, I told him how Heywood Broun used to operate—just the opposite of Mr. Pegler. Broun usually turned out his 600-word column in twenty minutes, or maybe fifteen, polishing it off just as rapidly as he could get the typewriter to run. (Notice how I am now referring to Mr. Pegler as "Mister." My past is all filled with low crimes and misdemeanors and I'm in no condition to be Peglerized.)

After I had yammered along for a while about the writing habits of other people, the young man finally said:

"Well, it sure sounds terrible. I'm sorry to hear you don't like to write."

"Who said I didn't like to write?" I came back at him. "I've just been telling you about other people. Me, I love it. I can't understand these other guys who howl about their horrible jobs. Why don't they take up some other trade? With a couple of years' training they might qualify as short-order cooks. Why don't they do that?"

A few years back I worked on a newspaper with a fellow named Joe, one of the nicest guys in the United States and one of the most level-headed. Then a publisher trapped him into writing a book and Joe became an author. He quit the newspaper business and disappeared from his customary haunts. His old friends didn't see him for a long time and then he came back for a brief visit. We were gathered around the pinball machine in Dominic Settiducatti's tavern when Joe walked in.

He said not a word to his old cronies, strode to the rear of the room, and picked up a straight-backed chair. Still ignoring everyone, he placed the chair so it faced a blank wall and sat down in it. Then he started singing "There Is a Green Hill Far Away." Joe is no Tibbett, neither is he a Crosby, but he can make lots of noise when he sails into a hymn.

He was roaring away at the blank wall when Mr. Settiducatti came alongside the chair, hands on his huge hips and a deep scowl on his face. Mr. Settiducatti just stood there until Joe had finished the hymn. Then he spoke.

"Listen," said Mr. Settiducatti, "why do you got to come in here and act like a nut for?"

"I'm not acting like a nut," said Joe. "It just happens that the urge came over me to sing a hymn."

"Well, why didn't you go to some church somewheres and sing it, instead of favoring us with it in here?"

"Listen, Nick," said Joe, "when I feel like I want to sing a hymn, I'm gonna sing that hymn and I'm gonna sing it the way I wanna sing it and in the place I wanna sing it. This time I got the urge to sing a hymn to myself, so I sung it."

"Well," said Mr. Settiducatti, "it is just such things like this that is giving my store a bad name. People come in here and see a guy standing on his head or making like they are a Ferris wheel or singing a hymn to themselves against the wall, and they ask me what kind insane asylum I am running around here anyway. The next time you feel like favoring yourself with a hymn, be so kind as to go holler it down a manhole somewheres else. Anyway, I personly think you are crazy."

"To be frank about it, Nick," said Joe, "I *am* crazy."

Whereupon he turned back to the wall and lit into "It Came upon the Midnight Clear."

Some years earlier I worked beside another author, a fellow named Paul, who had written a short novel. His book had been published almost in secrecy and though he was proud of it and considered it to be immortal, he seldom talked about it. Paul was definitely daft. He worked at an editing job and at his elbow was a tall wastepaper basket, a cylinder made of some light composition. He never dropped any wastepaper or other rubbish into the thing, nor would he permit anyone else to use it according to its ordained purpose. It was his custom to throw wastepaper on the floor and use the receptacle for hollering down. Everybody in the office knew he was tetched and everybody was a little afraid of him, for he was a large muscular guy capable of maiming a mule with his fist.

Paul would labor away at his editing job, performing his duties quietly and intelligently most of the time. Then, about once in every forty-eight hours, he'd put down his pencil, swivel his chair around, seize the wastepaper basket, and holler down it. He always hollered the same thing. He'd place his face over the long cylinder and let go with:

"PUSSY CAFFAY!"

Just one time he'd holler it, then he'd pick up his pencil and resume his work. For a long time the people around him refrained from expressing any curiosity about his idiosyncrasy. He was touchy about his personal affairs and we figured that if he wanted to explain his hollering-down-the-wastebasket, he'd explain it. The thing went along for many months. Whenever that cavernous "PUSSY CAFFAY!" rolled in heavy waves across the office, we'd all glance at one another with perhaps the suggestion of a grin and then go back to our work. Nobody ever laughed out loud.

Then came an evening at a neighborhood bar when Paul walked in, took a stool alongside me, and began drinking. He grew more morose as time went along and after a while he began to get drunk. Suddenly he summoned the bartender and asked:

"Have you got a rain barrel around here?"

The bartender said he was out of rain barrels, and Paul lapsed into his gloomy silence. By this time I had mustered a few grams of courage.

"Did you say rain barrel?" I asked.

"Yes," said Paul. "I want to holler down a rain barrel."

I let it stew for a bit. I didn't want to be hasty. But finally I said:

"Why?"

It was his turn for the long pause. He sat and stared at his drink and then he turned around and looked at me. There was a glitter to his eyes.

"I'd give ten dollars," he said, "to have a rain barrel right now so I could holler 'PUSSY CAFFAY!' down it."

I was determined that I should get at the root of the thing, and as discreetly as possible I asked for his aims and motives. He drew out his wallet and carefully extracted a ragged clipping.

"I wrote a book," he said. "This is the only intelligent review I got. Read it."

I read it. The review was about ten lines in length and the last line was:

"This is a veritable pousse-café of a book."

I handed it back to him.

"That's the only nice thing that was said about my book," he explained. "I like the sound of it. It's music. So I like to holler it down a rain barrel. When I holler 'PUSSY CAF-FAY!' down a rain barrel, it comes back at me, louder and more beautiful. I certainly wish I had a rain barrel right now." He took another long swig at his drink. "Listen," he said, "I'll tell you a secret. I live in a little apartment down near Gramercy Park. I've got a rain barrel in it. I get up sometimes in the night, when I can't sleep, and holler 'PUSSY CAFFAY!' down it. If it wasn't for that I'd never be able to sleep."

Not long after that Paul got involved in some crazy argument with the boss and was fired. I ran into him on the street a year or two later. He looked the same, except that he was shabby, and he told me he had written three more novels and was at work on a fourth. Nobody would publish his later "pussy caffays." He put the bite on me for two dollars and that's the last I've ever seen of him.

Since the time of my brief association with Paul, I've known a lot of authors—authors of all sexes and all descriptions—and, as I've suggested, a composite picture of all the authors in the world would frighten little children and send the beasts of the field fleeing into the forests. Let a man get his name on the cover of a book and something happens to his head. He begins to gabble cosmic nonsense. I try to keep myself from thinking that I have become an author because simple realization of the fact overwhelms me with an affliction which, in horses, is called the blind staggers.

I am slightly acquainted with a novelist who appears to be normal in all respects but who has on two separate occasions revealed to me the burning ambition that is the motivating force of his life and labor.

He wants a pillow stuffed with belly-button lint.

In all seriousness he told me that he looks forward to the day when he gets enough surplus cash to hire a clever agent whose job it will be to collect the belly-button lint. It may take years, the novelist agrees, but it can be done. The agent will have the task of probing thousands of belly buttons before he is finished. He'll have to gain the confidence of the owners of belly buttons first—a terrific job in itself. I don't know for sure what I'd say to him if he came to me and asked me for the lint out of my belly button. I don't need it, but I might be inclined to consider my belly-button lint to be property of such an intimate nature that I wouldn't be willing to have it stuffed in a pillow.

The novelist has spent days on end thinking about the project and he has told me of certain angles that worry him.

First of all, he must be sure of his agent's integrity. He can't take a chance on hiring some guy who'd cheat—who'd disappear for a couple of years and then come around with a gunny sack full of stuff which he *claimed* was pure belly-button lint. Moreover, the agent would have to demand full co-operation from all prospects. He could never permit a prospect to go out of the room and then come back with the lint from his or her belly button. The prospect might cheat too. The extraction would have to be performed right there on the spot, with the agent removing the lint, or the owner of the belly button removing it before the agent's eyes and handing it over. You can readily see how it would take a long time to collect enough belly-button lint to stuff a pillow.

I've had a great deal of enjoyment myself, speculating over various phases of the project. I've even worked out a series of advertisements which the novelist and his agent might use to simplify their search. Offer five dollars per helping for belly-button lint. Startle the public with the information that their belly-button lint is valuable. Splash display ads around, in this manner:

> DON'T THROW IT AWAY!
> THE BELLY-BUTTON LINT MAN
> WILL BE AROUND TO SEE YOU!
> HAVE YOUR WHOLE FAMILY
> SAVE BELLY-BUTTON LINT
> AND ENJOY A VACATION
> IN BEAUTIFUL VERMONT!

As I said, this novelist is altogether serious and I feel sure that, if they don't back the wagon up to his door, he'll eventually get that pillow. He doesn't want the pillow for ornament. Nor does he want it for bragging purposes. I might be able to understand his ambition if he simply wanted to have such a pillow lying around, so he could startle guests in his home by saying: "See that pillow over yonder—the pink one? Stuffed with belly-button lint." But that isn't the idea at all. He wants that pillow for one reason and one reason only—to sleep on. Personally, I'd charge money to sleep in the same room with a pillow stuffed with belly-button lint.

I'll not contend that all authors, or even most authors, are as daffy as this fellow, or even as daffy as the man who hollered down a rain barrel. Yet I've never know an author who wasn't eccentric in one way or another. Steinbeck, for example.

Steinbeck came to New York back in 1938 after *Of Mice and Men* hit the best-seller lists. He fairly crept into town because he knew the New York interviewers would be after him and, at that time anyway, he was inclined to go all to pieces in the presence of an inquisitive newspaperman. I was then working on a newspaper and, having heard a rumor that Steinbeck was in town, I called up my friend George Joel, who was then an executive of the company which published the Californian's books. George approached Steinbeck and Steinbeck said NO. George kept after him, however, and finally beat him down, and Steinbeck said he'd meet me at the publishing house the next morning at eleven.

As I learned later, he arrived at his publisher's at ten. He walked in with an unopened bottle of brandy under his arm, entered Pat Covici's private office, sat down at a table, and asked that someone fetch him a pitcher of water and two glasses. From ten to eleven he sat there, drinking brandy. When I arrived I was ushered into another office and George Joel went to see if Steinbeck were ready. Steinbeck took one final snort of brandy, thumped the glass down on the table, and said:

"Bring on the son of a bitch!"

He had two thirds of the bottle of brandy inside of him by that time and it was a delightful interview. He answered any and all questions that were put to him, and every few minutes he'd take another sip and cry out:

> *With lecherous howls,*
> *I deflower young owls!*

Toward the end of the interview my photographer arrived and Steinbeck seemed to regard him as a sort of savior. He all but embraced the cameraman, posed for eight or ten different pictures (including two with the brandy bottle), and then wrote an extensive inscription in a copy of his latest book for his new friend.

Not long ago I ran into this same photographer on a subway and during our conversation I asked him if he still had his Steinbeck book.

"My what?" he said.

"That book Steinbeck—John Steinbeck—autographed for you that day—the guy with the bottle of brandy."

"Oh, that!" he said. "You mean that book he give me. Nah, I don't know what happen to it. Funny thing about that. I *read* that book. Had one of these unhappy endings to it. Only had one dame in it and she was a broad. What the hell's a guy wanna write a book like that for? Where do you dig up these screwballs, anyway?"

One of my best friends among authors is James Street, whose typewriter erupts novels, short stories, movies, magazine articles, and indignant letters. Mr. Street is forever working himself into an elevated dudgeon, usually over some fatheaded Yankee's gross misinterpretation of the War Between the States. He is from Mississippi, and most of his writing is about the South, and he spends long hours worrying over the Dred Scott decision, the Missouri Compromise, and Harriet Beecher Stowe. When he has achieved a proper degree of anger, he leaps to his typewriter and lets go with a long letter full of bitterness and invective. He seldom mails one of these letters. He writes them, signs them, thrusts them into envelopes, puts stamps on the envelopes, then lays them on a table and sits and glowers at them for an hour. Then he tears them up.

Like myself, Mr. Street attends the movies regularly. Whenever he happens into one involving the habits or history of the South, he comes away in a tremendous fury. I remember when he went to see *Gone with the Wind*. He came out of the theater cursing David O. Selznick and everyone else connected with the production. Mr. Street's violent dissatisfaction with the picture was based on one single detail: he said that in the burning of Atlanta the fools had the smoke blowing in the wrong direction.

He is a neighbor of mine and works in a room where he

pursues one of his hobbies—collecting potted plants. He has a couple of hundred plants, of all shapes, colors, and sizes, in that room, and on entering it a visitor sometimes finds difficulty in locating Mr. Street and his typewriter. Whenever I find myself in the place I unconsciously begin making Tarzan noises and start peering through the foliage for Dorothy Lamour.

I first met Mr. Street in the winter of 1933 at a Santa Claus convention. He had just come up from the South and was writing feature stories for the Associated Press, whereas I was doing the same for the United Press. One day a note came in the mail saying the department-store Santa Clauses of New York City would hold a convention at Grand Central Palace the following afternoon. This was the period of the NRA Blue Eagle codes and the Santa Clauses were assembling for the purpose of drawing up a program of ethics. A novel spectacle! By the very nature of his calling a department-store Santa Claus has to be a proficient liar—a man as fundamentally dishonest as a real-estate agent. Moreover, I know it to be a fact that the average department-store Santa Claus hates and despises his customers—the little ones—and would enjoy nothing so much as running amuck in a crowd of tots.

At Grand Central Palace I wandered around in the various exhibition halls, finding no Santa Claus convention, and at last I sat down near the elevators to rest my feet. I was sitting there when an elevator door opened and a short young man stepped out. He glanced all around and then approached me.

"Begya pahdon, suh," he said, "but I'm lookin' for a bunch of dad-blamed Santy Clauses."

It was Mr. Street, and soon we were sitting down comparing notes and swapping newspaper experiences, and after a while we went wandering and found the convention. The Santa Clauses were in a little room far off in one corner of the building. There were about a dozen of them, and they had a keg of beer on a table. They were dressed in their Santa costumes, all but their whiskers which had been laid aside to facilitate the taking in of beer. If you have ever seen such an assemblage of Santas, minus their whiskers, you have seen something. And if you have ever heard them talk, you have heard something. They came in all shapes and sizes and there wasn't a jolly one in the group. Since that day I have never believed in Santa Claus.

So that was the beginning of a long and interesting friendship. Mr. Street and I sometimes go adventuring together, and while our roamings occasionally prove trying to organized society, sometimes even offending the body politic, we have fun.

There is one story I want to tell about Mr. Street but to get into it I've got to bring up the matter of the round chickens. One day in 1942 I chanced to meet a citizen of Peoria, Illinois, who was visiting in New York. He turned out to be a chicken fancier, and he said he had come East to acquire some round chickens.

"Round chickens," he said, "come originally from India. They got practically no necks and almost no legs. A hen will weigh as much as fifteen pounds and a caponized rooster will weigh as much as twenty. If they scrooched up a little and bounced, you could almost dribble them like a basketball. The poultry growers of this country are going to get wise to these round chickens. They got almost as much meat on them as a hog, and it's wonderful white meat. Once we get going with them, you won't go into a restaurant and order fried chicken or half a broiled chicken. You'll order a chicken steak."

It is the clear duty of a writing person, when he hears such a thing as this story of the round chickens, to get to work and find out all the facts, so I got to work. After a couple of hours at the Public Library I concluded that the Peorian had reference to the Cornish game chicken, or one of its kinsfolk.

Next I telephoned the Department of Agriculture's poultry division. They dug up their best chicken expert and I told him the story.

"Well," he said, "I think the man from Peoria is pulling your drumstick. If he says these hens grow to fifteen pounds, he must have hens with some ostrich blood in them. And the roosters—if they got to weigh twenty pounds—would be unmanageable. You'd have to build a steel-and-concrete fortress to hold roosters that big. They'd tear down an ordinary chicken house and they might even turn on their owners and murder them."

On my way home I stopped at Mr. Street's house, having remembered that in his early days he had been a chicken fancier. If these round chickens existed anywhere on earth, I figured Mr. Street would know about them. Having swallowed a good dose of quinine, I took my machete and hacked my way through the jungle of his study until I found him at his desk. We made our way back over the perilous trail until we reached the living room, where I laid the results of my research before him and did him the honor of asking his opinion.

He grinned at me and said he had never heard of round chickens and that, moreover, he was willing to make a confession.

"I was never actually very handy with chickens," he said. "It all dates back to an unhappy experience I had with chickens in Mississippi."

It appears that when Mr. Street was first married, down in Mississippi, he was a preacher—the youngest clergyman in the country, known as "The Boy Preacher of the South." Under provocation he can still let loose a sermon that'll curl the wallpaper. As a preacher he had a house and time on his hands so he decided to raise chickens. He built his own chicken house and made an elegant structure out of it. He bought a tribe of Rhode Island Reds and a flock of Plymouth Rocks, and then somebody told him that he should be careful never to let the breeds mix. He should never, they said, permit the Rhode Island Red rooster to raise dust around the Plymouth Rock hens, and the same went for the Plymouth Rock rooster and the Red hens.

So Mr. Street constructed his chicken house carefully with an eye to segregation. The building had two sections and there was a long chicken run with a fence between. This was certainly all correct, and he moved his flocks into their respective quarters.

He was extremely careful to keep Rocks separated from Reds at night. In the daytime he simply let all the chickens out into the yard together.

"Somehow," he said, "the notion was in the back of my mind that if I kept them apart at night, everything would be okay. I had this idea in my head that they only did that sort of thing at night. Before I knew it the whole thing was a mess. That's how much of a chicken expert I am."

CHAPTER X　*How to Become a Book Author*

CONSIDERING the nature and quality of the book authors I already knew, you might think I should have taken warning. Yet I didn't, and the first time a publisher came along singing sweetly of the Independent Life, I whooped and groveled like one of Aimee McPherson's sheep.

My first misadventure came in 1939, when I wrote a biography of a man about whom nobody ever heard. Nobody has ever heard of him to this day. The book was a bastard project from the start. It was about a man named Robert Gair and it was financed by the company which Robert Gair founded, hence it had to be written in a manner that would make Robert Gair stand out as a hero, a genius, and a benefactor of mankind. I even revised the history of the War Between the States to make it appear that Robert Gair, who wore kilts into battle, won it. I had to give Robert Gair a character that was warm and lovable and I had to pretend an enthusiasm for him that didn't exist. The little biography was brought out by a Fourth Avenue publisher and sold a total of forty-one copies after the Gair Company had given away 1,500 copies—including one to J. P. Morgan, who probably threw it at a photographer.

A year after that I wrote a short novel called *Mr. Klein's Kampf*, which was an attempt at satire, and the last I heard I owed the publisher $11.70. Now I was not only a biographer but a novelist, and I was beginning to learn a few things about the Literary Life.

One of the first shameful things I did after becoming a novelist was to make an ass out of myself in a bookstore. The thing wasn't premeditated. I stopped into a small bookstore near my home. Actually, it was a greeting-card store with books on the side. I was looking for a Thorne Smith novel I had missed. The proprietor of the store was a small, round man with thick glasses and a slight accent. He didn't have the book I wanted but he wasn't letting a customer get away. He tried to sell me a Thomas Wolfe novel which I already had.

"I got every kind book you want," he assured me, "except that one you said. Give me the name and I'll order it up. I got everything else."

Right at that point I did it. I looked at him a minute and then said:

"You have a book called *Mr. Klein's Kampf?*"

He stood for a moment in thought, then hurried to the rear shelves and began searching. At last he found it.

"Ha!" he cried. "What is it I tell you? Look! Brand new! I wrap it up for you."

"Never mind," I said. "I didn't want to buy it." He looked as though one of his adrenal glands had exploded. "I just wanted to know if you had it in stock," I went on. "You see, I *wrote* that book."

You should have seen the way I said it, the languid manner in which I tossed it off. He stood and looked at me, and then at the book in his hand, and then back at me, and finally a startled, happy expression swept over his face and he let out a yell.

"MOMMA!" he cried.

Out of a back room came a woman of exactly the same dimensions as the bookseller.

"Momma!" he said. "Look! This book! He wrote it!"

It seemed a perfect audience for my asinine posturing. I acted nonchalant. I got out a cigarette and, so help me, I *tapped it on the back of my hand* before putting it in my mouth, and when I put a match to it, I tried to remember how William Powell looked lighting a cigarette in the movies.

The bookseller and Momma stood there looking at me. Then the man walked completely around me, surveying me carefully from head to heel. When he had completed the circuit, he looked me straight in the eye and said:

"*I'm* gonna write a book."

His inflection made it all too clear what was in his mind.

He was saying to himself: "If this dopey-looking guy standing here can write a book, then anybody can write a book. *I* can write a book."

Having declared his intent, he leaned forward and tapped me on the shoulder.

"Know what about my book's gonna be?" he asked.

I assured him I had no idea.

"How lousy people are!" he said.

This recollection of my ignominious behavior in the little bookstore leads me to a pet proposal. I think there ought to be a law barring all authors and all relatives of authors from bookstores. Relatives of authors seem to abandon their senses the moment their man has a new book out. I remember back a dozen years when a newspaper friend of mine wrote a biography which didn't sell. During the first two weeks after its publication, the author's sixteen-year-old daughter took it upon herself to make a best seller out of it. Her technique was simplicity itself. The book had a bright dust jacket with the title and the author's name in big lettering. The girl spent from six to eight hours every day riding the New York subways. She'd perch herself on the edge of the subway seat ("it'll keep you on the edge of your chair") and hold her papa's book up level with her face, opened, of course, so people could see the title and name of the author. She'd pretend she was reading it eagerly, with her eyes bugging out. Occasionally she'd change position, turning to left or right in order that everyone in the car could see the name of this engrossing volume.

When my own novel was published, I went through much the same sort of thing. I recall that on a Sunday afternoon my wife and I took a walk down Fifth Avenue. We wanted to look in the windows of the big bookstores and see if my masterwork was being displayed.

At Scribner's we found a lone copy stuck down in the corner of the window. To me it loomed as big as the Lincoln Memorial, and I could easily have spotted it at a distance of one hundred yards. We stood and admired it for a while and I was ready to move on. Just then another couple came up to the window and began looking at the books. Suddenly my wife let out a yip.

"Oh, look!" she cried. "There's that book, *Mr. Klein's Kampf!* Oh, I've heard *so much* about that book! They say it's *marvelous!* We've got to get that book, *Mr. Klein's Kampf,* first thing tomorrow! Don't you remember, darling? Maxine just *raved* about it! Funniest book she ever read! See it there? *Mr. Klein's Kampf!*"

I couldn't stand it any longer. I grabbed her and dragged her off down the Avenue, and when I started to raise hell about such behavior, she simply said:

"Why, you know very well those people will buy it tomorrow."

Meanwhile, in Washington my brother Sam was in action. I didn't know about it until later. On his way to work each morning Sam passed a big department store. The book department was on the ground floor and it didn't take him long to perform his morning chore there. In this particular book department there was one shelf, set off from the others, bearing a sign: "Recommended." Every morning for ten days my brother would walk in, pretend to browse a bit, locate a half-hidden copy of *Mr. Klein's Kampf,* and quietly place it on the "Recommended" shelf. It wouldn't be there when he arrived the next morning, but he'd go through the same routine, and he tells me they never caught him at it. I don't know what the clerks thought. They probably figured I was in town.

Sam's behavior in Washington was by no means unusual for an author's relative. Booksellers have told me of many similar performances. I was telling a novelist acquaintance about Sam's one-man job of promotion. He had a story to match it.

He said that immediately after one of his first novels was published his girl friend flung herself into action. Three times she walked into the book department at Macy's and went to a shelf, almost hidden beneath a table, where they had a dozen copies of the novel. She'd boldly carry the books to another table, build a pyramid display with them, and then walk out. The third time she tried it they caught her, and the lady who interrupted her pyramid-building, being wise in such matters, simply said to her:

"The author's wife?"

Due to the infinite wisdom that characterizes my every act, I'd like to point out that I didn't want to write *Low Man on a Totem Pole*—the only thing I ever did that made good money. I was determined that I would become a novelist if it killed me. It is one thing to say you're going to write a novel and it's another to dredge up an idea. During the summer of 1940, while working on the New York *World-Telegram*, I was spending perhaps five minutes a day in quiet contemplation—hoping a plot would jump up and smite me. One afternoon I had an assignment that took me into a corset factory occupying part of a building on Union Square.

The proprietor of this establishment proved to be an interesting personality. He was a designer of corsets and girdles as well as a manufacturer. He took great pride in his accomplishments and told me he was an authority on the female form. He'd drag out corsets and girdles and yank them around in all the variations of the two-way stretch. Then he'd yell for a model, and a girl wearing a corset would come in and he'd use her to illustrate what he had been talking about—grabbing hold of her here and there as impersonally as he might grab a fire hydrant.

He made it clear to me that as a designer of corsets and girdles he was an artist.

"Night and day," he said, "I'm on the kwee vivvy. I am always doing research, keeping abreast of the times. That's a line I always use—a gag—keeping abreast of the times."

I asked him the precise nature of this interminable research. He said it involved constant study of female anatomy.

"Most of my research," he said, "I do on the street. I just walk around the street looking for girls and women. I get behind a girl and walk along and watch her rear. I take mental note of all the strains and stresses. I suppose if anybody noticed what I was doing, they'd think I was an old letch. But, after all, it's my business."

When he had finished giving me the information I sought, I started to leave, thinking that maybe I had missed my calling. On my way out I passed a door which led into the Cutting Department and I stopped to survey the busy scene.

Near me was a young man working at a wooden table. He was using pressboard patterns and a short-bladed knife to cut several layers of fabric. I stood and watched him for a while and then I noticed what he was cutting. He was turning out the upper parts of corsets—bust pockets, as I later learned they were called. This young man and his job gave me pause. Here, maybe, was a character for my novel. He was a nice-looking, sturdily built young man and, to my way of thinking, he had an unusual sort of a job. I visualized my fictitional character—a young man just such as this one, spending his long days cutting bust pockets, trying to keep his mind off the items that ultimately would go into them, dreaming at night perhaps of oceans of billowing busts pressing in upon him, smothering him.

Knowing that novelists are supposed to do some research, that they try to achieve accuracy in all technical details, I stepped into the room and approached the bust-pocket cutter. I introduced myself and told him the boss had given me permission to look around and asked him if he'd mind telling me about his work. He didn't mind. He cut a few sample bust pockets to show me how it was done, and demonstrated how the knife could handle twenty-four layers of fabric consisting, as he put it, of "twelve lefts and twelve rights."

I asked him about the matter of sizes and he said there were about ten different capacities, and then I asked him if the workmen in the place had any slang expressions to distinguish one size from another.

"Sure," he said. "The smaller sizes we call teacups. The mediums we call grapefruit, and the big ones we call hammocks."

"What do you think about all day while you're cutting these things?" I asked him.

"Oh," he said, "lotsa things. Mostly about stamps. I'm a stamp collector."

He gave me some more technological information about his work and I went on my way. Soon after that I started writing my novel with a bust-pocket cutter as my chief character. I turned out two sample chapters and an outline and submitted them to George Joel, editor of the Dial Press. To this day he says it was the worst piece of manuscript produced since Christopher Sholes invented the typewriter.

Jerome Weidman also recommended that I take my fiction and feed it to the nearest goat. Mr. Weidman suggested that I do a book based on my adventures interviewing people. I said no. I said it had been proved conclusively that such books don't sell. He argued the point at great length and finally I went to work on the book that was to become *Low Man on a Totem Pole*.

The actual writing of that book was a minor industrial project compared to the mad brain-rummaging that followed when it came time to give it a title. The search ended only after nine weeks of luncheons, round-table conferences, sessions at the bar and, finally, a sort of title tournament held in the Doubleday, Doran offices.

All my friends and relatives joined in the quest. Fred Allen spent a couple of evenings bouncing titles at me. He is a strong man, but in the end he achieved such a state of brain fag that he was crying out such things as, "The Two Sams—Flot and Jet."

My wife was determined that she would find the right title. She spent days prowling through Bartlett's Quotations. She made my homecomings hideous, for she would meet me at the door and begin assaulting my ear with the day's accumulation of phrases. Her participation reached a climax on a Sunday afternoon. She had finished with Bartlett and was going through Shakespeare. Occasionally she'd mutter a line from the bard and I'd shake my head no. Then suddenly she let out a happy cry. She had it!

"My Quill Is Too Short," she exclaimed.

It was one of the most humiliating things that has ever happened to me.

Personally, I was worn out early in the game. In desperation I finally asked that the thing be titled "Book." There were more than three hundred and fifty title suggestions on the list when the tournament finally was held. Nobody invited me. A dozen men shut themselves into a big office and quarreled and quibbled and called each other idiots. At last one of these men, glancing down at a proof of Fred Allen's introduction to the book, noticed a line and whispered hoarsely, "Low Man on a Totem Pole."

They telephoned me and told me about it and I said I didn't give a damn one way or the other. "Low Man on a Totem Pole." It didn't make sense. I tried to make it make sense by doing some research on the subject of totem poles.

Totem is an Ojibway word. Pole isn't. You don't have to be an Indian to have a totem. The idea behind totems is somewhat like the idea behind the organization of Boy Scout patrols. The essential difference between the Scout system and the totem system is that once you belong to a certain totem, say the anteater totem, you can't ever change your membership. Once a Potato Bug, always a Potato Bug.

Generally speaking, a member of a totemic group will not kill or harm the animal which represents his clan. It might be his grandfather. (There are, incidentally, all kinds of clan divisions. The Ponkas, for example, have moieties which are divided into phratries.) An Australian whose totem is the witchetty grub (it says this in the Encyclopedia Britannica) will respect and venerate the witchetty grub, but won't stop his friends from eating it. I'm glad I'm not a witchetty grub man. On the other hand, maybe it would be pleasant to be a witchetty grub man, serene in the knowledge that never, so long as I lived, would I ever have to eat one.

In my research I came across mention of the Aruntas of Australia, who are divided into totemic groups, membership in which depends upon the position of the mother at the moment of realization of pregnancy. That isn't very clear, is it? But that's what the book says. The Aruntas were people who practiced head-biting. I don't get it.

These are some of the things I learned about totems and totem poles. They leave the matter as confused as ever. I've had a number of booksellers tell me that *Low Man on a Totem Pole* was the best book title of 1941. And I've had publishers tell me that a title is always a wonderful title if the book sells well, and a lousy title if the book flops.

One thing about *Low Man on a Totem Pole*. It doesn't make sense, like the title of this book does.

After publication of *Low Man on a Totem Pole* people began writing me letters demanding to know the secret significance of the title. It was a question that didn't worry two song writers—Frank Ryerson and Grady Watts. They produced a song called "The Bottom Man on the Totem Pole," and it was recorded in two parts by the Casa Loma Orchestra.

The moment this record was issued and played on the radio, people began calling me up and saying, "Sue! Sue 'em! Git a lawyer!" I had no such notions. I was flattered. I bought the record and played it a couple of times. The man who sings it says he is the bottom man on the totem pole and that he can't move around to save his soul, and that if he happened to slip he'd be in a hole. He says his back is breaking because of the weight of the people up above. He remarks that if he were up high on the pole he would be able to get a good view of the sky, but who wants to look at the sky when the purty girls go by? He has a squaw which he sends for, and he declares himself an enemy of all skunks and other animals. All in all, it's quite a song, and makes sense.

After the sale of the book had fanned out over the country, I began getting large bundles of mail. A woman in Los Angeles wrote and asked me if I would think up a name for her Sealyham. And a pile of manuscripts came in. Typescripts of books ranging from novels to biographies arrived with requests from the authors that I please arrange to have them published. One man sent in a manuscript with the title: *Low Plum on a Fruit Tree*.

There were requests from unsuccessful writers that I collaborate with them. One of these was from a man I had met casually ten years earlier. He wanted me to help with the writing of a book in which he would survey the entire political development of the United States. To prove to me that he was no fly-by-night he sent word that he was already an author, enclosing a copy of his book: *Asphalt: Origin, History, Development—Its Relation to Petroleum*.

I turned down all collaboration requests. I've never been able to understand how two men can write together without, in the end, shooting each other dead. I tried it once.

Back in 1931 Henry McLemore and I set ourselves up as a writing team. It was our custom to meet at my apartment. We'd put a sheet of paper in the typewriter and then forget it for a while. We'd sit down with a bottle of gin and talk until the bottle was there and not the gin. Then we'd start to work. Within half an hour we'd be quarreling, calling each other names, and threatening each other with multiple contusions.

One of these quarrels finally ended the collaboration. We were shouting abuse at each other. I was sitting in an easy chair and Henry was pacing the floor. He was in a mighty fury. Suddenly he whipped around, leveled a finger at me, and shouted:

"You (censored) (censored) (censored)! You don't deserve to live with that nanny-goat brain you got! I'm gonna throw your whole god-damn apartment out the window!"

That's how mad he was. He had to have physical action.

"Go ahead and throw it, you (censored) (censored) (censored)!" I said.

He decided to start with the contents of the refrigerator. He opened one of the living-room windows, giving on an alleyway. Out went the eggs. Out went the bacon.

"Every stick of furniture in the place goes out!" he yelled.

The stuff that was in bottles and dishes made a frightful racket when it hit the pavement five floors below. Henry had finished with the contents of the refrigerator and was headed for the window with a floor lamp when the building superintendent came crashing into the apartment.

We had a time of it keeping that superintendent from calling the police, and we had to waste half a bottle of gin on him to pacify him. When he had gone, Henry sat down across from me and grinned.

"You think I didn't mean it," he said. "I'd have done it. I'd have thrown everything out and that includes you personally."

"Like hell you would've!" I said.

He jumped up and was ready to renew the job when I decided to temporize, yield, arbitrate, and surrender.

I want no more collaboration. Not with the price of eggs like it is.

CHAPTER XI   *Memoirs of an Ex-Columnist*

UNLESS HE POSSESSES the resistance of a razor-back hog, a man who writes a book quickly takes down with a sort of gumma of the brain. His affliction is one which no sulfa drug will cure.

A man who becomes a writer of a column, however, is much worse off. His brain achieves such a state that no respectable gumma would ever attach itself to it. He becomes a straightforward paranoiac. He suffers first from headache, tinnitus, palpitation, digestive disturbances, and incapacity for mental exertion. After that come intense egotism, selfishness, conceit, overbearing pride, violent temper, and moroseness. How do I know this? I was a columnist.

My own favorite columnist is Walter Winchell. Around newspaper offices, where it is fashionable to scoff, Winchell gets very little outspoken applause. Your omniscient, swaggering newspaperman greets his name with a sneer. I never did. I wouldn't sneer at a man I admire even though such sneering would make me appear to be sagacious, sardonic, and as sharp as a tack. The thing that has always amused me is the spectacle of newspapermen snorting through their noses at mention of Winchell and then fighting over possession of the *Mirror* when it arrives in the office—fighting to get page ten.

I've often contended that Winchell is a better writer than nine tenths of his newspaper critics, even though he didn't put in the usual years of apprenticeship. Day in and day out, his stuff has sparkle. He can turn a phrase with the best of them, and nobody can deny that he's one of the great reporters of our time. Alongside Winchell his multitude of imitators, male and female, are drab and dopey. Most of them are such bad reporters that they give themselves away. Getting an item right is so rare with them that when, by chance, they do get hold of something that's correct, they proudly mention their accuracy in another column.

Walter Winchell didn't become a newspaper gossip columnist until 1924. I was one in 1923. During the spring of that year the Huntington *Press* began running a feature under the signature, "By Miss Ella Vator." The first of Ella Vator's columns was a sober essay on how to build birdhouses, with special emphasis on birdhouses suitable for martins. After that Miss Ella Vator gained confidence and began dabbling in personalities.

Within a very few weeks I was in trouble. A man named Till Priddy was hopping mad at me for having disputed his claim to being champion mushroom hunter of Huntington County. Mr. Priddy's anger was mild, however. In one of the Ella Vator columns I made mention of a local hotel proprietor and his wife. Owing to the circumstance that his wife was a blonde, I referred to her as "Blondie." I didn't seem to know it but in Huntington, twenty years ago, to call a woman "Blondie" was almost the same as calling her a whorelady. The hotel proprietor telephoned the paper, canceled his advertising contract, announced that he was going to sue, and said that if he ever caught that snotnose Smith on the street he'd stomp him to death. My boss saw only one way out for me and the paper. I had to go down to the man's hotel, face him in his own lobby, and apologize to him—taking my chance of being stomped to death. He accepted the apology graciously, but that was the termination of my early career as a columnist. Miss Ella Vator disappeared at once and forever.

Let the curtain drop, now, to denote the passage of eighteen years. It is 1941 and again I have become a columnist. In that year I signed a contract with the United Feature Syndicate under which I was to produce a 600-word essay six days a week for ten years with no vacations. I lasted exactly six months.

Up until that time I believed that the column-writing business was almost exclusively in the hands of heels—some of them being born heels, others having acquired heelhood after becoming columnists.

Every columnist I know has a multitude of enemies. There have been times in my own life when, if Congress granted me permission to shoot ten citizens of the United States without fear of prosecution, the first eight on my list would have been columnists. But no more. They spew out hog-wash and sheep-dip from day to day, and they accept large sums of money in exchange for their daily drool, and they brazenly further their own private enterprises in their columns. They do these things, and yet my heart goes out to them. I've tried column-writing and I know what it is.

During the period when I was a columnist, a New York paper contracted for my daily output. The paper, however, used my column only about half the time. This was depressing to me at a time when I was already as depressed as a she-elk deprived of her young. One noontime a couple of prominent Broadway press agents invited me to have lunch with them. They wanted me to interview one of their clients. They also had another scheme up their sleeves. They knew how to make my column a rousing success.

"Listen," said one of them, "we'll do this job for you. You don't even need to know what's going on. We've got a dozen people working in our offices. They live in every part of New York and some of them live in the suburbs. We'll start a campaign right tonight. Every person in our office will write ten or twelve letters a day, praising your column. The letters will be mailed in to the paper—from different points in and around New York. That's all it takes. That much mail, day after day, will put you in solid."

I said no, thanks.

Vanity impels me to report that my column was not a failure. It was making money when I quit and was being used in the key cities throughout the country. But it was the biggest headache I ever took on. I got a chance to cancel my contract through a technicality and I canceled it. Writing a column is no job for a lazy man.

It seems unlikely that physical energy will ever be mentioned in connection with me. I am about as dynamic as a sea squirt. A sea squirt is a small gelatinous creature shaped like a tiny sweet potato. It attaches itself to a rock and stays there until it dies. It has two orifices at the top. A current of water passes into one orifice and out the other, and the squirt takes up, from this water, the small particles on which it subsists. Throughout its adult life the sea squirt shows no sign of animation unless a fish or a scientist approaches it.

Then it contracts and squirts water out of itself in two violent jets. If you don't believe this, look it up.

I have much the same inclinations as a sea squirt, but you just can't sit on a rock and turn out a column. The actual writing of the thing is no problem. The big worry is finding something to write about. I'm well aware of the fact that most of the columnists get a large portion of their stuff from the press agents. Which reminds me that I once had occasion to investigate an establishment called Hanson's drugstore— one of the most colorful hangouts in the Times Square neighborhood.

Hanson's drugstore operates around the clock. It is a hangout for press agents, Broadway detectives, showgirls, bookies, song pluggers, and outcasts from café society. It serves as headquarters for about a dozen Broadway press agents. They are chiefly free-lance artists engaged in publicizing unheard-of dance teams, strippers, Staten Island comedians, and ethical clip joints.

Some of these press agents confess that they have no offices, that Hanson's store serves them for a business address. One admits that he once had a letterhead listing his address as 780 Seventh Avenue, which is the drugstore, and giving three telephone numbers to make it appear that he sat behind a desk covered with phones. The three numbers were for the three pay booths in Hanson's.

The drugstore is an important institution to these boys. They gather here from midnight on and swap small talk and think up gags. This is the place where they usually make contact with the Broadway columnists.

Several of the columnists stop regularly at Hanson's, usually around three or four in the morning. The press agents will be there, but there is a rigid etiquette governing their behavior when a columnist shows up. They may nod and say, not loudly, "hello"; but they must never be so brazen as to approach a columnist and engage him in extensive conversation. The thing is done in a more subtle fashion, with something of the air of international espionage. A taxi driver named Sam Gross serves as liaison man.

During the evening the press agent will collect little news items and small flashes and bits of gossip. He will write these on a sheet of paper. The paper is handed over to Sam Gross. Gross is cabdriver by appointment to the royalty of Broadway —the columnists. So he collects the sheets of paper from the various press agents and sometime during the night hands them over to the columnists. Let's make this wonderful system a little clearer. The press agent has a client. The client is, say, a dance team known as Gomez & Marberry, currently performing at Chez Henhouse. The press agent will be paid regularly by Gomez & Marberry provided their names pop up occasionally in the Broadway columns. So the press agent goes to work.

He gathers all manner of items that have nothing whatever to do with Gomez & Marberry, and passes those items along to the columnists. After he has turned in ten good items, he is entitled to turn in a plug for his client. Accordingly, it comes out in the column something like this:

"If you really want an ill-thray, see Gomez & Marberry in their breath-taking routine at Chez Henhouse."

I had traffic with the press agents but I couldn't horn in on this system. My column kept me on the move. Some people may be able to sit at home, read the papers, then write learnedly of mankind and his affairs. Not me. I've got to get out and move around among the folks.

There were some pleasurable moments during my career as a columnist. I got to listen to a lot of talk from unique personalities. Thinking back over the six months, two names pop into my mind: H. L. Mencken and Tallulah Bankhead.

Mencken has been one of my favorite authors for a long time. During the nineteen-thirties whenever he was in New York I was always getting under his feet. I'd interview him once a month if I could get an okay from the boss, and the boss usually approved because Mencken was always good copy.

Now that I was a columnist, choosing my own assignments, I decided it was time I did another Mencken interview—this time in his native habitat. I got on a plane for Baltimore and, because of a policeman, made the trip without ever having to look at New Jersey. Criminal instincts have always dominated my inner life and for this reason I've never regarded a cop as being quite human. The man sitting next to me in the plane was a New York City patrolman.

He was not in uniform but wore a costume which made him look like a major-league umpire. We had a long conversation during the flight, and I found out that he was human. He hates New York City firemen, and he told me that all cops hate all firemen.

"Them firemen," he said, "are crooked as a dog's hind leg. They'd steal off their grandmothers. They go to a fire and wear these big hip boots that are wide at the top. I'd like to see the day come when the Federals would catch a bunch of firemen coming out of a store where there's been a fire. If you turned them upside down and shook them, half the moichandise in that store would fall out of their boots. I don't see why they don't let cops have boots like that. Them dirty firemen got it all over us, wearing their boots. A cop's gotta carry enough junk around in his pockets without finding a place to put loot. It's not fair."

He told me that firemen are so dishonest they even tell lies to their wives. He said the classic story in the New York fire department concerned a young fireman who was accustomed to reach his home on payday with maybe half his pay left. This fireman had not been married long, and he had convinced his wife that he, as well as all other firemen, were paid by piecework. He told her that members of each company got paid so much per fire, and to cover up his fortnightly deficit he'd sit around and complain about how slow business was.

One day this fireman's wife met the wife of another fireman, who worked at another company.

"How's business been lately over at your husband's place?" asked the deceived one. In no time at all she learned of the fraud that had been put upon her. According to my cop friend, she went straight to the station and asked the man on post at the door if her husband were in. The man on post yelled, and the double-dealer came down the brass pole. At the same instant his feet hit the floor his wife hit him—square in the teeth.

I found Mencken waiting for me at the offices of the Baltimore *Sun*. It was a steaming day—104 degrees in the shade. I had not seen Mencken in six years. I was startled when he walked into the room—shocked at the swiftness with which age had taken hold of him. He still seemed robust and alert, but age was showing in his face. He was well aware of it too. Several times during our long talk he spoke of the short time he had left.

I have at least one reason for hoping to outlive him. I have been written into his last will and testament. Readers of the Mencken memoirs will recall the story of the great Baltimore fire of 1904. At that time Mencken was city editor of the *Herald* and with the rest of the staff had to flee the newspaper's building when the flames took hold of it. Sometime later he returned to the gutted structure and managed to reach the floor where his desk had been. The desk was now no more than a layer of ashes on the floor but, prodding around in this mess, Mencken found his old copy hook—black and twisted but still intact. That copy hook has been one of his cherished mementos of the old days and, with all the audacity of an autograph nit, I once asked him if I might have it when he is finished with it. By letter he notified me:

That copy hook will become yours the day I am translated to bliss eternal. I have left orders that my carcass is to be stuffed and deposited in the National Museum at Washington. I had planned to ask the taxidermist to put the copy hook in my hand, but that request is now canceled and you will get it in due course.

We had planned to go out to the Mencken house in Hollins Street, but it was altogether too hot to move around so we settled down in an office there at the *Sun*. Mencken has written extensively about the three-story brick house, sandwiched in between buildings of the same approximate design, where he has lived almost all his life and where he has always done the major part of his work.

"The neighborhood has been going down steadily," he said. "In the last few years the Okies have been moving in. They are the mountain morons from Appalachia, and most of the old-timers of the neighborhood are moving out as these morons come in. Not me. I've lived in that house since 1883, save for the five years of my marriage. I intend to stay as long as I last. I may not last long, but that's where I intend to finish out my days."

He lives at the house with his bachelor brother, August, an engineer who is about ten years younger than Henry. August looks a good deal like "Harry" and is an author in his own right, having produced a recent book concerned with famous hangings. The brothers keep a couple of household servants and Henry has a secretary—a lady of middle years who comes in mornings, takes dictation, and goes home to write it. Mencken describes her as possessing asbestos ears.

He's a prodigious worker and his home is a veritable warehouse of raw materials for his labor. His mother never threw away any piece of paper with writing on it, and her literary son, engaged in recent years on autobiographical projects, has had a stupendous cargo of source material to aid him in setting down his reminiscences. It has not been necessary for him to visit the public library or the newspaper morgues to ascertain the price of hominy in 1883. He even dredged up the doctor's bill for his own birth. A certain Dr. Buddenbohn assessed the Menckens ten dollars for fetching Henry Louis on a September Sunday evening in 1880. I contend that was the biggest ten dollars' worth this country ever got.

During the last few years Mencken has been furrowing through these acres of material and writing his autobiography in sections. Thus far three volumes have been finished —*Happy Days, Newspaper Days,* and *Heathen Days,* and any person who can read those books and succeed in disliking their author—well, that person has a hive of maggots for a brain.

There in Baltimore I was interested, chiefly, in the kind of life Mencken is leading these days. He said he's still having fun.

"The chief pleasure I get out of life is my work," he said. "I get no pleasure in games. I hate sports. The one thing I love to do is travel, but a man can't travel any more. I don't want to see South America. I might get down there and get stuck in one of those rattraps. I've been everywhere and I think I know people in every town in America. It becomes a tough proposition for me to go to a town and try to see it and soak it up. People I know in each town want to entertain me and it's hard to get out of such things. What I really like to do is just wander around the streets and look at the morons."

Mencken is still the moving spirit of the Saturday Night Club—a small group of amateur musicians which has been holding weekly meetings since 1905. They gather in a room in a downtown office building and start playing their music at 8:15 P.M. Mencken plays second piano and they usually keep going until ten o'clock, at which time they adjourn to a beer resort for the remainder of the evening.

"I'm the only original member left," he said. "There are no written regulations and no officers. To become a member a man has to meet with unanimous approval. No guests are permitted to wander into our concerts. A member may bring a guest but he's got to be sure of his man and he's responsible for the guest's behavior. A guest is not permitted to criticize the music. He can sit and listen to it, but he can't say he likes it or dislikes it. If he says anything at all about it, we throw him the hell out."

Mencken no longer writes regularly for the *Sun,* though he is on the board of directors. He has no office at the newspaper and my meeting with him took place in the office of the publisher, Paul Patterson. Mencken generally rides a trolley car from his home to the *Sun* building. Many years ago he owned an automobile, but something happened. . . .

"It was in 1918," he explained. "I drove my car up in front of the *Sun* building one morning and stopped at the curb, just as I had been doing for months. A cop came up and said, 'Hey, you can't stop here.' I said, 'Like hell I can't!' He said, 'Like hell you can!' I said, 'Why the hell can't I stop here?' And he said, 'We got new rules. We got a parking law went into effect this morning.' Well, I looked at him a minute and then I said, 'Nuts to that,' and got in the car and drove it around the corner and sold it. I've never owned a car since that day."

After a couple of hours the time came for me to leave. I had to catch an airline coach at the Lord Baltimore Hotel across the street from the *Sun.* Mencken went with me. In the elevator he spoke almost affectionately with the Negro operator, asked about his health and the health of his family, and said, "I missed you around here the other day. I thought maybe you were in Europe fighting the Huns."

We walked across the street and stood at the entrance to the hotel.

"I'd go in with you while you make the arrangements about the coach," he said, "but maybe you already noticed that the chiropractors of America are having their convention in this hotel. You know how I have handled the chiropractors down through the years. I wouldn't be safe in there. They'd ambush me in thirty seconds if I stepped into that lobby. They'd throw me to the floor and dismantle my spinal column and play marbles with my vertebrae."

So we stood there and talked for about ten more minutes and then he left, swinging briskly up the street, nobody paying him a bit of mind. I stood and watched him. To me he was the greatest man in Baltimore, in Maryland, perhaps even in the United States. Yet there in the heart of Baltimore scores of people passed him without giving him a second glance. He had on a flat straw hat and a dull business suit and there was a black cigar stuck in his face. He didn't look like a great man. He might have been a plumber, taking a day off and heading for a Rita Hayworth movie. He stopped at the corner where the traffic light was against him, and turned around and saw that I had been watching him. He raised his arm and waved good-by, and I tingled all over like a high-school girl being introduced to Victor Mature.

I went into the hotel and up to the transportation desk where I had to wait a few minutes. A Baltimore taxi driver was standing at my elbow. I asked him if he knew H. L. Mencken.

"Sure," he said. "Newspaper guy. His column ain't as popular as it used to be, though. He's again Roosevelt."

☆   ☆   ☆

Tallulah Bankhead sent word that she didn't want to be interviewed. She said she was sick of being interviewed. She said that people come to interview her, then go away and write mean things about her—things that cause her to lose sleep.

I'm glad I didn't give up at that point. I argued and insisted and finally she said it would be all right for me to come and visit her in her apartment. But no interview. Just a friendly visit.

She turned out to be one of the most invigorating personalities I have ever met in my life. She is, at bottom, a beauty, and she talks like a machine gun. She talks about all the people she loves and admires, about the fabulous members of the Bankhead clan, about clothes and shoes and the war and dogs and maids and broadcasting and whisky and everything under the sun. I didn't take any notes, because, remember, it was not an interview. But I remembered a lot of things she talked about.

She told about the time she met Wendell Willkie. Impulsively she said to him that she considered him to be the third greatest man in the United States. Naturally, he asked her to name the first two.

"Franklin D. Roosevelt," she said, "and Joe Louis."

That story started her—an unvarnished Southerner—on the subject of Joe Louis.

"There's a man who has everything," she said. "He's a gentleman if I ever saw a gentleman. I'll never forget the fight with Conn. Joe was losing on points. He knew he was losing. He had to knock Conn out to win, and it looked bad. There were only two rounds to go. I sat there with chills running down my spine, suffering for him. Then Billy Conn's foot slipped and he almost fell. In that long moment Billy was wide open. Joe could have stepped in right then and finished him. But he saw that Billy had slipped, and he stepped back and gave Billy time to recover his balance. It was a magnificent thing. It was a beautiful thing to see. No trainer could ever have taught Joe Louis that. What he did was inside of him."

She went on and on, talking for what seemed hours and never uttering a dull sentence. Occasionally she'd stop for a sip of Dixie nectar—Coca-Cola. Tallulah quit drinking hard stuff at the time of Dunkerque and swore that she'd never touch another drop until Hitler was licked. She's been true to her oath.

She said that all the Bankheads have been great talkers. Not long ago her aunt Marie was hurt in an automobile accident. Her kneecap was broken and her tongue was so badly cut that she couldn't utter a word. She is past seventy and, by all accounts, one of the liveliest of all the Bankheads. When the doctor came to patch her up after the accident, he turned his attention first to the injured knee. The venerable lady quickly seized a pencil and scribbled.

"Forget the knee, you fool, and get to work on my tongue. A Bankhead without a tongue is unthinkable."

Under Tallulah's eloquent enfilade I found it next to impossible to sort out the stories, to untangle them, to remove them from the major oration and consider them as single pieces. I was on my way home before the main story—the best Bankhead story—suddenly took shape out of the torrent of words. It is the story of Eugenia Sledge's picture.

Tallulah talks a lot about Eugenia Sledge, who was celebrated as one of the most beautiful women in the South. There are photographs of Eugenia throughout Tallulah's apartment, because Eugenia was Tallulah's mother. Tallulah never knew her, for Eugenia died at the time her daughter was born.

It has been a tradition throughout Tallulah's professional career that a picture of her mother shall stand on her dressing table at the theater during every performance. The custom has become almost a superstition.

Back in 1933 Tallulah came home from her successes in London. Her first stage appearance in New York was to be in a play called *Forsaking All Others*. She backed the production financially and went into it with all the spirit and determination at her command, which is more than considerable. Yet everything seemed to go wrong. All the manifold woes and tribulations that can beset a theatrical company descended on this one. Not the least among these was the bank holiday, which almost coincided with the opening performance.

In the final rehearsals no less than four of the understudies were in action. Illness overtook some members of the cast. One of the chief performers was taken down with the alcoholic botts. Sets collapsed. People sprained ankles. Costumes caught on nails and were ripped wide open. And Tallulah, with both her money and her reputation at stake, came fairly close to nervous prostration.

The entire company was jittery when opening night arrived. There was a tense, stricken atmosphere about the theater. Everyone was on edge. Everyone believed that the production was hoodooed.

Tallulah arrived at the theater accompanied by Rose, her colored maid. One hour to go until curtain time. Troubles were still accumulating. Things were still going wrong. The stage-door keeper reflected the general pessimism when he remarked that failure was so heavy in the air he could smell it. Tallulah went wearily about the business of making up.

Then she missed it.

"Rose," she said to her maid, "Rose, where's the picture? The picture of Mother?"

Rose hadn't seen it. They had forgotten to bring it.

Tallulah got up from the dressing table and dropped heavily into an easy chair.

"This is the end," she said.

Rose got on the telephone. She called the Bankhead apartment. Miss Bankhead's secretary might still be there, and she could rush the picture of Eugenia Sledge over to the theater. But there was no answer at the apartment. Curtain time was now fifteen minutes away, and there was no way of getting the photograph of Eugenia Sledge from the uptown apartment to the Times Square Theater.

So Tallulah surrendered.

"I can't go on now," she said. "Go tell the others it's all off. Tell them we're not opening."

Rose was heading for the door when a knock sounded. A man with a package for Miss Bankhead. Under ordinary circumstances she would not have admitted him but now, stunned by the ill-fortune that had fallen upon her, she simply nodded. A stranger walked into the dressing room.

"Miss Bankhead," he said, "I've got something for you in this package—something I've been wanting to give you for a long time. I knew your mother when I was a child. We were kids together. She gave me this, and I've kept it all these years, and now I want to give it to you."

He unwrapped his small package and handed Tallulah a miniature of Eugenia Sledge, done when Eugenia was a child.

Forsaking All Others opened on time and, in spite of bank holidays and all that, ran for one hundred and ten performances. And the critics said Eugenia Sledge's baby was magnificent.

CHAPTER XII   *New York Is Mostly People*

ONE OF THE CHIEF sources of material for present-generation comedians is the transaction through which the Island of Manhattan was obtained from the Indians. People who never encountered the story in history books have heard it in jokes—how Peter Minuit, the Dutchman, bought the island from the Indians for sixty guilders, or twenty-four dollars.

That transaction was a bald swindle. Mynheer Peter was flimflammed. I have the true story of the deal in a history called *Mann-hatin.* This book was published by a big bank and has a prefatory note by James J. Walker, therefore it must be reliable. It informs us that Peter Minuit paid the sixty guilders to the Canarsie Indians, and the Canarsie Indians had no more right to sell Manhattan than the Pelew Islanders have to sell the Ozarks. It didn't belong to them. They didn't even hold a mortgage on it. But they sold it to the Dutchman and made off with their guilders and later on, after the fraud had been discovered, a new deal had to be negotiated with a tribe of Indians living at the north end of Manhattan—the rightful owners.

Since I learned of this redskin game I've taken considerable enjoyment thinking back to those days—picturing the benighted, ignorant, uncivilized aborigines lurking in the forests, waiting for another ship from Europe to come in sight, and when the ship does appear in the Narrows, I see those hapless Indians leaping up and down for joy, and crying out to one another: "Ugh! Ugh! Oh, boy! More suckers!"

Thus the heritage of New York—her history opens with a swindle. Today the little people of the city scheme and connive and finagle. More than that, they have made a precise science out of the wangle. They wangle this and they wangle that and they get it for each other wholesale. Petty larceny dwells forever in their hearts, and when they ask you the nature of your business or profession, they say, "What racket you in?"

In New York newspaper offices there is a large volume called a cross-index telephone directory. It lists telephone subscribers and their numbers by streets. For example, you could take the cross-index book and begin at the lower end of Fifth Avenue and find the names and numbers of telephone subscribers house by house and store by store, clear to the end of the street. This book is invaluable for getting quick coverage on such things as large fires, explosions, shootings, collisions, and so on, when those things occur close to edition time. Suppose a flash comes from police headquarters that there has been an explosion at Throggs Neck Boulevard and Dewey Avenue. Dead line is ten minutes off. Rewrite men take the cross-index book, turn to Throggs Neck Boulevard, find the telephones listed in that immediate neighborhood, and start calling, asking whoever answers if they know what exploded, whether there's a fire, if anybody has been killed or injured, and such other details as might be available.

The rewrite men sometimes come up against peculiar situations in making such calls. One of them, I think it was Bill O'Brien, once telephoned to check on an apartment-house fire and, by chance, got the phone in the apartment where the fire started. The occupant of this apartment talked on and on, describing the progress of the flames, the splashing of water around him, the yelling of the firemen, and finally said he thought he'd better hang up, as he was now personally on fire.

There was the day of a big holdup in Brooklyn, and Carl Randau got the phone number of a small store across from the scene of the crime. In some manner Carl was connected with a pay phone on which a policeman was giving in his official report of the stickup. Carl just kept saying, "Yep. Yep. Yep. Yep," and taking notes until the cop had finished the full and complete story.

Joe Mitchell telephoned about a shooting in upper Manhattan one afternoon and got a Chinese laundryman on the wire. The Chinese couldn't understand what Joe was trying to say and while Joe was exasperated and angry, he stubbornly insisted on getting his point across. He employed English as clearly and as simply as it is possible for a native of North Carolina to speak.

"I . . . am . . . a . . . newspaper . . . reporter," he would enunciate. "There . . . has . . . been . . . a . . . shooting . . . with . . . a . . . gun . . . you know . . . bang, bang, bang . . . shooting . . . did . . . you . . . hear . . . any . . . bang, bang, bang?"

From the other end of the line came:

"Okay. Bling laundlee."

I have made hundreds of these cross-index calls and I know what the most common response is. Usually the little people are at the other end of the wire. They listen to your brief statement concerning the incident in their neighborhood, and when you ask them if they know anything about it, their first words are these: "What's in it for me?"

The petty avariciousness of the little people is irritating to many critics of New York, but somehow, to me, it affords a pleasant spectacle. It's fun to watch a couple of them trying to beat each other out of a nickel.

Speaking as a pure-bred hon-yock out of the Middle West, I would like to go on record as an admirer of New York City. Whenever I get away from the place a certain vague unhappiness settles upon me. The chief complaint I have about living in the Big Town is the necessity now and then of showing it off to my kinsfolks or other unreasonable citizens from the Edgar Guest country.

I know a lot of other transplanted Middle Westerners in New York and they all agree with me. People from back home come to New York with their hearts full of suspicion and hatred. They really look upon New York as a separate country. It is almost impossible to keep out of fights and loud arguments when you have a visiting fireman in tow. In the first place, they usually come into town on their vacations. They are out for a big time. They want to stay up all night every night, drinking everything in sight. They don't realize that most of us in New York lead the same kind of life that a citizen of St. Louis or Seattle or Scranton might lead. For the most part we stay at home nights and read or listen to the radio. Once a week, maybe, we go to the neighborhood movie. Occasionally we visit a legitimate theater, and on rare occasions we take leave of our senses and go to a night club.

Our visitors come into town whooping and yelling. They get off a train and get into a taxicab and their first argument is usually with the taxicab driver. To them he is in and of New York and, therefore, he's a crook, ipso facto, per se, and across the board. I suppose there are crooked cabdrivers in New York but I never encountered one. These visitors, however, consider the hackmen to be swindlers from the very beginning. They not only argue about the fare; they work the argument around to the point where they are able to leave the cab and stomp away without tipping. Their behavior from then on follows the same pattern. Everybody in New York is trying to hornswoggle them.

It's a difficult matter trying to figure out some reasonable method of entertaining such people. Left to myself, I think I could give a visitor a pretty good time. But they are always headstrong and omniscient and they know what they want. They want to get lit and go to Leon & Eddie's and play the drums in the orchestra and goose a chorus girl and insult people in the streets and spit on the RCA Building.

Not long ago I had a guest from Indiana. There were several places I wanted to take him. For one thing I wanted him to see the gents' room at the Radio City Music Hall. Here is one of the most noble prospects in the Western Hemisphere. It is, beyond doubt, the biggest and most magnificent can on earth—a veritable Taj Mahal of toilets. Looking at it for the first time, a man's credulity is put to test. It is almost too purty to use. Yet when I suggested to my friend that I'd like to show it to him, he said:

"Listen, fer Crisakes! You think I come all the way to Noo Yawrk to look at a toilet? C'mon! Le's go! Whereabouts is Bill's Gay Nineties at?"

It's not much fun seeing New York with such people. I prefer to go it alone. Times Square remains the best show on earth and if you know your way around in the district,

you'll find life at its daffiest there. Times Square has been
the theatrical center of New York for upward of fifty years.
Before show business moved in, the neighborhood was occupied by carriage makers, harness shops, and livery stables.
The livery-stable atmosphere survives in many of its present-
day institutions, yet the place has its points.

I propose now to take you on a little pedestrian tour of
the neighborhood and introduce you to a few of the inhabitants. Now, put your wallet in your coat pocket and keep
your hand on it and we'll stroll around and look at things
and call on people.

Broadway, between Fiftieth and Fifty-first. A skinny little
guy in a derby hat comes up the street. He is handing out
pamphlets when he can get close enough to people who will
take them. Most people shy away from him because he has
a demented look. His pamphlets are religious tracts, poorly
printed, and as he makes his way up the street he keeps
singing out:

"God gonna getcha! God gonna getcha! God gonna
getcha!"

Here's the Capitol Theater Building. Let's step in. Joe
Curtin runs the elevator in this building.* He has an un-
fortunate name for his job because wisecrackers who know
him are always yelling, "Curtin going up!" Let's tell Joe
about the God-gonna-getcha man. He says yes, he's seen the
little guy lots of times. Joe knows I sometimes go on the
prowl for unique humans.

"They's another one I wish you'd go investigate," he says.
"It's a woman. She's got a whole neighborhood scared to
death—the neighborhood where I live down in Chelsea. She
must weigh over three hundred pounds and nobody knows
where she lives at or where she comes from. She turns up
around noon almost every day and begins walking around the
same block. She always carries a club—a big old club honest
to God you could stun a horse with. She just walks around
the block, swingin' that club and scowlin' at everybody she

---

*Mr. Curtin heard that I was going to mention him in this book.
He requested that I not refer to him as an elevator operator. I asked
him how I should describe him. He said: "Say I am a former third
baseman."

meets. Never hit nobody that I know of, but people cross the street to get out of her way."

We haven't time for a side trip to Chelsea, so let's take the elevator to Ben Serkowich's office. Ben is an ex-newspaperman who has devoted his latter years to various phases of show business. He possesses one of the most phenomenal imaginations I've ever encountered. Here he is. Meet Ben Serkowich. As usual he has a story to tell. He says it's true. Listen to it, and judge for yourself. Go ahead, Ben.

Well, my friend, it looks like I'm in the money at last. Amazing thing has happened to me. You won't believe it, but you never believe anything I say, anyway.

About ten days ago I was taking a walk through Central Park. About eleven o'clock in the evening. I was away from the road, off in a sort of wooded place, when I heard somebody sobbing. There was a bench under a tree and on the bench sits this guy. He was drunk as a goat and crying his head off.

I went over and sat down on the bench and asked him what was the matter. He raised his head up and looked at me. He was a nice-looking guy, around forty. Good clothes. He had a quart bottle in his lap, about three fourths finished. He didn't say anything but handed me the bottle and I took a belt at it. Then he took one, and looked at me again, and finally he started talking. Here's what he said:

"Brother," he says, "I'm the unhappiest one human you ever saw in your life. I'm rich. Got all the money a man could want. Got enough money I can have all the dames and all the whisky I want. But I'm unhappy.

"About twelve years ago I was just a working guy. Worked in an office on a salary. One night I bought a bottle of whisky and put it in my pocket. Then I came into the Park and started wandering around, taking a drink now and then. Finally I came to this bench. I sat down and drank some more. I got drunk. I was sitting here with my chin down on my chest. It was about this time of night. Suddenly I happened to look up, and I saw the god-damnedest most beautiful thing I ever saw in my life. This whole Park was going around. Slow. It was just circling. And all the buildings over there—the big ones with the lights—were going around. It was beautiful! Most beautiful thing a man could ever hope to see. Just kept going around, slow, sort of drifting and dipping, God! What a sight!

"Well, things happened to me after that. I left New York.

Went to South America. Got involved in business. Next thing you know, I'm rich. So I come back to New York. I say to myself, from now on I'm gonna have fun. I'm gonna enjoy life.

"For a while I did have fun. Had me a hell of a good time. Then, just a few weeks ago, I began to miss something. I really wasn't having a good time. I was lying in bed one night when it dawned on me. I knew what it was I wanted. I wanted to see Central Park go around again.

"Well, I figured that was easy. I got a bottle and came over here and found this bench—the same bench—and started drinking. Drank a whole quart, but the god-damn Park wouldn't budge an inch. I found a cabdriver and sent him for another bottle and when he came back I drank half of it. Not a move from the Park. Then I passed out and the cabdriver took me home.

"I've been coming over here every night since then. Drinking myself to death. But the Park won't circle. I've gotta see it once more. It sounds crazy, but it's something inside of me. I've got to see it go around or I'll go nuts."

He sat there and stared at the ground. It sounded crazy and then again it didn't sound so crazy. I smoked a while and looked at him. He kept drinking, and every now and then he'd raise up his head and look over toward Central Park South and groan. Then it hit me. I knew the answer, or thought I did. I asked him when it was that the Park whirled for him. He said it was 1930 or 1931. That was it! I told him I thought I could make the Park go around for him again. I told him it would have to be the next night, and he said that was okay, and then I got him into a cab and took him to his apartment. I wrote out my name and phone number and instructions for him to meet me on the same bench the next night at ten o'clock.

Next morning I went to see Milt, the guy who runs that saloon around the corner. I told Milt I wanted to get hold of some pre-repeal liquor. Prohibition stuff. Milt said he thought he might have some at home. We got in his car and drove out to Forest Hills to his house. He rummaged around in the basement and finally found a couple of bottles.

"How much?" I asked him.

"Well," says Milt, "this is genuine stuff—sort of antique liquor. Hard to get. I'll have to charge you seven bucks a bottle for it."

"How do I know it's genuine?" I asked him.

He says, "You can take my word for it."

Well, I wouldn't take a saloonkeeper's word for anything. I had to be sure about it. I told him I'd have the stuff tested, and, if it turned out to be genuine, then I'd buy both bottles. We drove back to town and I took the bootleg whisky over to a chemist I know on Eighth Avenue. I told him I wanted him to give it a good test and find out if it was genuine Prohibition stuff.

He did all kinds of things with it—Bunsen-burner stuff and test tubes and all that. Finally he says:

"Ben, you got something here. This is genuine. No question about it. It's the real stuff—pure Prohibition rotgut. It's the McCoy."

That night the guy was there on the bench when I arrived with my package. He was hung over and he seemed to be a little ashamed of himself.

"Listen," I says, "I wasn't fooling you. When you told me about the Park whirling twelve years ago, it suddenly dawned on me. The night the Park whirled, you were drinking Prohibition liquor. I think if you drank some Prohibition liquor tonight, she'd go around. Maybe so, maybe not. I had to dig for it, but I've got you some prime old speakeasy stuff here, and you owe me fourteen bucks. Now, get going on it."

He started on one of the bottles. He almost gulped the stuff. He handed the bottle to me and I started to take a drink, thinking maybe I'd like to see the old Park whirl, but the smell of the stuff hit my nose and I said, "No, thanks." He kept on drinking. He was cockeyed by the time he had half the bottle down. He started to mumble and slobber a little, but he kept on drinking. Then, just like I thought, it happened. He let out a yell. He stood up and right there in front of me he started turning around, whooping his head off and flapping his arms like a chicken.

He kept yelling: "There she goes!" He made about six turns and then fell over on the ground—out like a light. I took him home again and put him to bed.

Next morning he called me up and had me come over. He told me I had saved him from going crazy. He said he was sinfully rich and I could have anything he had. You know what I said to him? I said:

"I don't want any of your money. I'm glad I was able to do you a favor. I wouldn't take a cent of your money. But—if you want to do it, there's one thing: I always had a hankering to own a toll bridge of my own. Maybe you'd like to make me a little present of a toll bridge."

So, there it is. He's buying me a toll bridge. The papers are being drawn up this week.

I suppose you don't believe me. You never believe anything I tell you.

Let's say we believe him and get on out of here before he starts another one. Not far away is a theater. The sign outside says: "The One and Only Margie Hart." The man at the stage door is gruff and insulting, but you've got to expect that. He takes the message and Miss Margie Hart invites us in. She is sitting in her dressing room wearing a knickknack or two and maybe a bangle. She takes a couple of pokes at her carrot-colored hair, tilts back in her chair, and puts her feet on a make-up shelf.

"Excuse me," she says, "but I've got to have my feet up like this to get any rest. I just came offstage. Listen to that out there."

She has reference to a mob noise in the theater's auditorium where the gentlemen customers are whistling, shouting, stamping their feet, and hammering on the chairs. Obviously the customers had enjoyed Miss Hart's four-minute turn.

"I don't know what's come over them lately," she says. "In the last few weeks they have been more enthusiastic than ever before in the ten years I've been taking them off and letting them drop. You wouldn't believe it, but at one single performance of mine, just the other night, they broke more than a hundred seats. Just r'ared back and started kicking with their feet and smashing the seats."

We note with pleasure that there is no typewriter in Miss Hart's dressing room and then we recall how she was recently forbidden to make a speech before students of New York University. She had been scheduled to speak on "Agriculture," but the members of the faculty canceled her engagement. Apparently they suspected that Miss Hart was coming down to put on a mammae act that would be impossible for Al Jolson. Miss Hart informs us that she had the best of intentions, that she's interested in movements over and above bodily ones; for example, the back-to-the-earth movement. She's a legit farmer. She owns a one-hundred-and-twenty-acre place at Lathrop, Missouri, not far from the little town of Edgerton where she was born the daughter of a sewing-machine salesman.

"I bought the farm five years ago," she says. "Someday I'm going to get tired of all this. Not right now, but someday.

And when I get tired of it, the one thing I want to do is farm. Right now I'm a sharecropper. That is, I'm not a sharecropper. I'm being sharecropped on. You see, these people run my farm for me. I get one third of the corn, one half of the wheat, and one half of the oats. It's a nice arrangement and actually pays a profit. But it's not going to be like that always. Sometimes between shows I sit here and dream about the time that I'll be a full-time farmer.

"You see, I was a kid back in that part of the country and I love it. I love horses. I love mules. So many people don't know about mules. They think a mule is just something to make a gag about. I know all about mules because I've raised them. Why, the biggest mule barn in the world is right near Lathrop.

"I like to get out and put on an old straw hat and a pair of overalls and go fishing in the crick. I like to fish with a bamboo pole and a cork and a worm on the hook, and I put the worm on myself. And raise mules. I had these mares on my place, and a jack, and we got the cutest mules you ever saw. You know about how it works—mares and jacks and all that? There's a saying out there that when a mare drops a mule colt she drops a fifty-dollar bill.

"I like to climb trees and I like to go out and look for Indian arrowheads and I love to see the Watkins remedy man come around, with all the gossip for fifty miles in every direction. The Watkins remedy man is the Winchell of rural Missouri. I think I'd just pack up and get out of here next spring except for one thing. Chiggers. Chiggers go for me. A chigger will go for one person and leave the next person alone. My mother never gets a single chigger bite, but they climb all over me."

We suggest that if she goes back to the farm and conquers the chiggers, the day might come when she'll get a yearning to return to the footlights. What then?

"I've taken that into consideration," she says. "They've got a burlesque house in Kansas City. Forty miles from my farm. If I got the old urge to do a bit of public peeling, I think they'd let me do a few turns there. They've always been very nice to me back home."

So that's Margie Hart. Now, let's cross Broadway and have

a look in at Harry's Palace Bar & Grill on Forty-fifth. I've got to show you this establishment because they have a caricature of me on the wall right next to the gents' room. I won't say anything about it at first, hoping you'll notice it yourself, but if you don't, I'll get Harry or somebody to mention it. Getting your caricature painted on the wall of a saloon is the very last word in fame.

Here's the place and here's Jimmy Collins at the bar having a beer. Jimmy is a small, slender, bald guy. At one time he was a prominent jockey. He founded the Jockeys' Guild, an organization which now has seven hundred members weighing an average of one hundred and eight pounds. Jimmy doesn't talk in the manner you'd expect from an ex-jockey. He knows the language and in late years has developed into something of a writer. Let's get him talking on the subject of jockeys.

"Jocks," he says, "are strange people. Take this fellow Paul Keiper. He's a fine rider but he has peculiar habits. He eats razor blades and drinks ink. It's a fact. I lost a bet on it. He ate a razor blade right in front of my eyes and then drank half a bottle of ink. The other boys told me they saw him eat an electric-light bulb one day and they say he eats flies all the time. Just reaches out, grabs a fly, and pops it into his mouth and eats it. They tell me he even ate a bumblebee once."

One of the most peculiar traits of a jockey, Jimmy says, is his method of educating himself. Most jockeys grow up around stables and race tracks and, consequently, miss out on formal schooling. Then when they get in the money they are thrown into the company of people who are well educated. They sit around in restaurants with high-class people and they listen to the high-class people talk about history and politics and literature and art and so on. And the jockeys, knowing nothing whatever beyond how to stay on a horse, can't take part in such conversations.

This sort of thing finally begins to worry a jockey. He becomes self-conscious about his ignorance and he decides to remedy it. So he buys a book and reads it. Maybe it's a biography of Bach. Okay. He reads the biography of Bach, then he gets more books about Bach and studies hard, and finally he knows virtually all there is to know about Bach.

After that the jockey will sit with the high-class people and in some manner he'll manage to jockey the conversation around to music and then, quite casually, he'll let go a little remark about Bach.

"Bach!" the high-class people will say. "What the hell do *you* know about Bach?"

"Everything," the jockey will say. "I know more than you do about Bach."

And he'll proceed to prove it.

"This thing," says Jimmy Collins, "is true of a great many jocks. Take my own case. It happened to me just that way. I picked a subject and went to work on it. I began to study the ballet. I've read everything ever written about it. I'm an authority on it. The ballet people themselves are always calling me up and asking me questions involving ballet history. And I always have the answer.

"But I didn't stop at one subject. Most of the jocks concentrate on a single subject. One of them is an authority on Freud. He could discuss Freud with a college professor, but, at the same time, he couldn't subtract two from four. He knows all about Freud, but otherwise he's so dumb he couldn't find his butt with both hands. I decided I didn't want to be shooting off my face about the ballet all the time, so I studied Chinese mortuary jade. That's a very interesting subject and I'll tell you all about it some time. The Chinese use small pieces of jade to close up the nine orifices of the body after death and naturally that jade is very rare and very precious stuff.

"Well, here I was, an expert on the ballet and an authority on Chinese mortuary jade. Was I contented? Absolutely not. I still wanted more to talk about when I was with the high-class people. So I made a study of periodic ophthalmia. That's an affliction in horses and it's commonly called moon blindness. It's called moon blindness because it is recurrent. It comes every twenty-eight days and it's a very mysterious ailment. I know all there is to know about it—everything."

Jimmy says that some jockeys are lazy and pick a simple subject for their conversation piece. One rider, for example, sits with the high-class people and listens to their high-class talk until embarrassment comes upon him. Then he'll hit them in the eye with the one beautiful piece of knowledge he possesses.

"I'll bet," he'll say to them, "that none of you guys can spell the name of the guy that assinated McKinley."

He seldom finds a taker and he usually startles his auditors by spelling Czolgosz. The high-class people have only one consolation: maybe they can't spell Czolgosz, but they know the deed he committed was not "assinaton."

Here comes a fellow we know. Radio writer named Jerry Holland. "Hey," he says, "your old friend Stull's in town. Saw her this morning."

The hotel is near by so let's leave Harry's Palace Bar & Grill and call on Mrs. Nelle Brooke Stull of Elyria, Ohio. Mrs. Stull is probably the most vigorous mender of broken hearts operating today. She is president of the National Widows & Widowers Club, which she organized back in Elyria twenty-two years ago.

The first time I ever saw Mrs. Stull was an evening thirteen years back when she came into the Pulitzer building on Park Row wearing a golden crown, draped in forty yards of gauze, and singing, "Love, tra-la, Love, tra-la, O Love!" It was one of her own compositions.

This performance left an enduring impression, for Mrs. Stull is of approximately the same height and general consistency of Miss Elsa Maxwell. The passage of time, we soon discover, has not changed her much. This time she wears no crown and no gauze but she is carrying a lorgnette. One of the first things she does is show us her new letterhead—a magnificent job done in green and gold and containing her coat of arms. This heraldic device consists chiefly of four badgers in green and gold.

"A widower worked it out for me," she explains. "The gold speaks for itself. As for the green—well, I'm told that green stands for love of humanity. That is, I mean green on a coat of arm stands for love of humanity. Green on a tree stands for spring."

The significance of the four badgers is not stated and we let it pass because we want Mrs. Stull to tell us about her organization.

"My club," she says, "was purely social when it started.

Back in Elyria I asked all the town's lonely widows and widowers to come to a party at my house. Thirty-two of them showed up. Well, sir, before it was over all but two of them had remarried. One old gentleman died before he could get to the altar and one woman moved to Cincinnati. For all I know, maybe she got married there. I never heard.

"The theme of my club is not to think of the past, but just the things you have passed up. I have had a hand in more than 7,000 marriages. Out of these there has been only one divorce I know about. A woman seventy-six and a man eighty got married and he took her to Florida for a visit. He decided he liked Florida but she wanted to go back to Columbus. They got into a fight over it and wound up in the divorce court.

"The only trouble I ever got into was the time a woman tried to sue me. She joined my club on a Tuesday. Her rent was due on Friday. When I hadn't sent her a husband by Thursday night, she tried to sue me for the rent. She got no place, the dirty hussy."

Mrs. Stull tells us that she has received more than 6,000 proposals of marriage. Letters pile into Elyria by the bale.

"I get letters," she says, "addressed to 'Nelle B. Stull, United States.' Why, I ought to be on Ripley. What'm I talking about! I *have* been on Ripley! I am recognized as an expert on everything pertaining to love and marriage. I am an authority on divorce. There are, you know, only two basic causes for divorce. One is the man and the other is the woman.

"Of all the marriage proposals I ever received, I think the most touching was the one from a farmer in Ohio. He had seen a picture of me. He wrote to me and told me he had fallen in love with my left eye. He said he loved my left eye to distraction—that he loved my left eye so much he was willing to sell his big farm and bring the money to Elyria and marry me on the spot. It was a very lovely and touching sentiment, but I had to turn him down."

She had to turn him down, of course, because Nelle Brooke Stull is no widow. Back in Elyria she has had a husband for more years than she cares to mention.

So that was Nelle Brooke Stull and here we are heading

up Broadway and yonder comes Leo Lindy. He is known to readers of Damon Runyon as "Mindy," and as we spot him he's following his stomach down Broadway, headed for his celebrated herring shop. Let's fall into step beside him and say something about what a nice day it is. It takes him a while to recognize me, then he says:

"Ha! How's Low Men of Tuttem Pole?"

We stop for a traffic light and Lindy remarks that he is feeling exceptionally good of late.

"Is because," he says, "Broadway Rose shows up missing."

Lindy put up with the Broadway Rose nuisance for a number of years. She was certainly a nuisance, and she has been at least partially abated. She isn't seen around much any more, having been tossed in the can a couple of times for her hideous antics. The cops no longer tolerate her because of her hatful of mean little rackets. It was her custom to prowl the theatrical district each night, looking for celebrities. She is an unattractive creature and, coming upon a celebrity, she'd fling herself at him. She'd throw her arms around her victim with shrieks of undying love and hysterical tales of lost diamond rings. No matter how much her victim struggled, he couldn't get away. Such shenanigans naturally attracted crowds and her victim could not slug her, no matter how deep the urge. He knew that there was only one way to get rid of her—to reach in his pocket and pull out a bill and hand it to her. Then she'd fade off into the crowd.

"The cops," says Lindy, "crecked down. But if the cops didn't creck down, I think I would have wore her out ewentually. I could get rid of that bum every time. I know her two wicknesses. Squirt seltzer water on. She hates water and if you squirt at her she'll hit the road. Also stemp on her feet. Stemping on her feet—that drives her crazy."

Lindy has been involved in Broadway restaurant life for thirty years. One of the loveliest things about him when it comes to reminiscing is that he doesn't say a word about Jim Brady. He never waited on Diamond Jim Brady and never saw Diamond Jim Brady shovel it in and has nothing whatever to say about Diamond Jim Brady's appetite.

"The biggest eaters I ever knew," says Lindy, "were Carl Laemmle and the understudy to El Jolson, name of Harry

Wardell. Carl Laemmle was a little fella but, boy, how he could eat! When he would come East he would stop the train at Harmon and telephone me and say, 'Get it on the fire.'

"But Harry Wardell. There was a man could eat. I remember the time he made a hundred-dollar bet he could outeat anybody, so they brought in some fella from out New Jersey.

"Harry looked him over for a while, then he says, 'Okay, I spot you one turkey.' Then Harry sat down and ate a whole roast turkey. When he was through with it he said he was ready to begin the eating contest. Then, with a turkey under his belt already, he goes to work and outeats this Jersey fella with no trouble at all. He had one hundred crullers for dessert."

Lindy tells us he hates to confess it but that he's getting old.

"The way I can tell," he says, "is about the kids. I love to see little children come in my store with their papas and mamas. Every kid comes in gets a piece candy. Looie Sobel has been coming in for years, and for a long time he always brings his little girl and always I am waiting for her to give her a nice piece candy. Not long ago Looie comes in again with his daughter. Do I give her a piece candy? No. I give her a slug gin."

Let's leave Lindy to his work and go back down Broadway to Forty-second. I just happened to think about Jack Pfefer. Mr. Pfefer is the wrestling impresario who was once manager of a traveling opera company. On a previous occasion I went to his office to talk with him on the general subject of wrestling. I began by asking him for a definition of a wrestler. He recited it this way:

"Wrestler—a bom. A gorilla. A at'lete."

Mr. Pfefer in person is a small man weighing less than four poods. A pood, in Russia, is forty funt; in America, thirty-six pounds. Mr. Pfefer looks like Willie Howard. He is of a size with Willie and he behaves as Willie might behave with a fever of 104 and the rent due.

During that previous visit in his office Mr. Pfefer introduced me to half a dozen of his wrestlers. He has a small room in which these "boms" and "gorillas" and "at'letes" are allowed to loaf. They sprawl around on top of desks and even on the floor, staring at comic sheets and picture magazines. Mr. Pfefer always keeps a supply of funny papers on hand for their intellectual amusement, and each week he buys a new batch of picture magazines. A wrestler will sometimes open a copy of *Look* and stare at a single picture for twenty minutes without moving a muscle.

Among the wrestlers present that day was a Jap—one Oko Shikina—my visit having been prior to Pearl Harbor. Mr. Pfefer introduced me to Oko and to the others.

"This one," he said, "is Count Carl von Zuppe. He is a Austrian nubbelman."

"An Austrian what?" I said.

"Nubbelman. Nubbelman, like with a title. Put in your eye your monocle, Count."

The count, already wearing a waxed mustache, fixed a monocle into his face without changing expression.

"And this one," said Mr. Pfefer, "is Zim Zam Zum. Zim is my Hindu champeen with the faz on." True enough, Zim Zam Zum was wearing a fez.

After the introductions Mr. Pfefer and I started back toward his private office. At the door he turned and showered the wrestlers with cuss words.

"That," he concluded, "is in case any you boms gets drunk tonight."

In his own office Mr. Pfefer talked at length of wrestling, Life, and other matters.

"All my life," he said, "I am with show business. I can tell you wrestlers is easier to handle than actors. The bigger is the brute in the ring, the more like a rabbit easy to handle outside. Like a gorilla is a wrestler in the ring, when people want to lynch him on a rope, but outside he is like a little kitten.

"These wrestlers got all kinds habits. One wrestler likes to go all day to the movies. One movie right after another movie. One likes to read in books. One likes to read in magazines. One likes to eat. Some is good cooks. Likes to cook for the wifes instead the wifes cook for him. Some is great drinkers of milk. That is good. Makes healt'y. Zim is a strict wegetarian, eats only wegetables. No meat.

"This business I am in is a wonderful life. All kinds writers come to interview me. Joe Mitchell, Joe Liebling. Den Parker writes much about me. He is the one that crowned me with the name Halitosis. He calls me Jack Halitosis Pfefer. He is a great writer, that Den Parker."

This, then, is the gentleman we're going to call on. Let's phone him first to make certain he's in, and tell him we want to talk with him about Japs. He says come on over.

As we walk into his office Mr. Pfefer is indulging himself in his favorite pastime—talking on two telephones at one and the same time, using both ears. Into one phone he is shouting Russian and into the other he is murmuring sweet nothings in a language which he believes to be English.

When he has finished his talk, or talks, concluding each conversation simultaneously as befits the artist that he is, Mr. Pfefer executes a double hangup. Then he rises, drawing himself up to his full and impressive five-feet-four, counting his hair.

"You are the smart one," he says. "You are the smart one to come here because I give you all you want to know about the Japs. With no hassitation I tell you: the Japs is strickly snicky.

"My last Jap I have seen the last of, thank God. He was —you remember him?—Oko Shikina. Oko was a big Jap, two hundred and ten pounds, which is unusual for a Jap. But he was like all the rest snicky. All my life I have had dillings with Japs and all my life I know one thing. Japs is strickly snicky and werry suspicious. Even Japs that weighs two hundred and ten.

"But what I know about the snicky Japs is not all wrestling. I have spent much time in Japan and both China. That is back when I am traveling with the opera company. In Japan is wrestling not like in the United States. In Japan is wrestling big hosky guys, weigh four, five hundred pounds, what they call samurai. These big hosky guys wrestling like dopes. Push each other around is all they do, no catch-as-catch-can scientific. As soon as they totch the ground they are beat.

"These big snicky slobs is the national heroes of Japan. You cannot indentify between them and their wifes. Both dresses the same—the wrestlers and their wifes, and the wifes are big and hosky like their husband. Both wears a kimono and fixes the hair up on top and you cannot indentify between them."

We ask Mr. Pfefer to give us some specific instances in which Japs employed by himself had been sneaky.

"Listen," he says. "With me they cannot be snicky. When they work for me it is impossible they should be snicky. The reason for this is I am snicky myself when I want to be. I can be snickier than a Jap morning, noon, and night. They try plenty times to be snicky with me, but I am always better.

"The Chinese—that is a different color horse. I know the Chinese too. They are not to be compared. The Chinese is good-natured. Werry smart, but good-natured. That's why the Japs take adwantage all the time. If you ask me, it is just coldbloodness. And if you ask me, no more snicky Japs do I want in all my life except maybe to hit on top the head with a klob."

And that ends our tour for the present. We could keep going indefinitely. We could call on Harry the Horse and hear him brag about the "muriels" that decorate the walls of his saloon; we could stop in Ralph's and watch the actors standing at the bar, staring at themselves in the mirror for hours at a stretch; we might even go over and look at that Radio City Music Hall john. But let's not do it. This chapter's too long already.

CHAPTER XIII   *Report on a Quest for Culture*

AT THE TIME this book was being put together I discovered my first gray hair. It is on my left temple, out toward the front. The normal reaction to such a discovery, I've been told, is one of depression. With me it is different. I rejoiced. I live in anxiety for that gray hair. It's in an exposed area and I'm afraid I'll get it knocked off some way. I don't want that to happen. I want to keep that gray hair because it serves to remind me that I'm too far along in life to acquire Culture.

That great thinker among modern men, Arthur Brisbane, who was known among fellow newspapermen as Old Double Dome, wrote in the year of my birth, 1907:

"A peasant is not to be censured for his ignorance, but when he glories in it and draws its limits as a dead line for his betters, he is the least pleasing of all the beasts in the field."

Old Double Dome, who believed that the horse with the largest heart is the inevitable winner of any race and who argued that a man needs to have blue eyes to be a genius, surely didn't know that I was being born that year. Yet I sometimes feel that he had me in mind. I've spent half my life glorying in my ignorance. I'm definitely on the side of the stenographer who stood with her girl friend in Rockefeller Center, contemplating the sideways statue of Prometheus.

"Who's it supposed to be?" asked the girl friend.

"Don't be a dope, Hazel," said the stenographer. "That's Promiscuous."

There have been times when I've made halfhearted gestures in the direction of Culture. For example, I once went to the Metropolitan Museum of Art and spent two full hours trying to discover a reason for it. Again, I attended the first performance of Gertrude Stein's opera, *Four Saints in Three Acts*—the one in which the pigeons were on the grass, alas. I have gone to a French-made movie, a symphony concert, and a party at which New York City's leading debutantes, all creatures of Culture, rode kiddie cars around a dance floor screeching like commoners and showing their hams. Once I bought a copy of Joyce's *Ulysses* and applied myself to it three evenings in a row. After that I put it in the back corner of a clothes closet to drive off moths. When, at last, the fact finally bore in upon me that I was not made for Culture, I gave it up and devoted myself from there on out to being an unpleasant beast of the field. All things considered, I am about as genteel as an assistant beachcomber. I have only had one tailor-made suit of clothes in my life and it was given to me as a present. When I was standing there being taped and chalked and sighted at, the tailor suddenly asked me: "What side do you dress on?" I didn't know what he was talking about. I said: "You mean which side of the bed I dress on, or which side of the ocean?"

When Jimmy Collins, the former jockey, related how he had become an authority on the ballet, I thought for a time that that might be the cultural field for me. Through the intercession of a friend I was able to arrange a luncheon date with a girl named Tamara Toumanova, ballerina with the Ballet Russe de Monte Carlo. Tamara is pronounced to-morrow, as tomorrow is pronounced in my native Illinois, or, tuhmorra. Tamara is a striking girl—a sort of small Zorina. She talks at a fearful clip and is all full of animation, and she dilates her nostrils a lot, the way Valentino used to do it in the silent movies to indicate that he had ants in his pants.

I told Tamara that I was a little on the idiot side, that this fluff-and-thistledown style of dancing always struck me as being silly; that these here-we-go-gathering-nuts-in-May dancers impressed me as less graceful than a heel-and-toe walker, and would she be so kind as to instruct me in the Art? Would she explain it to me so I'd be able to appreciate it?

Well, she made a noble effort. She took a specific piece of ballet business—a thing called *The Labyrinth*. She said it was created especially for her by Salvador Dali. The way she explained it, Salvador Dali dreamed up the story, then got together with Leonide Choreographer, the eminent massine. Well, Leonide Choreographer found some music that would fit the story and then he got Tamara and they worked out the movements, and all the time Dali was designing costumes and sets and when it was finished, there it was. Of course, said Tamara, I really should have seen it to appreciate it. She mentioned that it was full of pigeons, roosters, dragons, and dolphins.

This was a little too heady for me—too big a dose to be taken all at once—so I got her away from ballet talk for a while. She said that she dislikes her first name—Tamara. The reason she dislikes it is that there are three or four other gals going around using the name of Tamara.

"I tried to cot it off Tamara and be only one name Tou-manova," she said, "but it would not work."

Tamara is a Russian name so I asked her its equivalent in

America—the American name which corresponds to Tamara.

"Susie," she said. "It is just like Susie."

We drank some coffee and then she made a valiant try at explaining ballet some more. She talked about *grands jets* and *tours en l'air* and *arabesques* and *acembles,* providing the spellings of same. And she talked about *entre-chats.*

An entre-chat is where the dancer jumps straight up in the air as high as he can go and, while in the air, begins wagging his legs so that his feet cross and uncross, keeping it going until he hits the floor again. Here was something I could remember having seen. She spoke of entre-chats as though entre-chats were something out of this world. I tried to get myself into a receptive frame of mind because I wanted so much to appreciate the beauty of an entre-chat, but I couldn't do it. Remembering entre-chats I had seen, I could only think: What a hell of a thing for a grown man to be doing!

Tamara went on to say that some men can entre-chat ten times, meaning that they can wag their legs that many times in a single jump. Women never get beyond six.

"Ten times," she said, "that's for the men. We do not try—the girls. We do not try after six. The men try to go better than ten sometimes and they almost break the legs. They hit the floor while the feet are still going, and that is bad. A girl can come down on the toes and not break the legs, but not the men."

I wanted to know if anybody was ever caught cheating—if, for example, some lowlife entre-chatter ever locked himself in a room and then came out whooping and yelling how he had entre-chatted eleven times with no witnesses. The very thought of such a fraud horrified Tamara.

Personally, I don't think I achieved much with Tamara. However, if you are a cultural lard head like myself, with an overwhelming desire to go look at a ballet, I think I can give you a solid tip. If you go to a ballet and if you see someone entre-chatting and if it's a man entre-chatting and he entre-chats more than ten times, cheer and whistle and stamp your feet. That'll show you know something.

☆   ☆   ☆

In my pursuit of Culture I made an attempt to understand Salvador Dali—the man who created that special ballet for Tamara. Whenever I'd get around arty people I'd make a point of asking them about Dali and invariably I'd get the same response. Dali is a genius, a great artist, a superb technician. Then I'd ask why he paints such cockeyed pictures and they'd give me all sorts of answers. They'd say it doesn't make any difference what he paints—it's how he paints it.

Dali was lionized when he was in Hollywood not long ago. Also he was fired. Fred Othman relayed the story of the firing. Dali had been engaged at Twentieth Century-Fox for a specific job. They were making a picture in which one of the characters had a nightmare and they wanted to show the nightmare in all its horrendous detail. Hiring Dali to design a full-bodied nightmare was almost automatic. They put him to work. He was to paint the nightmare, and after that his painting would be used as the model for construction of the nightmare set. According to Fred Othman, Dali painted a magnificent nightmare. Everybody thought it was swell, except the carpenters who were assigned to build it. They studied the project for a long time and then went to the boss and said they couldn't do it.

"We can't figure out where to start," they said.

During his stay in Hollywood Dali was guest of honor at a big garden party thrown by a prominent producer. During this party people swarmed around the chief guest and listened to him talk French. The prominent producer knew not a word of French, yet he didn't want to miss anything. His wife understood French so she served as interpreter on the sly.

The producer stood at the edge of the group surrounding Dali and occasionally he'd ask his wife in a whisper what the artist was talking about.

"What's he say now, Mama?" he'd ask.

"He says he's writing his autobiography," explained Mama.

Dali babbled on.

"Now what's he saying, Mama?"

"He says his autobiography is the greatest autobiography ever written."

"Tell me what he says next."

"He says his autobiography begins when he was in his mother's womb."

This was something! The famous producer cursed himself for his ignorance of French, which continued to flow from Dali's lip.

"Now, Mama! What's he say?"

"He says," said Mama, "that while he was in his mother's womb he remembers every minute of the time."

Dali did finish his autobiography and several publishers wanted to bring it out. He took it, however, to the Dial Press because Dial contains the same letters as Dali. I haven't read the book and don't intend to, but Dali's publisher told me it was marvelous.

"Craziest book I ever saw in my life," he said. "Tells how he likes to pick up a chipmunk and bite it on the head. How he once fell in love with a girl's runny nose. All kinds of stuff like that."

"Do you think he's crazy?" I asked.

"Who, that guy? He's crazy like I. J. Fox. Makes more money than me and you put together."

The only time I ever encountered Dali in the flesh was back in 1941, at a Fifty-seventh Street art gallery where some of his works were on exhibition. There were two rooms full of Dali monstrosities and I attended the press preview of the show. There was only one other reporter present—a tall, solemn guy with a crew haircut. He was going from painting to painting and scribbling acres of notes. I thought I'd fraternize. I eased alongside him and said:

"You from one of the papers?"

"Yes"—very coldly. He made it clear that I was bothering him.

"What paper?" I said, brushing off the brush-off.

"*Times*," he said gruffly, not even giving me a glance, suggesting in his manner that I ought to have enough sense not to bother a *Times* man in pursuit of his lofty duties. I didn't bother him any further. There wasn't a line in the *Times* the next day about the Dali exhibit. I was glad.

After having been put in my place by the *Times* man, I turned away and then I saw Dali. He was buzzing all over the place. He looks like something he painted. He has long, shiny black hair that keeps falling over his face and he moves around like a cat full of gin. He has a wild, feverish look in his eyes and he doesn't appear to be the gentle type. I had a feeling all the while that if I got near him he'd pull a knife on me.

I wandered into the back room and saw a startling object. The ceiling was about twelve feet high. Up on one wall was a desk, suspended from the ceiling by wires, high against the wall so that its writing surface was about ten feet above the floor. Standing before this desk was a chair— an ordinary straight-backed chair with four legs—the long-leggedest chair ever seen on earth. The legs on that chair were fully eight feet long and they brought it up to its proper position in relation to the hanging desk. I walked over to the thing and got another surprise. Each of the long chair legs rested on a turtle's back, each turtle being about the size of a bedpan.

I don't catch on to things quickly so I just stood there and looked at it, trying to figure it out. Then a young man came into the room carrying a crutch. He placed the crutch on a table, stood off and looked at it, moved it a trifle this way, then that way, then forward, then back, behaving in a very artistic fashion. He was an attendant in the place, and when he got the crutch fixed the way he wanted it, I called him over.

"What in the hell is this thing?" I asked. "Do you know what it means?"

"Sure," he said. "That's the desk and chair he used when he wrote his book. He invented it himself. Says he writes better up there."

"Well," I said, "I could almost but not quite understand that, but why the turtles? What are they for?"

"The way he explains it," the young man said, "is that it keeps him from wearing himself out. He says when a person sits at a desk for a long time, he tires himself out moving around, shifting his chair around to keep comfortable. The turtles are dead, but they are supposed to be alive. He says he gets a big stepladder and climbs up so he can get into the chair and then he starts writing up there near the ceiling. The turtles keep moving around a little all day long, and so he doesn't have to be shifting around all the time to keep himself comfortable. Saves his strength that way."

"And the crutch," I said. "What's that for?"

"Oh, that's the crutch he always uses for a model. He puts crutches in lots of his pictures. Crutches and grasshoppers. I saw one of his pictures where he had a crutch growing out of a woman's tit."

I went back into the main gallery. The *Times* man was still going around taking notes. Dali wasn't in sight. Standing in the center of the room was a glass case containing some jewelry—trinkets with tiny paintings on them. I was in front of this case, gazing at the trinkets, when somebody came up and stood alongside me. I turned and looked and my insides gave a little jump. It was Dali. He didn't have a dirk in his hand so I calmed down. We stood there together, staring at the painted jewelry. Finally I took a deep breath, poked a thumb at the glass case, and said:

"What's that?"

"Me paint," he said. Just like that. "Me paint." Just like Sitting Bull might have said it. And then he walked away.

I went around and found the man who was putting on the exhibit and asked him if Dali was crazy.

"Why don't you ask Dali?" he suggested.

"And have him bite me?" I said.

"Fiddlesticks!" said the man. "Lots of people ask him if he's crazy. In fact, almost everybody asks him that. He doesn't mind."

"Could you get him over here?" I asked. "And would you stand close by while I ask him?"

The man brought Dali over. I looked at him, swallowed a couple of times, and said:

"Are you crazy?"

"No," he said.

"There you are!" said the man. "There's your answer."

I've never discovered why Dali puts crutches in his pictures, but I've come on a story which explains the grasshoppers. The grasshopper is a symbol of Dali's father.

When he was a little boy in Spain he didn't like his father because his father thwarted him. His father didn't want him to be an artist. Frustration stuff. In those days, by his own account, Salvador enjoyed nothing so much as going out in the fields to lie on the grass and dream. Whenever he did this the grasshoppers bothered him and interrupted his dreams. So he got to thinking of grasshoppers whenever he thought of his father, and the grasshopper became the symbol for his father. Thus, whenever he gets the urge, he puts a grasshopper into his pictures. That's his paw.

Clifton Fadiman is a mighty smart man, intellectual and, I have no doubt, somewhat cultured. Mr. Fadiman and his Information, Please! gang represent the obverse of Old Double Dome Brisbane's picture. They put on a good radio show and Mr. Fadiman himself is a splendid spark plug. Yet they are as smug on their side of the fence as the rest of us beasts in the field. Mr. Fadiman enunciates quite a bit about democracy. He remains one of the most undemocratic of men, being an intellectual aristocrat from the Lower East Side who looks down his beautiful nose at most of his fellow men. I have been on the other end of that look a couple of times and I know its freezing qualities.

Oscar Levant is never smug, though he can be brilliantly impudent. I've never been able to recognize anything startling in the answers he gives to musical questions. Music is his business and has been his business all along. It would be alarming if he didn't know most of the answers. The thing that strikes me as admirable about Mr. Levant is his essential honesty, plus his general knowledge—his acquaintance with movies and politics and sports and literature, among other things. If he's dumb about something, whether it be the pronunciation of a word or the recognition of a piece of music, he comes right out and says so. The others don't perform that way—unless, perhaps, to say they don't know the answer and, in saying it, suggest that it is little short of a miracle that they don't. Take Deems Taylor. I remember one night when he was on Information, Please! A question came along involving the names of cities mentioned in certain songs. Roland Young, who is certainly not an intellectual snob, was a guest on the same program. The pianist played "Blues in the Night"—a number generally accepted as one of the best blues songs ever written. Nobody answered for a moment, but a listener could overhear Mr. Young whispering the lyrics to himself, trying to find a town name in them. At last he spoke up:

"Is there a town called Knee Pants?" he asked.

Mr. Fadiman said he did not believe there was such a town. Then Mr. Fadiman turned to Mr. Deems Taylor and suggested that Mr. Taylor, as an authority on music, should be able to answer. Mr. Taylor fairly dripped superiority as he responded. He was not acquainted with the number, "Blues in the Night." He never cluttered his mind with such stuff. Really, old man, you couldn't expect . . . Well, from that day forward it has been the custom in my house, when the name of Deems Taylor is announced as a guest on Information, Please! for all members of the family to rise and deliver themselves of unprintable noises.

Hey! What'm I saying! I started out on the subject of Clifton Fadiman with a definite thought in mind, and here I am acting as ladylike as Ilka Chase.

My quarrel with Mr. Fadiman concerns his enthusiasm for a book called *The Ox-Bow Incident*. Mr. Fadiman tooted his whistle all over the place for this book—called it the first Western novel to attain the level of literature. For having let loose such an ill-considered opinion, I consider Mr. Fadiman to be plumb loco.

It happens that I read *The Ox-Bow Incident* when it first came out in 1940. It struck me as being two degrees below dull. (I'm speaking here of the book, not the movie.) I had quite a struggle finishing it, but I did plug through to the end and then I took it back to the rental library and told the girl, "Double phooey."

Mr. Fadiman was born and brought up in New York City and his ideas about the cowboy are not to be trusted. He whooped for *The Ox-Bow Incident*, yet nowhere in that book does anyone say:

"Hold on thar, stranger, afore I make a lead mine outa yore guts. Whatta yuh a-doin' with that thar brandin' arn?"

It is apparent that Mr. Fadiman doesn't understand the

requirements of a Western story. He is a realist. He considers a cowboy to be nothing more than a field hand on a horse—which is true, maybe, but not for the purposes of Western novels and Western movies. Who wants to think of that old-time hero, the pony express rider, interrupting his grueling race across the prairies for a bowel movement? Not me. He had to do it, all right, but when I read about him in a book I want him to stay on that hoss and keep traveling.

The attitude of the New York movie critics toward the horse opera (known in *Variety* as mustang mellers and giddy-appers) has always been a source of chagrin to me. These critics scarcely recognize the existence of Westerns unless they are high-budget pictures with Gary Cooper playing the lead. I recall a review one of the critics wrote about the picture, *Wild Bill Hickok Rides*. It gave me a mild conniption, that review.

The critic was disgusted because the heroes of mustang mellers always walk down the middle of the street when they go gunning for the villain. The hero is, let us suppose, collecting his mail at the post office. Somebody dashes up and says Tin Whisker Pete has just rode into town with a mean look in his eye. The very presence of Tin Whisker Pete in town is enough to clear the main street of all traffic. Then out of the post office comes our hero. Down the very middle of the deserted street he strides, his jaw set, his steely eyes moving from side to side, his arms curved slightly, ready to draw.

This particular critic raised hell about it. He said that sort of thing is always happening in Westerns. He said it's illogical and silly and Tin Whisker Pete would always win if heroes actually behaved like that.

What on earth does the guy expect? Does he want our cowboy heroes to skulk? Does he want them to sneak up the alley? Or scrooch down the street underneath an old bathtub? That critic is plainly a sheepherder.

Once I wrote an attack on the critics, along these same lines, and it came to the attention of a Mrs. Polly Robichaud, of Mill Valley, California. Mrs. Robichaud wrote me a letter. She said that she and her husband were regular customers at a little movie house which plays nothing but giddy-appers. They like them. She said that their friends chide them about their low tastes, but the Robichauds are always amused when the lights go up in the little movie to find several of those same friends trying to sneak out, unseen. The next time they all meet at a party they sit around and discuss *Mrs. Miniver* and *For Whom the Bell Tolls* and *The Informer* and Hitchcock, and remark on "how utterly awful it is to sit through those utterly awful 'B' pictures."

Mrs. Robichaud said she'd quit going to the movies if they didn't have Westerns, and she told about a dandy she had seen the night before. I'm sorry I missed it. In this one the sheriff is sound asleep in his little bedroom. Suddenly the door is pushed open and in comes a horse. The horse goes over to the bed and begins nudging the sleeping sheriff with his nose. Finally the sheriff awakens, sits up in bed, stares at the intruder, and then says:

"Wal, I swan! Th' crittur wants me tuh foller him, I reckon!"

That's what it was! The sheriff strapped on his guns and the horse went ahead of him—leading him to an abandoned mine where the hero was hanging by one foot directly over the mine shaft and the sputtering fuse was within two inches of the dynamite.

That, pardners, is the way it should be. There's no room for the Hemingway treatment in Western movies or Western books. There's no room for realism because a real-life cowboy is a pretty dull citizen. I know.

In the summer of 1941 Jim Street and I spent a week at Bill Bell's dude ranch at the eastern end of Long Island. All the cowboys on the ranch, save one, were Long Island cowboys. They came from Sag Harbor and Easthampton and they behaved exactly as movie cowboys behave. The one exception was a tall, lean, taciturn cow hand from western Canada. The first day Jim and I were at the place, half a dozen of us were gathered in the living room of the main ranch house. The Canadian cowboy was slouched on a divan. He hadn't said a word all day.

I got up and wandered to the far end of the room to look at the contents of a gunrack. While I was standing there, I heard Jim doing a little bragging on me, in a low tone. He was telling the people that I was an author—author of a book that was a best seller. He was trying to impress them, knowing that later on I would do some bragging on him, telling them that *he* was the author of a best seller.

Dead silence followed Jim's little speech about what a great man they had in their midst. Then I heard the drawling voice of the Canadian cowboy. All he said was this:

"Never read but one book in all muh life . . . book called *Riders uh th' Purple Sage* . . . never gonna read another'n long as I live."

That's a real-life cowboy for you. A fine kind of citizen! I'll take the movie kind every time. I'll take the cowboy that Tom O'Reilly told me about. Here's Tom's story:

Out in west Texas is a ranch that lies one hundred and fifty miles from a town of any size. On this ranch lived two dozen cow hands and not one of them had ever seen a football game. They had read about football in old newspapers but they couldn't figure out the difference between a halfback and an offside or anything else about the game, and they were curious.

One day they heard that a football game had been scheduled in the town one hundred and fifty miles from their ranch. Obviously they all couldn't go so they pooled up their money and drew lots and one cowboy, named Ike, was chosen. He was to get on his horse and ride the one hundred and fifty miles and see the football game. Then he was to get on his horse and ride back and tell the others all about it.

The cowboys were gathered at the gate when Ike came riding back. They swarmed around him when he dismounted. What was it like? How was it played? Was it exciting?

Ike called for quiet and then told his story, which went something like this:

"Fellers, this football is a caution. All I gotta do is tell yuh how the gol-dang thing started off. They's a bunch of fellers in funny rig out on this here field. They's a guy in a cook's outfit totin' a pig bladder that's been blowed up and kivvered all around with cowhide. Well, these fellers all spreads out over the field and the cook puts the bladder on the ground and then one feller comes a-runnin' and kicks that bladder a helluva kick, clean up in the air.

"When it comes down they put it on the ground again.

Then one great big feller walks up to the bladder and bends over like if he's gonna pick it up. He hardly no more'n gits his hands on it when a little feller comes creepin' up behind him, all bent over, and this little feller gits closer and all of a sudden the little feller bites that big feller right squar' on the butt and it turns into the god-damnedest fight you ever saw in yore life!"

☆ ☆ ☆

Gentility is probably a nice thing, serving the excellent purpose of covering up the operations of a scoundrel, but unless a man is born to it his prospects of acquiring it are very remote. I can eat soup without making whistling noises, but sometimes I can't remember to stand up when a dame comes into the room. I have a tuxedo, which I wore for the first time at a party given by Ely Culbertson at the conclusion of l'Affaire Culbertson-Lenz. This party was a stag dinner and brannigan and toward the end of it we played a weird game of charades. Heywood Broun took the part of a racehorse named Gallant Fox and I was his jockey. I rode Mr. Broun piggyback while he tried a heavy version of the gallop, going around the long table two or three times before the others started throwing salt cellars at us. That was probably no proper way to break in a new tuxedo. I wore it once after that under more genteel circumstances and felt like a man being held incommunicado.

As for manners—I'm a little on the side of Lou Holtz's celebrated character, Sam Lapidus. Maybe you've heard Lou tell about the time Sam took a friend to a fancy restaurant. When they had completed their meal the waiter brought finger bowls. Sam's friend sat and debated the purpose of the little bowl of water. It was not to drink, he concluded, because they had already been served with water in glasses. It was not to dilute their coffee, for they were finished with their coffee. At last Sam's friend screwed up his courage and called the waiter over to get an answer to the vexatious problem.

"The little bowls," said the waiter, "are to wash your fingers in."

"Ha!" said Sam Lapidus. "So you're esking a foolish kvestion, you're getting a foolish enser."

My own manners are not exactly bestial, nor are they suited for display at a tea dansant or an afternoon musicale. I think I am better versed than the Philadelphia publisher who habitually addressed Cardinal Dougherty as "Your Immense." Yet the entire field of high-grade etiquette confuses me because it is so complex. Take a small matter such as answering the telephone. It happens that whenever I answer the phone I start off by saying, "Hello." This, according to my wife, is an abuse of etiquette.

When she picks up the receiver she always says, "Yes?" She says that is correct—that when she went to college she belonged to a wedge-letter sorority and in the sorority they taught poise. They always told the girls to say, "Yes?" when they answered the phone.

The thing bothers me. The phone rings. You pick it up and you say, "Yes?" Yes what? What is yes? Yes is an affirmative response. Okay. You mean, when you say it, that somebody on the other end of the line is wondering if it is you, and you are saying "Yes," it is you. No, that wouldn't be it, because the way you say "Yes" is with a question mark after it. You say, "Yes?" and mean "Yes, I'm here, whatta you want?" It couldn't be the other way because if you meant to say, "Yes, this is I," you would be assuming that the person on the other end had the right number and, sometimes, that is not the case, so there would be no point in your saying, "Yes," when you might actually mean, "No."

You can see very readily that when you get into a discussion on this point you are likely to get confused. That's what happened to me, so I decided to call up Emily Post and find out what she says when she answers the phone. Well, I couldn't get her—couldn't even find out her phone number. She is privately listed, and I don't blame her, because if her name were in the book, people would be calling her up all hours of the night and saying, "Which fork?"

There are a surprising number of people who say neither "Yes?" nor "Hello" when they answer the phone. I have one friend who always, after picking up the receiver, holds the phone a couple of feet from his face and sings out:

"Mr. Watson, come here, I want you."

There are others who answer the phone by saying, "Commence" or "Start the conversation." Then there is the Southern lady of my acquaintance who snatches up the receiver and exclaims, "Hey, theah!"

The boys who slay me, however, are the ones who have set pieces to recite when they answer the phone. There is, for example, a former New York newspaper executive who now works for the Government and who delivers a little spiel whenever he takes a call at his home. He pitches his voice eight notches above its normal level and says:

"Bide-a-wee Pet Shop, home of the birds that sing and the multicolored goldfish, where we will be happy to supply you with a black widow spider or an affectionate orangoutang; where your dog may be shampooed, clipped, purged, and have his toenails trimmed at a reasonable fee; where animal is king the clock around, and parrots converse in eight separate tongues, all refined, Elmer speaking, who's this?"

He has been going through this routine for years, but lately his wife has grown weary of it. This dissatisfaction on the part of the wife grew out of a call which came from a Park Avenue society woman. The pet-shop routine made the society lady sore and she decided she didn't want these people for dinner after all. Since that day the wife has forbidden the phone to her husband. He is, however, a man of strong will, and whenever the bell rings he makes a dash for the instrument. Usually she beats him to it, but now and then he gets there first and gets to have his fun. Wives can be terribly unreasonable at times.

I didn't, as I mentioned, get Emily Post's slant on answering the telephone, but a couple of months later a famous thing happened to me. I had lunch with Mrs. Post.

It was an intimate, cozy little affair, this luncheon, with only a thousand people attending. It was held in the grand ballroom of a New York hotel and I was told in advance that I would be seated at Mrs. Post's table.

I always did want to watch her shovel grub. One of the great disappointments of my life was the fact that I missed a dinner a couple of years ago at which Mrs. Post got all thumbs and spilled a plate of food all over herself and her immediate neighbors.

This luncheon was given for magazine people and at one end of the ballroom were three long tables, set in tiers and occupied exclusively by writers. In order to forestall fist fights, hair-pulling, and public biting (writers being what they are), the guests were seated in alphabetical order.

They had no A people so Libbie Block, the short-story writer, was in No. 1 position. The line-up then proceeded through the three tiers, through such people as Will Cuppy, Walt Disney, Dr. Morris Fishbein, Paul Gallico, Margaret Case Harriman, Eric Hatch, Elsa Maxwell, William Lyon Phelps, Jim Street, and right down to the last plate, where the place card said "Michael Strange." Michael Strange is the wild-haired poetess who is Diana Barrymore's mama.

Mrs. Post fell into place about midway of the table where I sat. She was between a Mrs. Moore and Channing Pollock. That doesn't make sense alphabetically, but that's the way it was.

Before all these people began feeding their faces, I made an earnest effort to chisel into one of the seats on Mrs. Post's flank, but sitting next to Emily Post was something both Mrs. Moore and Mr. Pollock wanted to brag about, and they wouldn't yield.

So I made my way down to the end and took my alphabetically correct seat next to Michael Strange, who immediately began talking about Life, Writing, Inspiration, and a piece of property she owns in Connecticut and would like to get rid of.

Well, I did everything but crawl up on the table trying to watch Mrs. Post in the act of taking on fodder. Occasionally, far down the line, she'd bob her head into view, but I couldn't see how she was deporting herself with her food.

Owing to the fact that I paid little heed to her conversation and kept knocking over glasses trying to improve my view of Emily Post, my poetic neighbor, Michael Strange, got bored with me and asked me to change seats with her. We shifted soup, and Life immediately grew livelier for Michael Strange, for she was now sitting next to Jim Street. I heard him ask her, slyly, something about John Barrymore, and she replied:

"Young man, I deem you impertinent. I ought to slap your face off."

Finally the party broke up and I hurried down the line to grab the people who had been nearest Mrs. Post. Mrs. Moore said that she talked with the etiquette lady all during lunch.

"Did she spill anything?" I asked. "Did she fumble her forks? Did she sneeze in her asparagus?"

Mrs. Moore said she hadn't noticed anything in the way of miscues. Channing Pollock had disappeared so I approached Libbie Block and Katharine Brush, who had been sitting in front of Mrs. Post, though facing away from her. Had they noticed anything?

"As a matter of fact," said Miss Block, "I tried to watch her for one reason. I wanted to see if she eats English style or American style. Over here, we cut a piece of meat, then put down the knife and change the fork into the right hand. In England they cut the meat as we do, but keep the fork in the left hand and carry the food to the mouth with the left hand. I never did catch her at the right moment. It wouldn't be polite to stare at Emily Post. So I only cast glances."

Thus my report on that luncheon is woefully incomplete. For all I know Emily Post may have burped and then fallen face forward into her string beans. If she did, I missed it. S is too far from P.

CHAPTER XIV *Containing One Kind Word for Hollywood*

IT BECAME MY PLEASANT DUTY one day ten or twelve years ago to interview Ernst Lubitsch. Mr. Lubitsch undertook to explain for me why the motion picture is superior to the legitimate theater. He demonstrated how the camera can extract drama from the slow turning of a doorknob, the slight movement of an actor's finger—things that are impossible on the stage. Mr. Lubitsch didn't need to convince me. I was already a movie man.

Your hidebound theatergoer usually sneers at motion pictures and in so doing afflicts me with all the symptoms of hydrophobia. I go to the legitimate theater two or three times a year, not to look at the people on the stage but to contemplate the deodorized ladies of the audience and the silk-hatted weregoats who serve those ladies as escorts. Thus the most interesting part of an evening at the theater, to me anyway, is intermission, when the customers gather in the lobby to smoke and to smell up the premises with their conversation.

I've never had a real hot yen to see but one stage play and it was never produced. It was written by a pleasant man named Frank White, who used to hang around the Denver Press Club. Frank White was a former newspaperman who played a good game of poker and, if pressed, would recite the play he had written. I don't remember the title of the opus but I do remember the way the script goes. Of it, Frank White used to say:

"No matter what anybody else has accomplished, I can always lay claim to one distinction. I am the author of the shortest play ever written."

The White drama has a single stage setting: the dreary living room of a New England farmhouse. As the curtain rises two characters are on stage. Lying in front of the fireplace is Eb, the son of the family. He is writing with chalk on the back of a shovel. Seated in the rocking chair is the daughter of the family, Marybelle.

Suddenly the door is flung open, revealing at one and the same time a blizzard and Paw. Paw holds the door open long enough for the audience to recognize the full fury of the storm outside. He is a tall geezer with chin whiskers. He slams the door, stamps the snow from his feet, crosses the room, and confronts Marybelle. He stares down at her a moment, then lifts his arm, points to the door, and says:

"Git out!"

Eb looks up from his shovel and says:

"Whatsa matter, Paw? She ain't done nuthin'."

And Paw replies:

"I know she ain't done nuthin', but it's a-snowin' out, an' out she goes!"

Curtain.

There's a play I could enjoy, though given my choice of seeing it on the stage or on the screen, I'd take it on the screen.

People who are stage daffy strike me as being of the same caliber as autograph bugs. If they ever go to a movie I have an idea they sit for ninety minutes, saying to themselves: "That's not really Joan Crawford up there. That's not anybody at all. Nobody. Only a bunch of photographs. No more Joan Crawford than I am. Joan Crawford's out in Hollywood." If they were seeing Joan Crawford on the stage, they'd apparently get a tingle from the fact of their being within a few yards of Joan Crawford in the flesh. I think such people suffer from the disease called Vicarious Vertigo. I know all about that disease because I've had it for years.

I am personally acquainted with Irving Berlin through Vicarious Vertigo. Know him well. I'll prove it as soon as I explain the disease. Vicarious Vertigo is a malady endemic in the United States of America and is characterized by pleasurable dizzy spells, swollen tongue, and, in some cases, loin twitch. Something also happens to the head. Both children and grownups suffer from Vicarious Vertigo, which is contagious, and the pill hasn't yet been pestled that will cure it.

Perhaps the most common manifestation of the disease is to be observed outside stage doors. Here the Vicarious Vertigo germ is joined by bacillus autograph, causing the victim to see spots before the eyes as big as basketballs.

If you are an observing person, you may see evidence of the disease all around you. Not long ago I was riding in a subway train when the chance arose to study an interesting case. The victim was a girl in her middle teens. The train was crowded and the girl was standing. Across the car was a middle-aged woman, occupying a vacant look. As it developed, the middle-aged woman was the dam of the teen-age girl. I was busy reading the works of Keats (Fred) when the girl, in that loud and unself-conscious manner of New Yorkers, yelled:

"Mommer!"

Mommer looked up.

"Mommer," yelled the girl, "you rememba that putchy kid lives uppen th' next block over tords Margie's name Freddie got the freckles all over him?"

"Yehr," said Mommer. "So what about?"

"Jus' think," yelled the girl. "You rememba that they had this memorial surface to Lou Gehrig up the Polo Grounds or somewheres and LaGardy and all them was there?"

"Where at?" Mommer called out.

"Well," said the girl, ignoring the question, "this Freddie he was the one played the taps on the bugle. Right there at the memorial surface to Lou Gehrig. Frunta all them people and LaGardy. Freddie, that lives over tords . . . You know, Freddie, got all them freckles on him."

"No!" said Mommer.

"Swearta God!" said the girl. "Margie told me he was the one."

The girl looked around at the other people in the car, smiling proudly.

There is a case of Vicarious Vertigo. Knowing the course usually taken by the malady, I realized that this girl would go around for weeks and months and maybe years, bragging about how she was "personly acquainnit with Freddie that played the bugle at the Lou Gehrig memorial surface in front of LaGardy." She was enjoying a sort of three-cushion celebrity herself and, no doubt, the disease soon took hold of Mommer. Mommer could now brag about how her own daughter knew Freddie that played . . . etc.

I have already confessed that the V. V. germ has had possession of my own carcass for years and I fear I have passed the disease along to my children. My daughter, who is in her teens, came dashing into the house a while back, crying:

"I think I saw Billy Gilbert!"

"Billy Who?" I asked.

"Billy Gilbert," she answered breathlessly. "You know, Billy Gilbert, the big fat movie star, the one that sneezes, got a little mustache."

"Where'd you see him?"

"Well," she said, "I was crossing the street, Northern

Boulevard, and the light was red and this car was stopped
and just as I got across I looked up and there were two men
in this car, the driver and this other man, and it was Billy
Gilbert. Honest it was! And he was looking *straight at me*.
And he *grinned* at me. It was Billy Gilbert. It couldn't have
been anybody else. And he acted like he almost *knew* me!"

Then she flew out of the house, headed for the homes
of all her girl friends, to brag about this earth-shaking thing
that had happened to her. I was left to sit alone and brood
over the appalling evidence. The fact stared me in the face.
My daughter had inherited V. V.

When I was a little heel around eleven or twelve I lived
in an Illinois town and was learning to swim at the Y.M.
C.A. One afternoon I was on my way to the "Y" pool and
was walking across a strip of ground back of the tennis
courts. Suddenly a tennis ball rolled across my path. I picked
it up and looked toward the court and saw a tall guy with a
racquet. Apparently he was alone and had been batting the
ball against the side of a building. He held his hand up and
smiled and I threw the ball at him and then I went on
toward the building housing the pool. At the door one of
the "Y" attendants stopped me and said:

"Hey, son. Know who that was you throwed the ball to?
That was none other than the great Bill Tilden."

Sure enough, it was Bill Tilden—not so great at that
moment as he later became but already a famous personality. The hell with going swimming after that. I headed for
home and, arriving there, set off on a bragging tour of the
neighborhood. The V. V. germ had me. At first I told a
story of having retrieved a ball for the great Bill Tilden, of
how I walked up and handed him the ball and chatted with
him about the weather. Within a few days I was telling
how I had joined Bill Tilden in a little game of batting the
ball against a building. By the time two weeks had passed I
was remarking, quite casually, that I had played a regula-
tion game of tennis with Tilden. And thereafter, for half-
a-dozen years, I went around talking about how I had engaged Bill Tilden in an impromptu *set* and had BEATEN
THE LIVING HELL OUT OF HIM!

That's the way the insidious malady works. The frightful thing about it is that people listen to its victims. Let me cite just one more instance before I get to Irving Berlin. As you doubtless know, the late O. O. McIntyre was, to millions of outland Americans, the First Citizen of New York. They worshiped him, particularly through the Middle West where he had his origin. Now, it happens that I had occasion to telephone O. O. McIntyre one day in connection with a newspaper story I was writing. I talked to him about thirty-eight seconds.

Some months later I was visiting my home town in the Middle West (I have at least four home towns) and was talking to a fellow at the Elks Club.

"Live in New York now, eh?" he said.

"Yep."

"Know people there purty well?"

"Well, I know some people."

"Know O. O. McIntyre?"

"Only slightly," I said. "Just slightly, is all. Talked to him not long ago on the telephone."

He was full of eagerness for the details—wanted to know how McIntyre's voice sounded, what he said, how he said it. And then he spread it all over town like this:

"Knows O. O. McIntyre, he does! Spoke to him on the phone. Says he talks regular, just like anybody else! Told me all about it at ten-eighteen by the clock last night at the third card table from the door on the left-hand side in the Elks Club."

By now you know Vicarious Vertigo and how it works, and I can demonstrate how intimately I know Irving Berlin.

One evening I was a guest in the home of the Carters in Greenwich Village. Mrs. Carter is employed by a large firm of interior decorators and has worked on many important jobs. Some time during the evening she began talking about her Easter bonnet. She had constructed it herself and it was unique beyond being simply a woman's hat. She had fashioned it of materials left over from three recent decorating jobs.

The main part of the hat was built from a slab of straw matting. This was left over from a table mat on the huge liner *America*, which Mrs. Carter had helped decorate. She had taken the fragment of matting and formed it into a shallow crown, and around the edges she had tacked on some yellow silk stuff that was left over from the bandstand of a leading New York night club.

Hanging down the side of the homemade hat was a small black tassel. This came from—here's the pay-off—this came from the home of Irving Berlin. Mrs. Carter had helped redecorate the Berlin home and had preserved a tassel left over from the drapes.

She got the hat out and let me look at it, even let me hold it. I held it in my lap for, well, maybe ten minutes all told. And I *fondled* the tassel that was left over from the drapes that were hung in Irving Berlin's house when Irving Berlin's house was redecorated.

Do I know Irving Berlin? Know him well. Known him for years. Practically pals, me and Irving. Know him almost as well as I know Bill Tilden.

☆   ☆   ☆

By hoary tradition newspapermen are supposed to be supercilious in the presence of fame. If I were a glittering Hollywood star, twice as big as I am now and possessing three times my present courage, and if I were subjected to periodic interviewing at the hands of newspapermen I would soon conclude my career on the gallows for mass murder. The ordinary reporter, when interviewing a movie celebrity, generally out-hams the ham. He puts on a pose of insolent superiority when, in actual fact, he's more than a trifle thrilled, even though thumbscrews would never bring him to admit it.

I used to be that way. I'd act haughty and superior in the presence of interviewees when I didn't really mean it. Right now I can confess that I get a wallop out of meeting most celebrities. That's why I enjoy visiting in Hollywood as a member of the press—a person with rare privileges, constantly being introduced to movie stars and even being invited to their homes. A visiting newspaperman, particularly one who has "circulation," is treated as royalty by the picture studios.

A newspaperman I know told me about his arrival in Hollywood and how he was taken at once into the presence of Louis B. Mayer. Mr. Mayer talked with him a while, made some discreet inquiries respecting the guy's following among newspaper readers, then informed him that he could have anything he wanted. As the visitor was leaving, Mr. Mayer glanced at the publicity man who had accompanied him and said:

"A."

Outside the door the newspaperman asked what he meant by "A."

"That means," said the publicity man, "that you're in luck. You get the 'A' treatment. You get a private car with chauffeur, always at your disposal. You get all the restaurants and night spots you want, on the cuff. And you get to date any of our actresses who are available. How would Linda Darnell suit you tonight?"

During my own two visits in Hollywood I never got the "A" treatment but I got better than that. I got Rufus Blair. Rufus Blair is a publicity man at Paramount. He is a master of invective, oral and written. He talks a good deal like H. L. Mencken writes. He is bitter and contemptuous toward most of Hollywood's institutions and never hesitates to express himself in that direction. When I come into Hollywood Rufus Blair is there to meet me. He was there at the airport when I came out of the plane and saw him for the first time. He stepped up, his hand extended, and said:

"You resemble a terrible baboon named Smith, so described to me by my New York office."

He stays with me for the duration and we make a determined effort to keep away from such places as the Brown Derby and Dave Chasen's and Slapsie Maxie's. We simply settle down in the Blair hillside residence, which is called Baskerville because of the presence of an entire herd of police dogs. Occasionally we invite Lou Smith or Blake McVeigh or Harry Flannery or Eddie Albert in to join us and we have a good time.

On the last visit I spent three weeks in Hollywood and I had a schedule of work laid out that was more exhausting than the love life of a galloping goose. I was appearing once a week on a sad radio program called "Swop Night," which required script conferences and interviews with yucks. *Yuck* is a word introduced into the language by Fred Allen.

A yuck is a dope who makes a practice of going around appearing on quiz programs. That was its original definition; it now means a dope of any description.

In addition to the radio show I was supposed to be collecting material for some magazine pieces about Bing Crosby. That was, in fact, my chief purpose in going to Movietown, although I also had to turn out a daily column containing, theoretically, something more than random thoughts on sunshine.

In writing the column from Hollywood I undertook an experiment in which I sought to avoid interviewing a single movie actor or actress during the entire three weeks. The publicity men kept my phone ringing constantly, offering appointments with the stars. One man wanted me to interview Gene Autry's horse on the subject of what a nice fellow Gene Autry is. I turned them all down because I knew that if I interviewed a star at Warner's, then I'd be compelled, in fairness, to interview stars at all the other studios, and I didn't have time for that. It amuses me to think back about the attention I got from the studios then. I was a columnist, an outlet for valuable publicity, and they courted me and sent gifts to my hotel and offered to take me to the fights and offered automobile service and all that. The next time I go out I won't be a newspaperman and they'll shun me as they'd shun a meat-eating Staphylococcus.

I intend to go out again, not alone for the pleasure of being ignored, but to achieve three small ambitions. I didn't have time for them before.

First, I want to visit Harry Carey's thumb. Harry Carey's thumb was my favorite movie actor when I was a kid. I went to all his Westerns and I was always fascinated by his thumb. He employed it dramatically whenever he was communing with himself. He'd place his thumb, cocked back from his fist, against his chin and just think, think, think, and what he was thinking was not healthy for the rustlers.

Second, I want to go out to Lola Lane's ranch, if she still has it. I interviewed Miss Lane in New York once and she told me about her ranch, which formerly belonged to Edgar Rice Burroughs. A big tree stands in front of the main house and it is this tree that interests me. Miss Lane told me that one summer night Edgar Rice Burroughs couldn't get to sleep in the house because of the heat so he dragged a mattress into the yard, placed it beneath the tree, and lay down on it. He was lying there, still unable to get to sleep, staring up into the branches of the tree, when he saw something. It was Tarzan. When I heard about this I told Miss Lane I'd dearly love to try that tree. She said that I could spend a night at her ranch, she'd fix me up with a mattress, and I could stare up into the tree all night if I wanted to, and that anything I saw up there I could keep and write about. I have no idea of what I might see, but I do know that if Edgar Rice Burroughs could see Tarzan, I'll be able to see something.

My third minor ambition is to sit on Lana Turner's stool. It appears that Miss Turner was a high-school girl in Hollywood and one day she was sitting on a stool at a soda fountain when a big shot happened in and "discovered" her for the movies. Subsequently, I'm told, the proprietor of the soda fountain had a metal plate attached to the stool, saying: "This is the stool on which Lana Turner was sitting when she was discovered." I want to sit on that stool. It's an urge I can't explain. I can offer no reason why I want to sit on it, but I do, and I will if I can find it.

When I resolved not to interview any movie actresses during that last visit, I forgot about Gerta Rozan. Five years earlier in New York I had done an interview with Gerta at the time of her arrival in America from Vienna. Gerta came to America as a refugee, unable to talk our language but possessing a good reputation as an actress. Before long she was swallowed up by Hollywood and nobody heard of her until a press agent talked her into performing her famous strip-tease picketing act.

She had been given a minor role in an Albert Lewin-David Loew film. When the picture was completed, Gerta's bit part had been scissored out. So one of Hollywood's press agents set her to picketing the studio, marching up and down in front of the entrance and taking off one garment each day. Her threat was that she would keep on picketing until she had taken every stitch of her clothes off, but of course it never got that far. She is a lovely blonde and, if the capitalistic bosses had kept the dispute in a deadlock, the effect would have been devastating.

So Gerta, the strip picket, was the only actress I saw. She told me she was sad. She had been sad for a long time. Back in 1932, she explained, she was dining in a Berlin restaurant. At the next table was a puny political ward heeler who looked like Charlie Chaplin.

"I thought," said Gerta, "that he looked so funny, and I giggled at him, right in his face, and he scowled very bad at me. It would have been so easy for me. I could have picked up a big bottle champagne and hit him on top the head and killed him. I kick my pants I didn't do it. I kick my pants all the time."

Though Gerta was the only actress I really interviewed I got to see many other citizens of Never-Never Land. I got to talk to my favorite movie actress—Joan Crawford. I was taken out to Jack Benny's house one Monday morning to have breakfast and to be shown over the Beverly Hills mansion by the master himself. I visited in the home of Hedda Hopper, a gracious battleaxe. I saw the inside of the homes of two of Hollywood's most genial geniuses—Mark Sandrich and Norman Z. MacLeod. I had a swell afternoon at Irene Rich's little ranch, which is on top of a mountain. And I even saw Dorothy Lamour.

One evening Harry Flannery and I were sitting in the cocktail lounge at the Hotel Knickerbocker. We were debating whether we ought to go upstairs and abuse William Saroyan. I had called on Mr. Saroyan the evening before and found him sitting on a divan in his living room, punching at a portable typewriter. I went in and sat down and after a while, pretending that I didn't know he was busy revolutionizing the motion-picture industry, I asked him what he was doing in Hollywood. He stood up, pointed a finger at me for emphasis, and said:

"I'm revolutionizing the motion-picture industry."

He usually talks that way but underneath it he is a nice fellow and, for all I know, a genius.

The cocktail lounge where Flannery and I were sitting is a colorful institution. You don't often see the aristocrats of Hollywood around the Knickerbocker but, sooner or later, you'll see everyone else. On this particular evening the door opened and in came Dorothy Lamour. She appeared to be in a hurry. She swished around a pillar and grabbed the lady who reads horoscopes at the Knickerbocker. They ducked into a corner and put their heads together and I could see the horoscope reader's jaw wagging at a furious pace. After about fifteen minutes Miss Lamour scampered out of the place. I went over and talked to the seeress, trying to find out what was troubling Dottie. She wouldn't talk beyond saying:

"Miss Lamour is a regular customer of mine. Sir, I cannot tell you the nature of the things that I have just told her. That is locked forever in my breast."

Miss Lamour works at Paramount and Paramount is the only studio where I know my way around. It is a lovely place for aimless wandering. You might run into anybody in the little studio streets. You might, for example, encounter Robert Benchley, wearing a large white button on his lapel. The button carries a cabalistic inscription: "W T F H A Y D O H I C?" You ask Mr. Benchley the meaning of this inscription and he tells you:

"What the hell are you doing out here in California?"

If you happen to get on the set where Miss Lamour is working in a jungle scene, you might run into Muk, the chimpanzee, during the trying period when Muk is getting his bottom lacquered. Muk's rear end is bare of foliage and gleams a fiery red in its natural state. Thus his backside could very easily dominate any scene in a technicolor picture unless something were done to dim its luster. His keeper has the job of neutralizing Muk's behind. Muk doesn't like it, as who would? Yet at frequent intervals he is compelled to bend over while the keeper smears him with black shoe polish. It is said that this rite is performed by order of the Hays office, but I don't believe it. I prefer to believe that the actors and actresses involved in Muk's pictures have demanded the paint job. If Muk were permitted to appear *au naturel* (look at me talk French!) his anatomical sunburst could easily capture an Academy Award for scene-stealing. It could even steal a scene from Dorothy Lamour.

The best Hollywood stories are those involving technical triumphs or technical mistakes. The men who work out the industry's technological problems are the real geniuses of Hollywood. Allyn Joslyn, the actor, has a collection of technological yarns and he tells them masterfully. My favorite among them is the story of the sunrise.

At one of the big studios a director was finishing a picture—a "B" product. As he neared the end of the job the director—a fellow with Art in his soul—decided his picture was more important than anybody thought. He discovered that his picture actually carried A Message.

Having reached this conclusion, he announced that he was going to film a brief epilogue. He wanted to crystallize The Message through this epilogue and he wanted it to be impressive. He would have the hero and the heroine standing against a beautiful setting, and they would talk to each other, and their talk would constitute a summarization of The Message. It would be nice. Maybe even terrific.

His mind made up, the director decided on the background for his epilogue. He would have the boy and the girl standing on a rocky promontory and, back of them as they talked, the great sun would rise slowly out of the sea. Oh, it would be lovely!

Such a shot as this is not actually made at the seashore. The sunrise at sea is photographed separately, then thrown on a screen in the studio. The actors stand in front of this screen and do their talking and the whole thing is photographed, and it comes out looking quite authentic.

So our director called in a camera crew and ordered his sunrise. He told the men to go down to the beach before dawn and get him a first-class sunrise.

The following morning they came back to the studio and said they hadn't been able to get it. They pointed out that the sun does not rise off the Coast of California. The director was nettled at having been a dope, but he covered his embarrassment and said:

"Listen, you guys. You shoulda been able to figure it out. Go back to the beach this evening and get me a beautiful sunset. Then we'll simply reverse the film, run it through backwards, and we'll have our beautiful sunrise."

The next day they were ready with their sunset picture. The film was reversed and thrown on the studio screen. The boy and the girl took their places on the hand-wrought rocky promontory, directly in front of the screen. They talked—talked The Message of the epilogue.

Even the workmen on the set stopped to watch, for it was a beautiful scene that was being shot. The boy and the girl surged along with their impassioned colloquy and as they talked, behind them the rim of a huge sun peeped over the waves. On went the talk, and slowly and beautifully the sun came up from the majestic sea.

Then someone let out a yell. Something was wrong. A mistake had been made.

It was all very lovely, except for one thing. In the picture of the beautiful sunrise all the sea gulls were flying backwards and the waves were going away from the shore.

One other little story involving a technical problem comes from Charlie Einfeld. This one involves a director who needed a couple of animals for a forthcoming sequence. The director got the name of an animal dealer and sat down to write him a letter. At the very beginning he was stumped. He wasn't sure about the plural of mongoose. He tried it this way first:

> *Dear Sir:*
> 　　　　*Please send me two mongooses . . .*

That didn't look right, so he threw the sheet in the wastebasket and started over again, this way:

> *Dear Sir:*
> 　　　　*Please send me two mongeese . . .*

That seemed even worse than the first try. The director sat and studied a bit, then got it figured out. On a fresh sheet of paper he wrote:

> *Dear Sir:*
> *Please send me a mongoose. By the way, while you're at it, send me another one.*

☆　　　☆　　　☆

It can be no news to the civilized world that Hollywood reeks with treachery and backbiting and malicious gossip and hatred. At almost any social gathering you'll find people who hate each other like Devil Anse Hatfield hated the McCoys. Hollywood's a feudin' town.

One of the most interesting feuds to be met with on the Paramount lot involves my friend Rufus Blair. For several years he has not been on speaking terms with a certain agent—a hulking fellow. He and Rufus Blair despise each other—all because of a goose.

Some years back, on a sunny afternoon, Rufus was having his shoes shined. The shoeshine man at Paramount had his chair outdoors, placed against a wall of one of the buildings. It was a matter of common knowledge that the shoeshine man, a colored gentleman, was the goosiest human being west of the Mississippi.

Even a mere gesture, the slightest threat of a goose in which no contact was actually made, was sufficient to give him the shrieks.

On this sunny day Rufus was in the high chair and the man was at work on his shoes. Sitting there in the sun, Rufus found himself getting drowsy and pretty soon he was slumped in the chair, sound asleep. The man was busy on his shoes, wielding the heavy wooden-backed brushes, swinging them back and forth in a rhythmic beat. Now the villain appears on the scene—the afore-mentioned agent. This man is not renowned for intellect and, to use Douglas Gilbert's phrase, possesses a magnificent grasp of the obvious. A goose, to him, represents the ultimate in humor.

The agent came down the street and spied the shoeshine man at work with the brushes. Creeping up behind the Negro, he managed to get within goosing distance without making his presence known. Then with tender and loving care he administered a masterpiece—a goose that had finesse to it; not too forceful, not too delicate, just precisely right.

That Negro screamed and went straight up in the air. When he came down, he landed squarely on top of the sleeping Blair. His wooden brushes were still going, by some sort of goose-induced reflex—still swinging back and forth and knocking against the sides of Rufus Blair's head.

Rufus says his awakening was the worst experience of his entire life. He came out of his pleasant doze with a colored gentleman in his lap and a pair of wooden brushes cracking against his noggin. He fought his way clear of the shoeshine man and the chair and found the agent standing there, convulsed with laughter.

"What a thing to do!" screamed Rufus, and flung himself at the malefactor with both fists flying. There was no great damage done because the thing was broken up before it had fairly begun. But to this day Rufus and the agent—to whom Rufus refers bitterly as The Gooser—pass each other without speaking, glowering as though murder inhabited their hearts.

That's one Hollywood feud. There are several thousand others. The Big People of the industry like to talk about how Harmony reigns in their sun-baked empire, where Intelligence sits on the throne and all men are Brothers. They know better.

One of the most intelligent men in the town, B. G. DeSylva, production chief at Paramount, has indirectly confessed the extent of the trust he places in the people around him. He was attending a luncheon with executives from several other studios. The talk got around to baseball. An executive from a rival studio remarked to Mr. DeSylva that he would like to get up a baseball team at his plant and challenge a team chosen from among Paramount employees.

"No," said Buddy DeSylva. "We'd better not try it. I can't think of eighteen men in all Hollywood that I could trust if they had baseball bats in their hands."

CHAPTER XV   *Of Bananas and Crosbys*

WHEN my father was in the vicinity of twelve years old he was unreasonable about bananas. He could never get enough of them. In those days bananas were almost as rare as rotolactors and Pop's passionate yearning for them became a source of irritation to his parents.

One afternoon his father summoned him to the front yard

of the Smith homestead. Hanging from a lower limb of the mulberry tree was a stalk of bananas, full and complete.

"Yonder's some bananas for you," said Caleb Smith.

The entire family, augmented by half-a-dozen neighbors, gathered in the front yard to watch Pop eat bananas. He vows to this day that he didn't move off the spot until he had consumed every one of those bananas. He has not eaten another during all of the ensuing fifty years. It nauseates him to be in the same room with a banana.

Something similar happened to me in 1941. I acquired a surfeit of Crosbys. There were times during that year when a mere whispering of the name was sufficient to send me to bed.

I mention this attack of Crosby allergy by way of preface to a short course in the art of writing for magazines. The story begins back in the summer of 1940 and has its genesis, properly enough, in a saloon.

At that time I might have been described as a warm admirer of Bing Crosby's style of singing. I attended his movies, sometimes listened to his radio programs, and occasionally bought his records. Still, I didn't like Bing Crosby as much as Pop liked bananas.

That summer afternoon, on my way home from work, I stopped in a record shop, looked over the new releases, and bought a couple of Crosby platters. Further along toward home I undertook the pause that refreshes. The bartender was a young fellow—a man I'd never seen before. I had the envelope containing the records lying on the bar beside me when he came up. He looked at me, nodded toward it, and said:

"See ya got some records."

"Yep," I said.

He studied me a moment, then leaned forward and remarked:

"Bet I know what records you got."

There was nothing printed on the big envelope to suggest what was inside so I said I bet he didn't know.

"Crosby," he said.

Naturally I was a trifle agitated, being a person who holds no belief in the occult and also being convinced that no human possesses X-ray eyes.

"How did you know that?" I demanded.

He grinned. "You got that Crosby look," he said. "You look like a Crosby man."

When I got home I spent quite some time with a mirror, but I couldn't figure it. I took to worrying about the thing. I began taking a deeper interest in the doings of Bing Crosby and I started talking about him whenever I was around the Broadway know-it-alls. Little by little I acquired anecdotes about Crosby, and after two or three months the fact dawned on me: if I hadn't been a Crosby man before, I was a Crosby man now.

The story of the guy's career and the peculiarities of his personality fascinated me. Then one day I encountered Stuart Rose, associate editor of the *Saturday Evening Post*, and started yammering Crosby at him. Within a week I had been given an assignment to do the story of Crosby for the *Post*. I was told that half-a-dozen writers had come to the *Post* from time to time with the same idea, but they had all been turned down. Now the *Post* editors had decided that I was the proper person to do Crosby. Apparently they looked at me as the bartender had looked at me and concluded I was a Crosby man.

I never got so sick of a thing in all my life as I did of that job. I scurried around New York for a while, digging up people who had known Crosby. I went out to Hollywood for the primary purpose of collecting Crosby material. Before I was finished I had talked to more than a hundred persons, and I had enough material on the Life and Times of Bing Crosby to produce a biography bigger than Sandburg's *Lincoln*. Part of this material appeared eventually as two articles in the *Post*. The rest of it—a bundle as big as last week's wet wash—occupies a corner of my workroom, serving me as a constant warning and reproach. It isn't a symbol of wasted effort, but rather represents a lesson I've learned—the same lesson Pop learned when he ate too many bananas.

During that assignment it seemed that every step I took I turned up a heel. I recall once having recommended a book about the Russian Romanovs to Fred Allen. Soon after that I had a note from him saying he was halfway through it.

He wrote: "I haven't come across so many bastards since I played in vaudeville." I feel much the same way about the Crosby job. Looking back on it, I can remember only a couple of men I actually enjoyed meeting. One was Dr. Simon L. Ruskin, who was operating an entire hospital virtually by himself but who took an hour off and favored me with a lecture on the subject of singers' nodes with particular reference to the nodes studding the Crosby larynx. The other was Jack Kapp, president of the Decca Company, which issues Crosby records.

Mr. Kapp turned out to be a noble creature alongside most of the others; yet he gave me a few bad moments. He asked me to dinner at his house, and the dinner went along nicely until toward the end when a dish containing *broiled* grapefruit was placed in front of me. It was one of those situations where I had to make conversation and maintain a sly reconnaissance on the others, waiting for someone else to start eating to see how it was done. Such things always throw me off balance, but I was recovering poise after getting my hands on the right tools, and then somebody brought in finger bowls, and floating in the finger-bowl water was a rose petal. A full hour elapsed after dinner before I was able to ask Mr. Kapp a sensible question about Crosby.

The quest for Crosby material furnished justification for Buddy DeSylva's remark that he didn't know eighteen men in all Hollywood who could be trusted with baseball bats in their hands. It soon became apparent to me that there is no such thing as a legitimate transaction in Hollywood— that everyone in the town is suspicious of everyone else. In its fundamentals, my job was simplicity itself. I was merely gathering material for the purpose of writing some pieces about Bing Crosby for the *Saturday Evening Post*. Yet virtually everyone I approached eyed me with skeptical distrust, asking either with the mouth or with the manner: "Okay. What's the angle?" Nobody could believe that I was simply engaged on a legitimate writing project. The theory appears to be that every man who comes around with a piece of business in hand is a double-dealer, a thimble-rigger, and a footpad.

The first Crosby I met was Everett, a muscle-bound man who is Bing's manager as well as his brother. Everett was in New York when I called on him at his office. I had been warned that he was a tough man to get along with so I put my case to him with gentleness and tact. He sat and stared straight ahead, and when I had finished telling him what I wanted to do, he grunted and said:

"Didja get Bing's permission to write about him?"

I said that Bing had indicated by telegram that he looked with favor on the project, whereupon Everett grunted again and growled:

"How much's th' *Saturday Evening Post* payin' Bing for this?"

From these two questions I quickly reached the conclusion that Everett is one of those fellows who are unhandy performing certain simple operations with a boot. I got away from him and went to Hollywood.

Personal business took me to the NBC studios on the first day I was in town. I was on my way to one of the offices, heading down a corridor, when I came upon Bing himself. He was sitting on a bench and I almost fell into his lap before I recognized him. I stuck out my hand and introduced myself.

"Oh, yeah," he said. "I heard you were comin' out."

"How've you been?" I asked.

"Fine," he said. "And you?"

"Fine," I said. And that was the last I saw of Bing.

Next on my calling list was Larry Crosby. Larry is the oldest of the Crosby boys and in theory is Bing's publicity man. I went to see him at the Crosby building on Sunset Boulevard and almost immediately I saw that he was suspicious of me. Before long I found out the nature of his apprehensions. It appears that Larry and another brother, Ted, wrote a biography of Bing back in 1927. They wrote it themselves (no question about that) and they published it themselves and they are proud of it. Bing must love them deeply to have ever permitted its publication.

Among other beautiful incidents the book tells of the time back in Spokane when Bing was a child and when his mother got word that one of her relatives had bought an automobile. This made Mrs. Crosby wistful, but little Bing toddled up to her and told her not to worry—that when he grew up they'd have a couple of automobiles.

"I'm gonna make a million dollars—just you wait and see —and you can have all kinds of servants," said tiny Bing, according to the book.

There's another occasion recited in the authorized biography in which Pop Crosby comes home with a gramophone and sets it to playing the "Merry Widow Waltz," which causes Mrs. Crosby to grow wistful again, and once more little Bing comes over to her and says:

"Gee, Ma. You like it, don't you?"

There in the Crosby offices Larry told me he suspected I was collecting material for a book about Bing, and that such a book would be put in competition with his own book, and he wouldn't stand for any such thing as that. In other words, I was traveling under false pretenses.

When I outlined some of the things I wanted to do, Larry told me I was taking too much for granted. It was foolish of me to think of spending any time at Bing's house.

"We'll arrange to get you together with him," said Larry, "but you can't ask him anything about his private life. You can talk to him about golf and you can talk to him about horses. If you try to talk about anything else, he won't see you."

"The hell with that all over the place," I said. "I don't want to talk to him about golf and horses. If that's the setup, I don't want to talk to him at all."

After that I bade him farewell and said good-by to Pop Crosby, who had been in the office with us, and then I went away. I didn't go back.

When I returned to New York I learned that Larry and Everett were quarreling by way of the mails, accusing each other of messing up my project, so I went to see Everett again. He practically bowed me into his office, gave me his own chair back of his desk, made a few remarks about Larry, and told me he'd give me anything and everything I wanted. And he did. During two long evening sessions he talked for hours at a stretch, telling me tales about his brother and about the whole Crosby family.

Subsequently, when he saw what I had written, my operatives tell me he let out a piercing scream.

"Whisky, whisky, whisky!" he cried. "You'd think Bing's middle name was Whisky from this stuff!"

"Well," broke in someone, "where did Smith get all those stories?"

"I gave them to him," shouted Everett, "but Jesus God, does that mean he's gotta put 'em in print?"

The Crosbys had other hysterical objections to my articles. By putting a lot of twos and twos together and cross-checking in the family's own book, I discovered conclusively that Bing was—at the time I was writing—forty years old. I could understand their objection to having this fact printed. Bing has a tremendous following among the ladies and, from that point of view, is one of the nation's champion kidney-weakeners. So I was willing to go along and say nothing specific about his age. I was willing until the Crosbys demanded that I describe him as being thirty-three. That, as Artemus Ward used to put it, wuz 2 mutch.

Gathering the material, I had interviewed movie people, radio people, advertising people, newspapermen, recording people, singers, musicians—everything but racehorses. And when I was finished, I figured I knew more about Bing Crosby than Bing Crosby did. Strangely enough, even though I overloaded on Crosby just as Pop overloaded on bananas, I came out of it still admiring the guy—still a Crosby man. When I say I'm still a Crosby man, I mean I'm a BING Crosby man.

The story of Bing's career remains to me an American epic because it is the reverse of the traditional success story. *Time* magazine once commented that Bing made a bum out of Horatio Alger, Jr., and that, approaching the apex of his career, he is "still falling uphill." He has been the antithesis of all that the Sunday schools and the Boy Scouts and the "Y" secretaries taught—and look at him! He has consistently violated all the rules and he still violates them whenever he chooses. His attitude toward me was the same as his attitude toward the rest of the press. Where most of the Hollywood stars look upon personal publicity as the life-blood of their business, stooping to inane invention and trickery to get it, Bing thumbs his nose at it.

There are other shining stars who back away from interviewers and who make no compacts with the chit-chat columnists, guaranteeing those columnists full and exclusive reports on future romances, marriages, prospective whelpings, divorces, changes in hair-do, and the like. Yet none of these brushes off the press because of sheer indifference as Bing does.

The Women's Press Club of Hollywood once voted Fred Astaire the most unco-operative actor in Hollywood from a publicity point of view. Crosby came in second—a photo finish. Astaire doesn't normally co-operate because he is a shy, sensitive man who suffers anguish in the presence of an interviewer, suspecting that every question is deliberately framed for the purpose of tricking him into an asinine answer. Crosby, on the other hand, is unco-operative because he just doesn't give a damn.

Privately he justifies his behavior toward the press with two arguments. He contends that he needs publicity—the kind of publicity that comes of being interviewed—about as much as he needs a hole in his head. He has three tremendous publicity outlets at his command: a weekly radio program, three motion pictures a year, and records. These instruments spread the Crosby voice and the Crosby personality to the ends of the earth, and he is in a position to control and direct them to suit his own whims. He cannot prevent a writer from twisting his phrases and making him look foolish or hammy, but in the production of his movies, of his broadcasts, and of his recordings, he is the boss. If Crosby wants a certain thing done, it's done; and if Crosby objects to something else, out it goes. Wherefore, what need has he of the kind of publicity the press has to offer?

His second argument is his answer to the sheep cry: "But you owe it to your public." All he owes to his public, in his own logic, is his best performance, whether on the screen, on the air, or on records. His job is to entertain and amuse the customers but not on street corners or in his bedroom. He makes a picture and the customers flock into the theaters to see it. If they enjoy it, if they like his performance, then he has done his job. It is not required that he be waiting outside the theater to hand them photographs of himself, sing a couple more songs, go into a rigadoon, sign their autograph books, and introduce them to his wife and kids.

His success has brought him everything he ever yearned for a thousand times over. He never yearned for much. He never believed in himself, save perhaps at the very beginning of his career when he felt he might, with help from on high, become a middling vaudeville performer.

His friends and his family have had to browbeat him and flog him up the road that led to success. Time after time, when things were beginning to break his way, he gave up, tried to disappear, announced himself a failure. He has been wheedled and bluffed and tricked into doing the things that, in the end, brought a golden torrent pouring into his lap. He achieved notoriety long before he achieved fame. Almost to a man the people who surrounded him in the early days held no hope of his ever getting anywhere. Whenever his name came up they'd shake their heads and agree that Crosby was headed for perdition. Yet the wild and irresponsible rhythm boy of 1929 has become one of the most respectable family men in Hollywood. He has assembled part of the Crosby clan about him and they help run his extensive business affairs, sometimes quarreling among themselves but always standing united when danger threatens from without. And drinking has long since ceased to be a problem with him. He still drinks but, in his own phrase, "never in self-defense." His story inspires me because he has proved that the rule books are crazy.

The Crosbys lived on the wrong side of the tracks in Spokane and traced their ancestry back to the *Mayflower*. Pop Crosby worked in a brewery and there was a house full of kids. Al Rinker, the piano-banger who was Bing's first partner on the stage, remembers the Crosby home in Spokane quite vividly. Rinker is now in the radio business in New York. He told me that the Crosby house was like a zoo where all the animals are mad at each other. The place was in a constant uproar with the kids quarreling and fighting, and it was all Mrs. Crosby could do to keep a piece of furniture intact. Pop Crosby was never a razor-strap man.

When one of the kids got out of hand it was his custom to grab up a stick of kindling wood and whack the miscreant alongside the head.

When Bing's larynx first began bringing in profits Everett was a truck salesman in Los Angeles and not doing well at it. Larry was barely getting along in an advertising agency up North. Pop and Kate Crosby still lived in Spokane. To-day Pop and Kate and one of the married daughters and Everett and Larry all live comfortably in Hollywood.

As I may have suggested Everett is not the most popular man in the movie capital. He is tough and he is cunning. A lot of people who have tried to best him in a deal now hate him and curse him in company. When he gave up selling trucks to take over as manager Bing was just another vaudeville and night-club performer. Granting him his due, he has done a good job of steering his younger brother up the hill.

Half the con men and crackpots of the nation have tried at one time or another to nibble at the golden flow of Crosby money. Everett is the man who throws them out. He doesn't just throw them out the door; he hurls them into the next county. He has probably scraped through the surface of more gold bricks than any man in Hollywood. One of his perennial customers is an inventor who wants to sell Bing a grandstand for the Del Mar race track. It is no ordinary grandstand. When the horses leave the barrier, the grandstand takes off with them, riding on tracks, and travels even with the pack right around to the finish line.

There's a legend in Hollywood about a certain actor whose relatives came down upon him in such numbers that he had to move out of his own home or make provision for the visitors elsewhere. He resolved his dilemma by purchasing a complete tourist camp on the outskirts of Los Angeles and installing his kinsfolk in the cabins.

Then there's the story of the minor executive at one of the studios who proudly announced his promotion from second cousin to first cousin. And there have always been vague whisperings about stars who have mothers and fathers and sisters and brothers hidden away in the garret as though they were physical monstrosities.

Among Hollywood families the Crosbys are unique in

that all of them work. Their universe revolves around Bing and their own fortunes are wrapped up in his, and they guard him as they'd guard a gold mine. If it can be said that any one member of the family rules the rest, that one is not Bing, nor Everett, but Kate Crosby. She is in her middle sixties and fully as alert and vigorous as she was twenty years ago. She and Pop Crosby live in a bungalow eight blocks from Bing's big house.

To this day Kate Crosby refuses to hire a maid and does all the housework herself. She still cooks and sews and knits and prays as she did in Spokane. From the beginning she has kept Bing's scrapbooks and preserved his letters. Bing himself has never paid much heed to clippings, although for several years he carried two ragged newspaper notices around in his wallet—one being a review of a Crosby movie in which his name was not even mentioned, and the other being a derisive commentary on his acting.

Kate Crosby is intensely religious and keeps her children posted, where it is necessary, on holy days and days of abstinence. Back in the Spokane days it was her custom, whenever trouble confronted any member of the family, to scurry for the Poor Clare convent where she would ask for prayers of intercession. She made such visits at all crucial moments in Bing's early career, and once when Bing was asked if he believed success came through luck, he replied that he preferred attributing his progress to "the workings of Providence." Nowadays, when troublous situations arise, Kate Crosby slips a $5.00 bill into an envelope and sends it off to the Poor Clares, asking for prayers.

She pays close attention to all of Bing's business affairs. Suppose the opening of a new Crosby picture is announced in the papers—with a photograph of Bob Hope and Dorothy Lamour but no Bing. She'd be on the phone at once, demanding of Larry why Bing was left out. She telephones for Everett at the Crosby offices and, failing to get him, keeps calling all day until he shows up. Then she laces him down. Does he expect some stenographer to run the Crosby business? Does he think he can fritter away his time on the golf course with all that business piling up?

Perhaps Everett is in New York. Kate Crosby reads an

item to the effect that Paramount has bought two excellent stories for Bob Hope. Off goes an air-mail letter to Everett.

"Why is it," Kate Crosby demands, "that Paramount is buying these fine stories for Bob Hope? Why aren't they buying stories like that for Harry? Get after them."

She has always called her famous son Harry.

Bing first achieved big celebrity just ten years ago, in 1933, when he was singing for CBS in New York. One of his tasks at the time was to fill out a "bio book." This is a twenty-four page folder containing a wide variety of questions with spaces for the radio artist to fill in his answers. The book is then used as source material for publicity releases. I succeeded in getting my hands on Bing's 1933 book and it contains several responses worth noting, including a voluntary declaration that he'd do anything for publicity, if only a squib in the Bronxville *Gazette*. This from the guy who, today, hides himself from interviewers and sometimes makes Donald Duck noises whenever a press camera is trained on him.

One question in the "bio book" asks what the artist would do if he had a million dollars. Bing's holograph on this subject:

I would go to California, buy a home, a boat, and a car; take up some light work, i.e., buy a piece of some prosperous business—travel abroad a bit, fish and golf in the interim—visit the various race tracks in season, and raise a small family. If a million bucks ever came my way, I could doubtless distribute a considerable amount to relatives, etc., in loans, and still have enough to carry out the program described. I'm pretty socialistic in this connection and really don't think anyone is entitled to or should have more than they need to live comfortably. My wants are comparatively simple and with half a million I could possibly scrape along somehow. In point of fact, if I ever connect with the aforesaid amount, I'll wash up.

During that same period Joe Mitchell called on Bing for an interview. The new singing star of radio and the screen was refreshingly candid with Mr. Mitchell, particularly when it came to a discussion of his past misdemeanors.

"They say I left a trail of broken hearts behind me when I left California for New York," said Bing. "Now, I wouldn't do a thing like that. The fact is—I left a trail of broken bottles and unpaid bills."

Then his mind carried him back to the days when . . .

"I was pretty bad," said Bing. "I got in fights and things like that. Whisky has ruined my career five times in five years. I studied law in college and I can truthfully say that the bar of the state of Washington is the only bar I was ever kept out of.

"People who compare me with Vallee and the other mugs are more interested in me than I am in myself. I'd like to be able to sing like the crooners. The reason is—a crooner gets his quota of sentimentality with half his natural voice. That's a great saving. I don't like to work."

It is not my intention to go back over all that ground again because every time I get within five feet of that bundle containing the Crosby material I become afflicted with the pip—that disease in chickens which makes them droop their heads and look as though they didn't have a friend in the world. I only wanted to show people who have ambitions to write for the magazines that it's not always so simple as it looks.

CHAPTER XVI   *Out of Many, One*

THE FIRST CELEBRITY I ever interviewed was an individual named Iron Man McArdle, who was built like a rhinoceros and had a faint facial resemblance to that creature. Looking back from a distance of almost twenty years, I'm not certain as to the geographical extent of his fame, but in Huntington he was a celebrity.

Iron Man McArdle was brought into town by an automobile company for the purposes of demonstrating the durability of a certain car. At high noon on a Monday the mayor of our town publicly handcuffed Iron Man to the steering wheel of the car, and Iron Man drove away on his endurance run while the populace cheered. Ostensibly the test was to demonstrate Iron Man's personal staying power, but the automobile company paid him for his pains and used the stunt as the basis for a later advertising campaign.

The car was to be driven up and down and back and across the county, night and day, always by Iron Man, until such time as he fainted from exhaustion. The newspaper where I was a fledgling reporter carried daily bulletins on the "grueling test," but these bulletins were furnished us by a publicity man—the first of 60,000 press agents I have met. I followed the thing with eagerness. To me Iron Man Mc-Ardle was a hero. And the day came when I was given the chance not only to speak to him, but to actually ride with him.

At the urging of several printers on the paper, I was sent out to make contact with Iron Man and ask him a question which, to the curious compositors, was more pertinent than anything else. Inasmuch as Iron Man was going day and night, always handcuffed to the wheel, and since the car never ceased moving at any time, the printers wanted to know his method of performing certain necessary functions. It was a poor beginning for a celebrity interviewer, but I went at it with zest and trembling. I was permitted to hop on the running board of the car as it came slowly down Jefferson Street and, in full view of many citizens, I interviewed Iron Man McArdle—performing remarkable acrobatic feats of my own in twisting my body around so everyone could see I was taking notes.

Iron Man's answer to the printers' question was never, of course, included in published reports of the stunt, nor will it be included here. It reminds me, however, of the day back in the nineteen twenties when one of the transatlantic flights was about to start from Roosevelt Field on Long Island. Going along on this ocean flight was an attractive young woman. The reporters assigned to the field grew curious, much as those printers in Indiana had grown curious, and they cut the cards to determine which man should approach the charming lady. The loser spent half an hour framing his question into the least offensive form he could think of. Naturally his compatriots stood by as spectators, expecting to see him get slapped purple. When, however, he finally got his point across to the lady flier, she merely gave him a winsome smile and said:

"What do you think that carton of lily cups is for?"

Iron Man McArdle was the first of a long line for me, and after the passage of a dozen years I acquired a small amount of self-confidence. This was true only when I was interviewing a person of moderate intellect, such as an actress or an evangelist or a collegiate goldfish-swallower. Whenever I came up against statesmen or financiers or great authors I usually suffered from hot flashes and palpitation of the knee-caps. Such famous figures could throw my head into neutral by simply looking at me.

The first author I ever interviewed was Rex Beach, who came to live in Sebring, Florida, when I was fumbling on the local paper. I was determined that I'd get a history-making interview out of this great genius—a story that would begin on page one and run into five or six columns inside. I sat down with him and instead of asking him legitimate questions, I started showing off. I had recently read a book called *The Americanization of Edward Bok,* so I started the conversation with Rex Beach by trying to demonstrate that I, too, was literary and bookish. I began this way:

"Well, well. How goes the battle with words? Oh, by the way, I just finished a corking good book last night. *Americanization of Edward Bok.* Wonderful piece of work. You've read it, of course?"

"No," said Rex Beach.

Something in the way he said the word shriveled my brain, and I never recovered. The conversation crawled from that moment forward, and though I managed to come up with a story of sorts, it was far from the grandiose journalistic triumph I had planned.

I've had many such embarrassments. Years after the Rex Beach interview the head of the National City Bank in New York, Charles E. Mitchell, got himself involved with a series of mathematical troubles, none of which made any sense to me, and finally was indicted in a case concerned with income-tax matters. Here was one of the great how-the-mighty-have-fallen stories, and on the evening of the day Mr. Mitchell appeared in court, my boss sent me to his house for the purpose of interviewing him.

The Mitchell home was one of those white-front mansions

on Fifth Avenue opposite Central Park, and when I got there, a press photographer was loafing around across the street. I asked him if Mr. Mitchell had come home yet and he said he didn't know. I went to the front door, hoping to God that Mr. Mitchell had not.

After a couple of nervous punches at the bell, the door opened and a man, obviously not a butler, stood before me.

"Is Mr. Mitchell at home?" I squeaked.

"No," said the man.

I knew it was Mr. Mitchell in person. Anybody would have known it since his photographs had been plastered through the newspapers for days on end.

"Well," I fumbled, "that's too bad."

"Yes, it is," he said.

"Do you expect him?" I asked.

"Who are you?" demanded Mr. Mitchell.

"I'm a reporter from the United Press and I'd like—I mean —that is, I came up to try to interview Mr. Mitchell, but if he isn't——"

"He's not home," said Mr. Mitchell, "and we don't expect him home for weeks."

"Well, in that case I guess I'll go on back."

"While you're at it," he said, "you can tell that photographer across the street he's wasting his time."

"Yes sir."

"You work for Karl Bickel, don't you?" said Mr. Mitchell. Karl Bickel was then head of the United Press.

"That's right," I said.

"Well, when you see him, tell him I said hello."

"Sure. I'll tell him. Tell him you said hello."

"Yes," he said. "Tell him Charlie said hello."

"Yes sir," I said. "Thank you."

He gave me a grin and then closed the door, and I went out and told the photographer and then went on back to the office. Dopey, wasn't I? But not *too* dopey. I wasn't dumb enough to go back and tell Karl Bickel that Charlie said hello.

There's a supposition on the part of many people that interviewers generally become fast friends with their interviewees. Many times I've returned from interviewing some celebrated glamor girl from Hollywood, to be greeted in the office by the less knowing members of the staff with the eager query: "Didja layer?"

Four out of every five movie stars I ever interviewed wound up the conversation with something like this:

"Now, don't forget. The minute you get to Hollywood, look me up. Be happy to have you come out to the house."

When I finally did get to Hollywood I made a few calls, but they didn't know me, never heard of me, treated me as though I were a *Book of Knowledge* salesman, and told me to go away. The only exception I can think of at the moment was Joan Crawford, who has only one fault that I know about. She sings opera songs in her spare time.

Out of the entire procession of celebrities, then, came but one friend. Late in 1939 I met Fred Allen in a hotel lobby, retired with him to a table in the dining room, and listened to him talk for a couple of hours. I had seen him once before, in 1933, when Helen Strauss asked me to do a story about a ten-foot figure of Fred Allen that had been constructed for display at the Chicago World's Fair. I went to a Manhattan loft building where this huge mechanical comedian had been mounted on a platform. At that time Fred Allen was no more than a vague name to me. Miss Strauss was with me and she introduced me to another young woman and we stood and looked at the monster, watching its arms work and its lips move. Mr. Allen himself was on the platform, inspecting himself and keeping up a steady flow of quips. Each of these gags caused the young lady who was with us to shriek with laughter. Finally I said to her:

"What's so funny? I don't see anything funny about that guy."

Miss Strauss managed to kick me on the shin and a bit later drew me off to one side.

"Ye gods," she said, "don't you know that's Miss Hoffa?"

"And who's Miss Hoffa?" I demanded.

"Fred Allen's wife," she said.

After that luncheon with him in 1939, however, it was me for Fred Allen. We began a correspondence which is one of the delights of my existence. Once every month or so Fred claws the world off his back and creeps off into the wilds of Queens for a bull session involving his good friend

Alton Cook and myself. The womenfolk generally gather at one end of the room and the menfolk at the other and the thing goes on interminably. The talk is never of the type known as intellectual, but it's the best talk I know about.

This is all bragging on my part, and I'm aware of it because I always brag about Fred Allen. I take great delight in opening a conversation with, "Fred Allen was saying to me the other night . . ." and that sort of thing. In this respect I am just like Jimmy Collins' jockey, who strives constantly to work the conversation around to the spelling of the name of the man who assassinated McKinley. I work the conversation around to a point where I can bring in the name of Fred Allen, and then I brag.

Fred occupies a unique position in show business. He's the only man on Broadway, to my knowledge, who has no enemy. In that territory where the stiletto is as common as the hatband feather, I've never heard anything but applause for him. This is all the more mysterious when you consider that Fred himself never pulls a punch. He is forever ridiculing the human race in toto and in its integral portions. He has cut down more people with a phrase than anybody I know, yet they don't seem to get sore about it. Maybe they think he's just being funny. After all, he's a comedian. But he isn't trying to be funny. Stupidity and pretense and hypocrisy in high places or low infuriate him and he unburdens his mind.

The world very likely lost a great writer when vaudeville got him. He has a genius for satire—a genius that is almost wasted in radio because his sardonic assaults on the antics of mankind are too swift for the Great Radio Audience. He is probably the most censored man in radio—not for reasons of bad taste but because he's always being told: "Yeh, it's good, it's wonderful, but they won't get it."

Away from the microphone, off the stage, he appears to be the unhappiest mortal on earth. He groans and complains, always eloquently, and if he can find nothing else to be unhappy about, he always has his physical condition to fall back on. He refers to himself as a crumbling ruin, and in the last few years he has seen almost as many doctors as he has panhandlers.

He even took himself to the Mayo Clinic, and when he got back there was a single note of cheer in his story of the trip.

"So far as I could see," he said, "I was the only person in that town who wasn't either on wheels or walking around with a string hanging out of his mouth."

The quips roll off his tongue like putty knives coming off the assembly line in a putty knife factory, yet he looks at the world with a sad and bitter countenance. He once leaped into the street to rescue a newsboy from in front of a truck and, having saved the boy's life, demanded roughly of him: "What's the matter, kid? Don't you want to grow up and have troubles?"

For the last half-dozen years he has always believed that his current radio contract would be his last. He walks forever through clouds of pessimism. Writing his own material as he does, he sometimes cries out in anguish over the multitude of restrictions placed upon him. He can't joke about politics. He has to be careful about religion and racial topics. His sponsor and various vice-presidents of advertising agencies and broadcasting companies have individual taboos that must be kept ever in mind.

In one of his rehearsals several years ago he was having more trouble than usual finding a joke to fit a certain spot. He would think of gag after gag, only to have it thrown out for one reason or another. Finally he thought he had it. He inserted a joke about a man with a glass eye. He had no more than uttered it when the program executives came piling out of the control room.

"Good God!" they cried. "Don't you know the sponsor's brother has a glass eye!"

He escapes this pall of censorship only when he writes letters or when he indulges in conversational orgies with his friends. In such circumstances he seldom utters a dull sentence and his spoken paragraphs are often little masterpieces of construction. In illustration, here is what he once told me about my noble profession:

"You newspapermen have a reputation for level-headed thinking. People believe you to be the most realistic breed in the world. That isn't true. Your entire attitude toward life is warped by the very business you're in. You are like vaudeville actors. Ask an old vaudeville ham if he remembers the Johnstown flood. You'll find immediately that he doesn't think of the Johnstown flood in terms of tragedy—of women and children dying and buildings collapsing. No. He says, 'Oh, boy, do I remember the Johnstown flood! That was the night Lil and me was playin' the Bijou in St. Paul and the manager come runnin' back and says we should go on next to closing in place of that old bag Trixie Dumont and boy! Did we lay 'em in the aisles! Brother, do I remember the Johnstown flood!'

"Now, you newspaper people contemplate the world and all its tremendous workings as just so many stories. You never look upon a human event as an event—it's a story. Tragedies are not tragedies to you—they're headlines and purple words. When you look at all these millions of people in New York, each one is a story—no more than that. A human being confronts you and you don't regard him as a human being at all. To you he's an item with skin around it."

He lives a simple, almost Spartan life. For years he and Portland were content with hotels, and Fred was always satisfied so long as he had a place to put a bridge table and his typewriter. A few years ago Portland acquired the understandable urge to create something resembling a home of their own. They moved into an apartment that lies midway between Times Square and Central Park, and Portland supervised the decorating and furnishing of the place. Fred has a study containing the first desk he ever owned and a wall lined solidly with bookshelves. He spends most of his time in that study and he is proud of his book collection, which is admirable for reference purposes. As you probably know his real name is John F. Sullivan, and his favorite book, which he came upon one day in a side-street shop, bears the title: *Never Hit a Man Named Sullivan.* The apartment contains a living room which answers the description of the "drawing room" you might see in a movie. It is long and has a fireplace and is expensively furnished and looks almost forbidding. Fred never goes into that room without first seeking out the colored maid and saying:

"Would it be all right if I go in the front room?"

Portland does most of her own cooking and they have always got along without an automobile. Fred has never owned a car and doesn't know how to drive one. During production of his last movie the script called for a sequence in which he was to step into a long black automobile and drive off. The Paramount people sent him into a barren section of the San Fernando Valley for an entire day of instruction in driving. Yet in rehearsal the following day Fred had just one chance to demonstrate his ability. The director decided it wouldn't do—that Fred would likely destroy five million dollars' worth of equipment and kill four million dollars' worth of talent if given his head at the wheel. They solved the problem by hooking the car onto a Ford by a thin, strong wire. The Ford was out of camera range. Fred stepped into the car, pretended to manipulate the ignition key, the clutch, the gear shift, and the wheel, and was dragged away by the Ford.

Fred has no cultural inclinations. He knows nothing about music. He has never been to an opera and admits that if he ever did go, even if he tried to understand and enjoy it, he'd spend all his time trying to figure out operatic "bits" for his program.

His letters, as I've said, are a major event at my house. He seldom writes a short one. He types them on a portable and never uses capital letters. This is not an affectation. Back in 1921 he bought his first portable while traveling in vaudeville. The machine was kicked around in theaters and hotels and acquired certain mechanical shortcomings. One of these was a stubborn refusal to capitalize. Fred's compositions from that time forward have been lower case from force of habit.

The publishers of this book have long been urging me to talk Fred into writing a book for them. I agree with them that such a book would be an event, but he has enough on his hands at the present. To assuage, in very small part, their yearnings for an Allen book, I'm going to append a few random excerpts from his letters. Ladies and gentlemen, Fred Allen!

On dandruff:

am in receipt of your semi-official communiqué and contents noted, including the two spoonsful, or spoonfuls, of dandruff which jiggled about noiselessly at the bottom of the envelope. the dandruff i am selling to people who keep other people's hair in lockets. most of these folks with hair in their lockets complain that people to whom the puberty by-product is shown generally say, "it may be so-and-so's hair—i'll take your word for it." these people who know so-and-so or did know so-and-so if the former owner of the hair is defunct, also know or knew that so-and-so when he had the hair on his person also had dandruff. through putting dandruff in all lockets, along with the hirsute strands, many arguments will be nipped at the source and the person to whom the hair is shown will be forced to exclaim, "it sure is old so-and-so's hair. that bum had plenty dandruff and there it is in the locket, plenty dandruff."

Making a date:

if it's convenient meet me next friday at 5:30 in my atelier (which until recently i thought was one of two things that spurted from a deer's parietal area). i don't know what i will be doing an hour from now, let alone friday, but 5:30 is angelus time. i always hear bells ringing at that hour. if one of the bells proves to be the doorbell i shall lift my weary head and open the door. if it is you, i give you advance notice that you may enter.

On the evils of drink:

the grape is a globule which, unlike trousers, does not improve with pressing. i can't drink any more. i had some brandy recently and it tasted as though sloan had merged with hennessy and had a beverage miscarriage. it was a sort of three-star liniment. i was sick for two days. didn't know what i was doing and wrote a hell of a script. it is too much trouble to get in that condition to write each week. with my essential hypertension i am supposed to report to a doctor every two weeks for blood pressure checkups. i am not permitted to have salt and a mere peek at a snapshot of lot's wife sends my pressure up.

On the Allen maid:

the maid sends regards. she is always sending something. today she baked a big batch of cookies to mail to her boy friend who is up in boston conducting himself provocatively at an open window on columbus avenue. hoping this finds you the same in jackson heights.

Of a certain Ben Pratt of the National Broadcasting Company:

knowing ben pratt i am not surprised at his observations. he is executive not only without portfolio; he is also without desk. he always seems to be roaming the halls of n. b. c. and i, along with thousands of others, have no idea as to his status with the organization. he may be bait for the radio city tours. as pratt's pratt disappears through various doors in the building the guides may shout, "there goes a friend of kate smith's!" or, "quick! there goes singing sam!" if you know what mr. pratt does there, in all fairness you should tell him. i am sure that he is in constant doubt himself.

On exercise during a vacation:

i am a bum at heart and may yet puzzle out a way to eliminate work and taxes and survive pleasantly seated on my gristle. the only effort being expended up here is in church. the man who passes the collection plate at our church has short arms and it is necessary for us to scale our offerings into the basket.

On a recording of a song titled "Cornsilk":

despite the fact that you played it over and over again i can't even remember how the damn thing goes. it proves that this is an oscar levant tune. i could hum "dancing cheek to cheek" the first time i heard it. after i had only heard "dardanella" twice i blew two cold sores off my upper lip whistling the melody, but that damn "cornsilk" i must have heard forty times in one night and i still don't know how it turns out melodically. either your ear for music has a hernia in the lobe or you are far ahead of this generation musically when you pick "cornsilk" for your hit parade.

On the "Pine Point Hermit" in Maine:

i'm enclosing a picture of the "pine point hermit." he spoke to me about appearing on our program when i was in maine last summer. i said that i would try to use him and, on the strength of this hapless non-promise, the hermit started to let his hair and whiskers grow so he would look wilder, if possible, when the call came. in a recent letter he takes me to task for not sending for him and says that the hair is now so long it is starting to grow up his nose, tending to make him very uncomfortable. if he is found dead, a victim of hirsute suffocation, i imagine that i shall be wanted in maine.

On humor:

you have to be a yuck to cater to yucks. you can't go through life writing with your tongue in your cheek. half of the world will think you chew tobacco and the other half will think you have bitten off the end of somebody's goiter. you have a much better chance with written humor than with oral humor. all humor is a matter of opinion. as for radio, i always feel that someone has just dropped a loaded privy into the air-conditioning system.

On Amos 'n' Andy:

i'm in agreement. in my estimation they are the cleverest team in radio today. their dialogue holds up better than any of the other shows which is really something when you realize that for fifteen years they have been grinding out five shows a week. their voice changes and the fading in and out of the characters as they come and go are uncanny. most people cannot appreciate the skill involved, which is to be expected. most people, knee deep in the little messes they call their lives, cannot appreciate much of anything.

The concluding letter was not written to me. It has attained wide private circulation. I had heard tell of it, but I didn't see it until a man in Hollywood gave me a copy. It had its genesis in the rude behavior of an eagle named Mr. Ramshaw. This eagle appeared as a guest performer on the Allen radio show in Studio 8-H and his performance proved to be one of the great off-the-record howls of the 1940 radio season. Fred's letter to an NBC executive follows:

am in receipt of your letter commenting on l'affaire eagle as they are calling it around the young and rubicam office.

i thought i had seen about everything in radio but the eagle had a trick up his feathered colon that was new to me. i thought, for a minute, i was back on the bill with lamont's cockatoos.

an acolyte from your quarters brought news to us, following the nine o'clock broadcast, that the eagle was to be grounded at the midnight show. it was quite obvious that mr. ramshaw, as the eagle is known around the falcon lounge at the audubon society rooms, resented your dictatorial orders. when his cue came to fly, and he was still bound to captain knight's wrist, mr. ramshaw, deprived by nature of the organs essential in the voicing of an audible complaint, called upon other anatomical regions to wreak upon us his reaction to your martinet ban.

toscanini, your house man, has foisted some movements on studio audiences in 8-h; the bulova company has praised its movement over your network, but when radio city is being torn down to make way for another mcguinness restaurant, the one movement that will be recalled by the older radio fans will be the eagle's movement on wednesday last. if you have never seen a ghost's beret you might have viewed one on mr. rockefeller's carpet during our sterling performance.

i know you await with trepidation the announcement that i am going to interview sabu with his elephant some week.

yours for a wet broom in 8-h on wednesday nights.

fred allen.

CHAPTER XVII   *Walla Walla Talk*

THE TITLE OF THIS CHAPTER is a term used frequently in radio. Whenever a director of a radio program wants a babble in the background, a subdued mumble to indicate the presence of a crowd, he calls for Walla Walla talk. This Walla Walla talk is provided chiefly by musicians who, if they can think of nothing else to say, keep repeating "rhubarb and rhubarb and rhubarb."

The origin of the expression Walla Walla talk is a mystery. Radio is an industry that is full of mysteries, full of scientific as well as biological confusions. Fred Allen is forever trying to evolve definitions to fit the people and institutions in the business. He calls a radio producer "an ulcer with a stop watch." And his description of an advertising agency is this: "Eighty-five per cent confusion and fifteen per cent commission."

When it comes to understanding radio I stand in the same class as Moses Saint Matthew Ashley. One day a couple of years back I came across a letter Moses Saint Matthew Ashley had written to the newspaper where I worked. He described himself as inventor of a remarkable radio attachment called the Atmoswitch and he concluded his letter in this way:

"Who are willing to Angel along this line of radio research? Have I made it clear? I hope so."

He hadn't made it clear altogether so I went to see him. I was not willing to Angel along his line, but I did want to get a more adequate explanation of the Atmoswitch and its functions.

Moses Saint Matthew Ashley turned out to be a Negro weighing two hundred and eighty-nine pounds. He lived in a single room at a Long Island boardinghouse—a mere cubby-hole of a room which he had piled so full of accumulations that no cat, however tiny, could have been swung in it. Mr. Ashley had strung clothesline back and forth across his room and from these lines were suspended several hundred colored pictures which he had cut from magazines. Almost all of them were pictures of movie stars.

"These are my company," said Moses Saint Matthew as he began clearing a couple of foxholes in the debris so we could each find a place to sit down. "I do not care for human company," he went on. "Yonder is a picture of Booker T. Washington. At one time I chopped stovewood for him. My papa chopped stovewood for him down in Alabama and I used to help my papa chop it."

I asked Mr. Ashley the nature of his business or profession and he said he was a former sandhog, retired at the age of forty-seven.

"I am a sick man," he said. "My joints swell up if I don't watch them. So I spend all my time in this room steddying."

Where, I wanted to know, was the Atmoswitch? He had quite a job of it getting the thing out from under his bed. It appeared to be an old suitcase with some wires and knobs fastened on top. The entire thing had been shellacked in some way to give it a metallic appearance.

"There it is," said Mr. Ashley at last. "I deem it so valuable that I don't deem to take out a patent on it. You can see what it is on the outside of the Atmoswitch. On the inside is the secret. That is what is patentable. The full name of it is the E-Attachment Adam Genesis Atmoswitch. I tried to get 'Reciprocity' in the name of it but I thought the name was long enough like I had it. There is reciprocity in it just the same. Now I want to show you the book that I steddy all the time."

He conducted another mining operation and came up with a book called *Understanding Radio*. Inside the front cover was written: "Bought on Good Friday, April 11, 1941 —at the 'Y' at 5 West Sixty-third Street, NYC. The sudden lift and tone repressioner."

I asked Mr. Ashley the meaning of that last line. He informed me that the moment he bought the book and glanced through its pages he decided to invent the Atmoswitch, and that on the instant he named his uninvented invention the sudden lift and tone repressioner. Later he changed it.

Mr. Ashley got down on the floor and began poking his fat fingers at the doodads on top of the Atmoswitch.

"Notice this little switch I got right here," he said. "You lift it sudden and you don't have to fidget and fengle with anything else. It's a sudden lift and it repressions the tone."

What had he done toward promoting his invention, beyond writing to the newspapers?

"I have already had the Atmoswitch tested out," he said. "I took it up to the NBC laboratories and while I was there I got Mary Margaret McBride's autograph, which I will show you.

"It is hard to explain what the Atmoswitch does. It increases the amplitude of the signal which is radio itself. That is one of the things it does. Radio sets used to get overhet and burn out, but now the Atmoswitch just seems to dreen it off like a lightning rod. It's a radical departure. Yes, you can say that. You can say that as a departure, it is radical.

"This device is doing something valuable, but I don't know rightly what it is. I am not all the way through the book yet. Let me show you about alternating arrows. The picture is in the book."

He began turning pages until he came to a page illustrating alternating currents, with little arrows indicating the direction of flow.

"Here it is," he said. "You see, the arrows go shooting off in both directions and that's why they are called alternating arrows. By the time I get through with this book and learn everything in it I'll know what the Atmoswitch does if I live that long. I figured out about alternating arrows before I ever got this book. Figured it right out. And then I got the book and opened it up and there it was. Alternating arrows.

"You have got to understand that the tubes in the radio have not been un-vacuumized or de-aired enough and this causes mechanical noises. The Atmoswitch gets rid of these. It's really a signal filterer.

"I made it out of an old traveling bag and one thing you can see right now. It is too big. My problem is to reduce the size of that old thing you see there. I am gonna take a correspondence course to cut down the size, if I can find the right one. Then when I get the size cut down and get the book finished, I've got my big job ahead of me. I've got to find out what the E-Attachment Adam Genesis At-moswitch does."

As I said at the beginning, I'm pure half-wit when it comes to scientific things, so all Moses Saint Matthew Ashley's talk was wasted on me. I look upon the entire institution of radio just as Mr. Ashley looks upon his Atmoswitch. It does something, but what it does I don't know.

I spent most of 1935 working in the press department of the Columbia Broadcasting System in New York. One of my duties at CBS was to take the telephone call that came again and again during the winter months from a woman known as "Mrs. Birdie." Each morning when snow was on the ground she called the broadcasting company, always with the same message.

"Now," she'd say, "I want you people to be sure and put the birdie announcement on the air every fifteen minutes today. Just tell the people to be sure and put out food for the birdies."

I'd always tell her that we'd take care of the matter and she never complained that we didn't.

Upon the attainment of full-fledged authorship, I became qualified as a radio performer and script writer. My first job was the preparation of an audition script for an advertising agency. The agency was trying to cook up a new half-hour program for a comedian and I was called in to work on the script for the first show. That was my introduction to script conferences.

A script conference is a conference in which people think out loud. Everybody in such a meeting is always thinking out loud.

For example, a man will say:

"Now look, fellas. I'm just thinking out loud."

He'll go on talking about the problem before the house and maybe he'll say something that someone else considers wrong. Somebody will jump on him about his lack of judgment, and he'll have a ready response.

"Good Lord!" he'll say. "I was just thinking out loud!"

We had more conferences over that audition script than were held over the construction of the Panama Canal. It didn't take long for me to see that I was getting involved in a daffy business, filled with shrieking and general hair-tearing.

The idea of the audition script was to prepare and rehearse a sample half-hour program, then stage it just as though it were being broadcast. It would be recorded, and then the records would be played for the tobacco company executives who, everybody hoped, would laugh until they fell on the floor and then order the thing produced regularly.

We were having final rehearsals in one of the big NBC studios. One of the features of the show was a new orchestra conducted by a young man named Edgar. It was his big chance in radio and he was understandably nervous. His job was to stand on the platform, facing his musicians, and simply direct the musical interludes.

Edgar was getting along beautifully in the rehearsals. The music was excellent. But suddenly in the middle of one selection the director's voice boomed from the control room.

"Edgar!" he shouted. "Don't beat your foot like that. The mikes pick up the sound."

Edgar looked down at his left foot.

"Okay," he said, and started over.

He got halfway through the number and then his left foot started tapping again. And again came the yell from the control room. Edgar was quite upset about it. Here was a young man who had been leading an orchestra for five years and he had always slapped out the beat with his left foot.

A recess was called and the director lectured Edgar about the foot.

"I try to keep it in mind," Edgar told him, "but when I keep my mind on my foot, then I can't keep my mind on the music."

"Well, you gotta stop it," said the director. "You gotta stop it, or else."

"Or else" in radio means much the same thing as it means elsewhere. Out.

Edgar applied himself to foot-thinking from then on. Came the dress rehearsal. Ten minutes of the show ran off smoothly. Then the mikes began picking up that faint, disquieting thump-thump-thump-thump. The dress rehearsal couldn't be stopped, so a man ran up to Edgar and started pointing excitedly at Edgar's hoof. Edgar stopped tapping.

Another few minutes and that foot started beating again. This time the man crept up to Edgar on all fours, seized Edgar's foot with both hands, and held it firmly against the floor until the rehearsal was over.

After that came the final script conference. Edgar was ashamed of himself. He apologized all over the place and everyone frowned at him. Finally one of the production men spoke up.

"I got an idea," he said. "Supposing we get a little pillow and put it under his foot. That'll sorta deaden the noise."

They all seemed to take that suggestion seriously, but I thought it was a gag. So I spoke up.

"I got a better idea," I said. "Let's have Edgar appear on the platform wearing full dress—white tie and tails—and he'll be barefooted. That'll not only solve the noise problem, but provide us with a novelty. People all over the country will start talking about the barefooted maestro."

So help me, they took me seriously! They spent twenty minutes discussing the proposition and then decided against it on the unique grounds that a barefooted band leader would detract from the dignity of the production. They finally wound up by using a rubber sponge under Edgar's foot and everything worked out splendidly. That is, everything worked out splendidly until the tobacco company executives heard the recordings. They said the show smelt.

Shortly after that misadventure I appeared on a morning radio program with a lady who tells people what to cook for supper. It happened that an independent radio producer named Douglas Storer heard this broadcast. It was early in the day and Mr. Storer probably was still half asleep, for he decided that I should be a regular performer on the air waves. And he had just the idea for me. He was getting up a program called "Swop Night" and he wanted me to be master of ceremonies, or Chief Swopper, on it.

Mr. Storer is a short, dynamic man who does his share of thinking out loud and who not only produces radio shows but manages talent. One of his clients is Dale Carnegie, and it is a beautiful experience to hear Mr. Storer talking to Mr. Carnegie by telephone. Mr. Storer's side of the conversation goes somewhat like this:

"No, Dale! I told you to stay away from that gang. You don't know how to handle people like that. Now, listen! Leave them to me! Whenever they try to approach you, simply tell them Doug Storer will do the talking for you. Let *me* handle them!"

Mr. Storer knows radio backward and forward. We became good friends, even though we had to sit together through many script conferences. For one thing, Mr. Storer taught me how to mark a script before a broadcast.

A radio actor usually carries a red pencil. He takes a script and goes through it, marking his cue lines and putting a red circle around his own name wherever it appears. Then, off in a corner by himself, he rehearses the lines he has to speak. He seldom reads what the other people on the program have to say. He only knows his cue, and then what he has to say. He might appear on dozens of dramatic programs and never have an idea what the show is all about.

I've never taken part in a so-called soap opera but I've encountered many people involved in these productions. Once I interviewed the woman who is supposed to be the champion author in this field. Her name is Irna Phillips, and at the time I talked with her, she was writing four or five different serials—all of them running daily on the networks.

She was in her hotel room with a secretary when I called, and I asked her how she managed to turn out such a mess of stuff every day. She said she dictated it. I asked for a demonstration. Miss Phillips got up and began pacing the floor. Her secretary sat at the typewriter. Then Miss Phillips went into a routine like this:

Music up and down. Helen: Yes, my dear, he'll be along any moment now. I do hope he brings Charlie. Beatrice: Is he really as wonderful as all that, darling? Helen: Oh, you've never . . . Sound: doorbell rings. Helen: Oh, here he is! Come in! Sound: door opens and closes. Helen: Med-

ford! It's you! Beatrice: You! Sam Medford! Sound: heavy
footsteps. Sam: Yes. It's Sam Medford. You didn't think
I'd come back. Sound: click of revolver. Helen: Stand back,
Sam Medford. Don't take another step. Sam: Put that gun
down, Helen.

I told Miss Phillips that was enough—I got the idea.

When my own affairs took me almost daily into the back
corridors of Radio City, I began meeting other people connected with these shows. One morning, soon after ten
o'clock, I got off an elevator and found myself in a large
quadrangular lobby. Around the walls were leather-covered
benches and all these benches were occupied. Between the
benches were other people, sitting on the floor. Still others
were leaning against pillars or standing off in corners. All
of them appeared to be reading scripts and talking at the
same time. As I walked the length of the lobby I passed
men and women who were uttering remarkable speeches.

A girl sprawled on the floor would be saying:

"John! I've had enough of this! Take me home this minute or I'll spill the whole thing to Judge Godfrey!"

Another step and here's a middle-aged lady, speaking in
a half-sob:

"Here, darlin'. Put your head here on my shoulder. Now,
now, now. Tell me all about it. You can always trust me."

All up and down the big room this sort of thing was
going on. Half-a-dozen different soap operas would be going on the air in the next few hours, and these were the
individual performers, busy perfecting their lines, reading
them just as they would read them at the microphones.
Nobody seemed to pay any attention to anyone else. From
various quarters little shrieks would arise, and now and then
a tone of hysteria would get into one of the voices, but
nobody looked up.

I had a definite sensation that I was in a nuthouse.

Radio is full of peculiar people and, at the same time, it's
possible to find intelligence scattered here and there. There
are hundreds of self-considered geniuses in the business—
guys who know it is only a matter of time until they become the new Orson Welles or the new Norman Corwin.

These people are permitted their tantrums—nobody seems to mind. And, for my part, it's fun to be around them.

My own small experience in the business was enlightening and pleasant. It had but one bad feature. It almost got me into the movies—as an actor. I say *almost*—but I'll let you judge the distance involved.

One winter night, with a blizzard blowing outside, I was sitting at home in my pajamas when the telephone rang. It was late in the evening. The caller said he was with Metro-Goldwyn-Mayer, that he had heard me on the radio, that he wanted me to act in a picture, and that it was an urgent matter requiring an immediate decision. Would I come right into town for a conference?

Thinking of the bitter storm outside, I said it would be impossible for me to come in. Then he asked if he could come out to my house. I said if he wanted to do it, to come ahead. I wouldn't have gone into town that night if Garbo had invited me to see her new etching.

As I say, I had on pajamas and a robe and I was unshaven. My wife insisted that I get dressed, but I refused to shave at that hour of the night. For her part she got into a pair of slacks which—at that time, anyway—was the equivalent of getting into the Hollywood mood.

In about an hour the taxi came up through the sleet and snow and two men piled into my house. One was a Mr. Morgan—the man who had called. The other was a dark, taciturn individual with burning black eyes. Mr. Morgan produced credentials to show that he was in charge of short subjects for M-G-M, and explained to me that his companion was a director of shorts.

They sat down, lit cigarettes, and went to work on me. Mr. Morgan explained the project. I'd have to appear before the cameras two days later. He talked about costumes and props. He asked me if I had ever faced a movie camera and I said no. He asked me if I'd be frightened or nervous in front of a camera and I said very likely.

Meanwhile, the dark man just sat there and stared at me. I'd wheel my head around slowly and there he'd be—just staring. I was being screen-tested, in a way. And what do you suppose I did? I turned ham. I began acting. Making little gestures, arching my brows, tossing off quips.

They talked on and on about this short-subject thing and I could tell that my wife was a little disappointed. I suppose she thought they were coming out to cast me for a part in *For Whom the Bell Tolls*.

All this time that dark guy just sat there and stared at me. Mr. Morgan would ask him how he thought I'd photograph and he'd say:

"Hmm-m-m-m-m-m-m."

So my wife spoke up.

"Oh," she said, "he photographs fine, except when you get him at a certain angle his head looks like a peeled egg."

The dark guy seemed to intensify his study of me now and after a time they got up and Mr. Morgan said he would give me a call the next day and tell me where and when to report.

The next day I jittered around the house, trying to get some work done but unable to concentrate on anything but my movie career. Occasionally I'd go into the bathroom, lock the door, and face the mirror. I'd simulate anger, nonchalance, chagrin, grief, hilarity, and a lot of other things. It didn't work very well.

The hours went by. Other people called, but not Mr. Morgan. The day ended and night began and still no call. I figured that maybe he always called after ten o'clock. But he didn't. And he didn't call the next day.

I don't know what happened. I don't know what ended my picture career before it ever got started. But I have a suspicion. I think maybe it was that crack about the peeled egg. That must have fixed it.

As I've indicated, my radio career didn't last long, but I do think I got a lot out of it. I remember attending a rehearsal once and overhearing a conversation between two musicians. One man said he had been rejected by his draft board.

"What's the matter with you?" asked the other.

"I got head murmurs."

Haven't we all?